Real-Resumes for Police, Law Enforcement & Security Jobs...
including real resumes used to change careers
and transfer skills to other industries

Anne McKinney, Editor

PREP PUBLISHING

FAYETTEVILLE, NC

PREP Publishing
1110½ Hay Street
Fayetteville, NC 28305
(910) 483-6611

Library of Congress Cataloging-in-Publication Data

Real-resumes for police, law enforcement & security jobs : including real resumes used to change careers and transfer skills to other industries / Anne McKinney, editor.
      p. cm. -- (Real-resumes series)
   ISBN 1-885288-25-5 (trade pbk.)
   1. Résumés (Employment) 2. Police. 3. Law enforcement. 4. Police, Private. I. McKinney, Anne, 1948- II. Series.

  HF5383 .R39588 2002
  650.14'2--dc21
                                        2002020591
                                            CIP

Printed in the United States of America

By PREP Publishing

Business and Career Series:

RESUMES AND COVER LETTERS THAT HAVE WORKED

RESUMES AND COVER LETTERS THAT HAVE WORKED FOR MILITARY PROFESSIONALS

GOVERNMENT JOB APPLICATIONS AND FEDERAL RESUMES

COVER LETTERS THAT BLOW DOORS OPEN

LETTERS FOR SPECIAL SITUATIONS

RESUMES AND COVER LETTERS FOR MANAGERS

REAL-RESUMES FOR COMPUTER JOBS

REAL-RESUMES FOR MEDICAL JOBS

REAL-RESUMES FOR FINANCIAL JOBS

REAL-RESUMES FOR TEACHERS

REAL-RESUMES FOR STUDENTS

REAL-RESUMES FOR CAREER CHANGERS

REAL-RESUMES FOR SALES

REAL ESSAYS FOR COLLEGE & GRADUATE SCHOOL

REAL-RESUMES FOR AVIATION & TRAVEL JOBS

REAL-RESUMES FOR POLICE, LAW ENFORCEMENT & SECURITY JOBS

REAL-RESUMES FOR SOCIAL WORK & COUNSELING JOBS

REAL-RESUMES FOR CONSTRUCTION JOBS

REAL-RESUMES FOR MANUFACTURING JOBS

Judeo-Christian Ethics Series:

SECOND TIME AROUND

BACK IN TIME

WHAT THE BIBLE SAYS ABOUT...Words that can lead to success and happiness

A GENTLE BREEZE FROM GOSSAMER WINGS

BIBLE STORIES FROM THE OLD TESTAMENT

Fiction:

KIJABE...An African Historical Saga

Table of Contents

Welcome to the Real-Resumes Series. The Real-Resumes Series is a series of books which have been developed based on the experiences of real job hunters and which target specialized fields or types of resumes. As the editor of the series, I have carefully selected resumes and cover letters (with names and other key data disguised, of course) which have been used successfully in real job hunts. That's what we mean by "Real-Resumes." What you see in this book are *real* resumes and cover letters which helped real people get ahead in their careers.

The Real-Resumes Series is based on the work of the country's oldest resume-preparation company known as PREP Resumes. If you would like a free information packet describing the company's resume preparation services, call 910-483-6611 or write to PREP at 1110½ Hay Street, Fayetteville, NC 28305. If you have a job hunting experience you would like to share with our staff at the Real-Resumes Series, please contact us at preppub@aol.com or visit our website at http://www.prep-pub.com.

The resumes and cover letters in this book are designed to be of most value to people already in a career change or contemplating a career change. If we could give you one word of advice about your career, here's what we would say: Manage your career and don't stumble from job to job in an incoherent pattern. Try to find work that interests you, and then identify prosperous industries which need work performed of the type you want to do. Learn early in your working life that a great resume and cover letter can blow doors open for you and help you maximize your salary.

This book is dedicated to those seeking jobs in the police, law enforcement and security field. We hope the superior samples will help you manage your current job campaign and your career so that you will find work aligned to your career interests.

Real-Resumes for Police, Law Enforcement & Security Jobs...
including real resumes used to change careers
and transfer skills to other industries

Anne McKinney, Editor

Introduction:
The Art of
Changing
Jobs...
and Finding
New Careers

As the editor of this book, I would like to give you some tips on how to make the best use of the information you will find here. Because you are considering a career change, you already understand the concept of managing your career for maximum enjoyment and self-fulfillment. The purpose of this book is to provide expert tools and advice so that you *can* manage your career. Inside these pages you will find resumes and cover letters that will help you find not just a job but the type of work you want to do.

Overview of the Book

Every resume and cover letter in this book actually worked. And most of the resumes and cover letters have common features: most are one-page, most are in the chronological format, and most resumes are accompanied by a companion cover letter. In this section you will find helpful advice about job hunting. Step One begins with a discussion of why employers prefer the one-page, chronological resume. In Step Two you are introduced to the direct approach and to the proper format for a cover letter. In Step Three you learn the 14 main reasons why job hunters are not offered the jobs they want, and you learn the six key areas employers focus on when they interview you. Step Four gives nuts-and-bolts advice on how to handle the interview, send a follow-up letter after an interview, and negotiate your salary.

The cover letter plays such a critical role in a career change. You will learn from the experts how to format your cover letters and you will see suggested language to use in particular career-change situations. It has been said that "A picture is worth a thousand words" and, for that reason, you will see numerous examples of effective cover letters used by real individuals to change fields, functions, and industries.

The most important part of the book is the Real-Resumes section. Some of the individuals whose resumes and cover letters you see spent a lengthy career in an industry they loved. Then there are resumes and cover letters of people who wanted a change but who probably wanted to remain in their industry. Many of you will be especially interested by the resumes and cover letters of individuals who knew they definitely wanted a career change but had no idea what they wanted to do next. Other resumes and cover letters show individuals who knew they wanted to change fields and had a pretty good idea of what they wanted to do next.

Whatever your field, and whatever your circumstances, you'll find resumes and cover letters that will "show you the ropes" in terms of successfully changing jobs and switching careers.

Before you proceed further, think about why you picked up this book.
- Are you dissatisfied with the type of work you are now doing?
- Would you like to change careers, change companies, or change industries?
- Are you satisfied with your industry but not with your niche or function within it?
- Do you want to transfer your skills to a new product or service?
- Even if you have excelled in your field, have you "had enough"? Would you like the stimulation of a new challenge?
- Are you aware of the importance of a great cover letter but unsure of how to write one?
- Are you preparing to launch a second career after retirement?
- Have you been downsized, or do you anticipate becoming a victim of downsizing?
- Do you need expert advice on how to plan and implement a job campaign that will open the maximum number of doors?
- Do you want to make sure you handle an interview to your maximum advantage?

- Would you like to master the techniques of negotiating salary and benefits?
- Do you want to learn the secrets and shortcuts of professional resume writers?

Using the Direct Approach

As you consider the possibility of a job hunt or career change, you need to be aware that most people end up having at least three distinctly different careers in their working lifetimes, and often those careers are different from each other. Yet people usually stumble through each job campaign, unsure of what they should be doing. Whether you find yourself voluntarily or unexpectedly in a job hunt, the direct approach is the job hunting strategy most likely to yield a full-time permanent job. The direct approach is an active, take-the-initiative style of job hunting in which you choose your next employer rather than relying on responding to ads, using employment agencies, or depending on other methods of finding jobs. You will learn how to use the direct approach in this book, and you will see that an effective cover letter is a critical ingredient in using the direct approach.

The "direct approach" is the style of job hunting most likely to yield the maximum number of job interviews.

Lack of Industry Experience Not a Major Barrier to Entering New Field

"Lack of experience" is often the last reason people are not offered jobs, according to the companies who do the hiring. If you are changing careers, you will be glad to learn that experienced professionals often are selling "potential" rather than experience in a job hunt. Companies look for personal qualities that they know tend to be present in their most effective professionals, such as communication skills, initiative, persistence, organizational and time management skills, and creativity. Frequently companies are trying to discover "personality type," "talent," "ability," "aptitude," and "potential" rather than seeking actual hands-on experience, so your resume should be designed to aggressively present your accomplishments. Attitude, enthusiasm, personality, and a track record of achievements in any type of work are the primary "indicators of success" which employers are seeking, and you will see numerous examples in this book of resumes written in an all-purpose fashion so that the professional can approach various industries and companies.

The Art of Using References in a Job Hunt

You probably already know that you need to provide references during a job hunt, but you may not be sure of how and when to use references for maximum advantage. You can use references very creatively during a job hunt to call attention to your strengths and make yourself "stand out." Your references will rarely get you a job, no matter how impressive the names, but the way you use references can boost the employer's confidence in you and lead to a job offer in the least time.

Using references in a skillful fashion in your job hunt will inspire confidence in prospective employers and help you "close the sale" after interviews.

You should ask from three to five people, including people who have supervised you, if you can use them as a reference during your job hunt. You may not be able to ask your current boss since your job hunt is probably confidential.

A common question in resume preparation is: "Do I need to put my references on my resume?" No, you don't. Even if you create a references page at the same time you prepare your resume, you don't need to mail, e-mail, or fax your references page with the resume and cover letter. Usually the potential employer is not interested in references until he meets you, so the earliest you need to have references ready is at the first interview. Obviously there are exceptions to this standard rule of thumb; sometimes an ad will ask you to send references with your first response. Wait until the employer requests references before providing them.

An excellent attention-getting technique is to take to the first interview not just a page of references (giving names, addresses, and telephone numbers) but an actual letter of reference written by someone who knows you well and who preferably has supervised or employed you. A professional way to close the first interview is to thank the interviewer, shake his or her hand, and then say you'd like to give him or her a copy of a letter of reference from a previous employer. Hopefully you already made a good impression during the interview, but you'll "close the sale" in a dynamic fashion if you leave a letter praising you and your accomplishments. For that reason, it's a good idea to ask supervisors during your final weeks in a job if they will provide you with a written letter of recommendation which you can use in future job hunts. Most employers will oblige, and you will have a letter that has a useful "shelf life" of many years. Such a letter often gives the prospective employer enough confidence in his opinion of you that he may forego checking out other references and decide to offer you the job on the spot or in the next few days.

With regard to references, it's best to provide the names and addresses of people who have supervised you or observed you in a work situation.

Whom should you ask to serve as references? References should be people who have known or supervised you in a professional, academic, or work situation. References with big titles, like school superintendent or congressman, are fine, but remind busy people when you get to the interview stage that they may be contacted soon. Make sure the busy official recognizes your name and has instant positive recall of you! If you're asked to provide references on a formal company application, you can simply transcribe names from your references list. In summary, follow this rule in using references: If you've got them, flaunt them! If you've obtained well-written letters of reference, make sure you find a polite way to push those references under the nose of the interviewer so he or she can hear someone other than you describing your strengths. Your references probably won't ever get you a job, but glowing letters of reference can give you credibility and visibility that can make you stand out among candidates with similar credentials and potential!

The approach taken by this book is to (1) help you master the proven best techniques of conducting a job hunt and (2) show you how to stand out in a job hunt through your resume, cover letter, interviewing skills, as well as the way in which you present your references and follow up on interviews. Now, the best way to "get in the mood" for writing your own resume and cover letter is to select samples from the Table of Contents that interest you and then read them. A great resume is a "photograph," usually on one page, of an individual. If you wish to seek professional advice in preparing your resume, you may contact one of the professional writers at Professional Resume & Employment Publishing (PREP) for a brief free consultation by calling 1-910-483-6611.

Part One: Some Advice About Your Job Hunt

What if you don't know what you want to do?

Your job hunt will be more comfortable if you can figure out what type of work you want to do. But you are not alone if you have no idea what you want to do next! You may have knowledge and skills in certain areas but want to get into another type of work. What *The Wall Street Journal* has discovered in its research on careers is that most of us end up having at least three distinctly different careers in our working lives; it seems that, even if we really like a particular kind of activity, twenty years of doing it is enough for most of us and we want to move on to something else!

That's why we strongly believe that you need to spend some time figuring out *what interests you* rather than taking an inventory of the skills you have. You may have skills that you simply don't want to use, but if you can build your career on the things that interest you, you will be more likely to be happy and satisfied in your job. Realize, too, that interests can change over time; the activities that interest you now may not be the ones that interested you years ago. For example, some professionals may decide that they've had enough of retail sales and want a job selling another product or service, even though they have earned a reputation for being an excellent retail manager. We strongly believe that interests rather than skills should be the determining factor in deciding what types of jobs you want to apply for and what directions you explore in your job hunt. Obviously one cannot be a lawyer without a law degree or a secretary without secretarial skills; but a professional can embark on a next career as a financial consultant, property manager, plant manager, production supervisor, retail manager, or other occupation if he/she has a strong interest in that type of work and can provide a resume that clearly demonstrates past excellent performance in *any* field and *potential* to excel in another field. As you will see later in this book, "lack of exact experience" is the last reason why people are turned down for the jobs they apply for.

> Figure out what interests you and you will hold the key to a successful job hunt and working career. (And be prepared for your interests to change over time!)

> "Lack of exact experience" is the last reason people are turned down for the jobs for which they apply.

How can you have a resume prepared if you don't know what you want to do?

You may be wondering how you can have a resume prepared if you don't know what you want to do next. The approach to resume writing which PREP, the country's oldest resume-preparation company, has used successfully for many years is to develop an "all-purpose" resume that translates your skills, experience, and accomplishments into language employers can understand. What most people need in a job hunt is a versatile resume that will allow them to apply for numerous types of jobs. For example, you may want to apply for a job in pharmaceutical sales but you may also want to have a resume that will be versatile enough for you to apply for jobs in the construction, financial services, or automotive industries.

Based on more than 20 years of serving job hunters, we at PREP have found that your best approach to job hunting is **an all-purpose resume** and **specific cover letters tailored to specific fields** rather than using the approach of trying to create different resumes for every job. If you are remaining in your field, you may not even need more than one "all-purpose" cover letter, although the cover letter rather than the resume is the place to communicate your interest in a narrow or specific field. An all-purpose resume and cover letter that translate your experience and accomplishments into plain English are the tools that will maximize the number of doors which open for you while permitting you to "fish" in the widest range of job areas.

Your resume will provide the script for your job interview.
When you get down to it, your resume has a simple job to do: Its purpose is to blow as many doors open as possible and to make as many people as possible want to meet you. So a well-written resume that really "sells" you is a key that will create opportunities for you in a job hunt.

This statistic explains why: The typical newspaper advertisement for a job opening receives more than 245 replies. And normally only 10 or 12 will be invited to an interview.

But here's another purpose of the resume: it provides the "script" the employer uses when he interviews you. If your resume has been written in such a way that your strengths and achievements are revealed, that's what you'll end up talking about at the job interview. Since the resume will govern what you get asked about at your interviews, you can't overestimate the importance of making sure your resume makes you look and sound as good as you are.

Your resume is the "script" for your job interviews. Make sure you put on your resume what you want to talk about or be asked about at the job interview.

So what is a "good" resume?
Very literally, your resume should motivate the person reading it to dial the phone number or e-mail the screen name you have put on the resume. When you are relocating, you should put a local phone number on your resume if your physical address is several states away; employers are more likely to dial a local telephone number than a long-distance number when they're looking for potential employees.

If you have a resume already, look at it objectively. Is it a limp, colorless "laundry list" of your job titles and duties? Or does it "paint a picture" of your skills, abilities, and accomplishments in a way that would make someone want to meet you? Can people understand what you're saying? If you are attempting to change fields or industries, can potential employers see that your skills and knowledge are transferable to other environments? For example, have you described accomplishments which reveal your problem-solving abilities or communication skills?

The one-page resume in chronological format is the format preferred by most employers.

How long should your resume be?
One page, maybe two. Usually only people in the academic community have a resume (which they usually call a *curriculum vitae*) longer than one or two pages. Remember that your resume is almost always accompanied by a cover letter, and a potential employer does not want to read more than two or three pages about a total stranger in order to decide if he wants to meet that person! Besides, don't forget that the more you tell someone about yourself, the more opportunity you are providing for the employer to screen you out at the "first-cut" stage. A resume should be concise and exciting and designed to make the reader want to meet you in person!

Should resumes be functional or chronological?
Employers almost always prefer a chronological resume; in other words, an employer will find a resume easier to read if it is immediately apparent what your current or most recent job is, what you did before that, and so forth, in reverse chronological order. A resume that goes back in detail for the last ten years of employment will generally satisfy the employer's curiosity about your background. Employment more than ten years old can be shown even more briefly in an "Other Experience" section at the end of your "Experience" section. Remember that your intention is not to tell everything you've done but to "hit the high points" and especially impress the employer with what you learned, contributed, or accomplished in each job you describe.

Once you get your resume, what do you do with it?

You will be using your resume to answer ads, as a tool to use in talking with friends and relatives about your job search, and, most importantly, in using the "direct approach" described in this book.

When you mail your resume, always send a "cover letter."

A "cover letter," sometimes called a "resume letter" or "letter of interest," is a letter that accompanies and introduces your resume. Your cover letter is a way of personalizing the resume by sending it to the specific person you think you might want to work for at each company. Your cover letter should contain a few highlights from your resume—just enough to make someone want to meet you. Cover letters should always be typed or word processed on a computer—never handwritten.

Never mail or fax your resume without a cover letter.

1. Learn the art of answering ads.

There is an "art," part of which can be learned, in using your "bestselling" resume to reply to advertisements.

Sometimes an exciting job lurks behind a boring ad that someone dictated in a hurry, so reply to any ad that interests you. Don't worry that you aren't "25 years old with an MBA" like the ad asks for. Employers will always make compromises in their requirements if they think you're the "best fit" overall.

What about ads that ask for "salary requirements?"

What if the ad you're answering asks for "salary requirements?" The first rule is to avoid committing yourself in writing at that point to a specific salary. You don't want to "lock yourself in."

There are two ways to handle the ad that asks for "salary requirements."

First, you can ignore that part of the ad and accompany your resume with a cover letter that focuses on "selling" you, your abilities, and even some of your philosophy about work or your field. You may include a sentence in your cover letter like this: "I can provide excellent personal and professional references at your request, and I would be delighted to share the private details of my salary history with you in person."

What if the ad asks for your "salary requirements?"

Second, if you feel you must give some kind of number, just state a range in your cover letter that includes your medical, dental, other benefits, and expected bonuses. You might state, for example, "My current compensation, including benefits and bonuses, is in the range of $30,000-$40,000."

Analyze the ad and "tailor" yourself to it.

When you're replying to ads, a finely tailored cover letter is an important tool in getting your resume noticed and read. On the next page is a cover letter which has been "tailored to fit" a specific ad. Notice the "art" used by PREP writers of analyzing the ad's main requirements and then writing the letter so that the person's background, work habits, and interests seem "tailor-made" to the company's needs. Use this cover letter as a model when you prepare your own reply to ads.

Date

Exact Name of Person
Exact Title
Exact Name of Company
Address
City, State, Zip

Dear Exact Name of Person (or Dear Sir or Madam if answering a blind ad):

With the enclosed resume, I would like to make you aware of my interest in exploring employment opportunities with your organization.

As you will see from my enclosed resume, I am currently excelling as Chief of Police with a 450,000-person community near Chicago, IL. I have advanced to the Chief job in a track record of promotion which has included serving with distinction as a Patrol Officer, Detective, Special Agent, Detective Division Sergeant, Patrol Division Watch Commander, and then Deputy Chief of Police.

I am held in the highest regard in the community and within the law enforcement community. I have served as President of the District Chiefs of Police Association, and I have been elected to community leadership roles which include serving on the executive board of the city's computer dispatching center that serves multiple fire departments and police departments. While managing a $2 million budget and 68 individuals, I have written grants that obtained $3 million in funds for modernizing the department, and I have provided leadership in developing new programs for teens, seniors, and others.

Although I am held in the highest regard in my current position, I am ready for a new challenge, and I am selectively exploring opportunities with organizations which can utilize a resourceful leader with strong programming skills as well as international project management experience.

If you feel you could use my creative programming ability, leadership skills, and expertise related to security and law enforcement, please contact me to suggest a time when we might meet in person to discuss your needs. I am available for worldwide relocation and/or extensive travel as your needs require.

Sincerely,

Kevin Q. Jackson

Employers are trying to identify the individual who wants the job they are filling. Don't be afraid to express your enthusiasm in the cover letter!

2. Talk to friends and relatives.

Don't be shy about telling your friends and relatives the kind of job you're looking for. Looking for the job you want involves using your network of contacts, so tell people what you're looking for. They may be able to make introductions and help set up interviews.

About 25% of all interviews are set up through "who you know," so don't ignore this approach.

3. Finally, and most importantly, use the "direct approach."

The "direct approach" is a strategy in which you choose your next employer.

More than 50% of all job interviews are set up by the "direct approach." That means you actually mail, e-mail, or fax a resume and a cover letter to a company you think might be interesting to work for.

To whom do you write?

In general, you should write directly to the *exact name* of the person who would be hiring you: say, the vice-president of marketing or data processing. If you're in doubt about to whom to address the letter, address it to the president by name and he or she will make sure it gets forwarded to the right person within the company who has hiring authority in your area.

How do you find the names of potential employers?

You're not alone if you feel that the biggest problem in your job search is finding the right names at the companies you want to contact. But you can usually figure out the names of companies you want to approach by deciding first if your job hunt is primarily geography-driven or industry-driven.

In a **geography-driven job hunt,** you could select a list of, say, 50 companies you want to contact **by location** from the lists that the U.S. Chambers of Commerce publish yearly of their "major area employers." There are hundreds of local Chambers of Commerce across America, and most of them will have an 800 number which you can find through 1-800-555-1212. If you and your family think Atlanta, Dallas, Ft. Lauderdale, and Virginia Beach might be nice places to live, for example, you could contact the Chamber of Commerce in those cities and ask how you can obtain a copy of their list of major employers. Your nearest library will have the book which lists the addresses of all chambers.

In an **industry-driven job hunt,** and if you are willing to relocate, you will be identifying the companies which you find most attractive in the industry in which you want to work. When you select a list of companies to contact **by industry,** you can find the right person to write and the address of firms by industrial category in *Standard and Poor's, Moody's,* and other excellent books in public libraries. Many Web sites also provide contact information.

Many people feel it's a good investment to actually call the company to either find out or double-check the name of the person to whom they want to send a resume and cover letter. It's important to do as much as you feasibly can to assure that the letter gets to the right person in the company.

On-line research will be the best way for many people to locate organizations to which they wish to send their resume. It is outside the scope of this book to teach Internet research skills, but librarians are often useful in this area.

What's the correct way to follow up on a resume you send?

There is a polite way to be aggressively interested in a company during your job hunt. It is ideal to end the cover letter accompanying your resume by saying, "I hope you'll welcome my call next week when I try to arrange a brief meeting at your convenience to discuss your current and future needs and how I might serve them." Keep it low key, and just ask for a "brief meeting," not an interview. Employers want people who show a determined interest in working with them, so don't be shy about following up on the resume and cover letter you've mailed.

It pays to be aware of the 14 most common pitfalls for job hunters.

STEP THREE: Preparing for Interviews

But a resume and cover letter by themselves can't get you the job you want. You need to "prep" yourself before the interview. Step Three in your job campaign is "Preparing for Interviews." First, let's look at interviewing from the hiring organization's point of view.

What are the biggest "turnoffs" for potential employers?

One of the ways to help yourself perform well at an interview is to look at the main reasons why organizations *don't* hire the people they interview, according to those who do the interviewing.

Notice that "lack of appropriate background" (or lack of experience) is the *last* reason for not being offered the job.

The 14 Most Common Reasons Job Hunters Are Not Offered Jobs (according to the companies who do the interviewing and hiring):

1. Low level of accomplishment
2. Poor attitude, lack of self-confidence
3. Lack of goals/objectives
4. Lack of enthusiasm
5. Lack of interest in the company's business
6. Inability to sell or express yourself
7. Unrealistic salary demands
8. Poor appearance
9. Lack of maturity, no leadership potential
10. Lack of extracurricular activities
11. Lack of preparation for the interview, no knowledge about company
12. Objecting to travel
13. Excessive interest in security and benefits
14. Inappropriate background

Department of Labor studies have proven that smart, "prepared" job hunters can increase their beginning salary while getting a job in *half* the time it normally takes. (4½ months is the average national length of a job search.) Here, from PREP, are some questions that can prepare you to find a job faster.

Are you in the "right" frame of mind?

It seems unfair that we have to look for a job just when we're lowest in morale. Don't worry *too* much if you're nervous before interviews. You're supposed to be a little nervous, especially if the job means a lot to you. But the best way to kill unnecessary fears about job hunting is through 1) making sure you have a great resume and 2) preparing yourself for the interview. Here are three main areas you need to think about before each interview.

Do you know what the company does?
Don't walk into an interview giving the impression that, "If this is Tuesday, this must be General Motors."

Find out before the interview what the company's main product or service is. Where is the company heading? Is it in a "growth" or declining industry? (Answers to these questions may influence whether or not you want to work there!)

Information about what the company does is in annual reports, in newspaper and magazine articles, and on the Internet. If you're not yet skilled at Internet research, just visit your nearest library and ask the reference librarian to guide you to printed materials on the company.

Do you know what you want to do for the company?
Before the interview, try to decide how you see yourself fitting into the company. Remember, "lack of exact background" the company wants is usually the last reason people are not offered jobs.

Understand before you go to each interview that the burden will be on you to "sell" the interviewer on why you're the best person for the job and the company.

How will you answer the critical interview questions?
Put yourself in the interviewer's position and think about the questions you're most likely to be asked. Here are some of the most commonly asked interview questions:

Q: "What are your greatest strengths?"
A: Don't say you've never thought about it! Go into an interview knowing the three main impressions you want to leave about yourself, such as "I'm hard-working, loyal, and an imaginative cost-cutter."

Q: "What are your greatest weaknesses?"
A: Don't confess that you're lazy or have trouble meeting deadlines! Confessing that you tend to be a "workaholic" or "tend to be a perfectionist and sometimes get frustrated when others don't share my high standards" will make your prospective employer see a "weakness" that he likes. Name a weakness that your interviewer will perceive as a strength.

Q: "What are your long-range goals?"
A: If you're interviewing with Microsoft, don't say you want to work for IBM in five years! Say your long-range goal is to be *with* the company, contributing to its goals and success.

Q: "What motivates you to do your best work?"
A: Don't get dollar signs in your eyes here! "A challenge" is not a bad answer, but it's a little cliched. Saying something like "troubleshooting" or "solving a tough problem" is more interesting and specific. Give an example if you can.

Research the company before you go to interviews.

Anticipate the questions you will be asked at the interview, and prepare your responses in advance.

Q: "What do you know about this organization?"

A: Don't say you never heard of it until they asked you to the interview! Name an interesting, positive thing you learned about the company recently from your research. Remember, company executives can sometimes feel rather "maternal" about the company they serve. Don't get onto a negative area of the company if you can think of positive facts you can bring up. Of course, if you learned in your research that the company's sales seem to be taking a nose-dive, or that the company president is being prosecuted for taking bribes, you might politely ask your interviewer to tell you something that could help you better understand what you've been reading. Those are the kinds of company facts that can help you determine whether or not you want to work there.

Q: "Why should I hire you?"

A: "I'm unemployed and available" is the wrong answer here! Get back to your strengths and say that you believe the organization could benefit by a loyal, hard-working cost-cutter like yourself.

In conclusion, you should decide in advance, before you go to the interview, how you will answer each of these commonly asked questions. Have some practice interviews with a friend to role-play and build your confidence.

STEP FOUR: Handling the Interview and Negotiating Salary

Now you're ready for Step Four: actually handling the interview successfully and effectively. Remember, the purpose of an interview is to get a job offer.

Eight "do's" for the interview

According to leading U.S. companies, there are eight key areas in interviewing success. You can fail at an interview if you mishandle just one area.

1. **Do wear appropriate clothes.**

You can never go wrong by wearing a suit to an interview.

2. **Do be well groomed.**

Don't overlook the obvious things like having clean hair, clothes, and fingernails for the interview.

3. **Do give a firm handshake.**

You'll have to shake hands twice in most interviews: first, before you sit down, and second, when you leave the interview. Limp handshakes turn most people off.

4. **Do smile and show a sense of humor.**

Interviewers are looking for people who would be nice to work with, so don't be so somber that you don't smile. In fact, research shows that people who smile at interviews are perceived as more intelligent. So, smile!

5. **Do be enthusiastic.**

Employers say they are "turned off" by lifeless, unenthusiastic job hunters who show no special interest in that company. The best way to show some enthusiasm for the employer's operation is to find out about the business beforehand.

Go to an interview prepared to tell the company why it should hire you.

A smile at an interview makes the employer perceive of you as intelligent!

6. Do show you are flexible and adaptable.

An employer is looking for someone who can contribute to his organization in a flexible, adaptable way. No matter what skills and training you have, employers know every new employee must go through initiation and training on the company's turf. Certainly show pride in your past accomplishments in a specific, factual way ("I saved my last employer $50.00 a week by a new cost-cutting measure I developed"). But don't come across as though there's nothing about the job you couldn't easily handle.

7. Do ask intelligent questions about the employer's business.

An employer is hiring someone because of certain business needs. Show interest in those needs. Asking questions to get a better idea of the employer's needs will help you "stand out" from other candidates interviewing for the job.

8. Do "take charge" when the interviewer "falls down" on the job.

Go into every interview knowing the three or four points about yourself you want the interviewer to remember. And be prepared to take an active part in leading the discussion if the interviewer's "canned approach" does not permit you to display your "strong suit." You can't always depend on the interviewer's asking you the "right" questions so you can stress your strengths and accomplishments.

Employers are seeking people with good attitudes whom they can train and coach to do things their way.

An important "don't": Don't ask questions about salary or benefits at the first interview.
Employers don't take warmly to people who look at their organization as just a place to satisfy salary and benefit needs. Don't risk making a negative impression by appearing greedy or self-serving. The place to discuss salary and benefits is normally at the second interview, and the employer will bring it up. Then you can ask questions without appearing excessively interested in what the organization can do for you.

Now...negotiating your salary
Even if an ad requests that you communicate your "salary requirement" or "salary history," you should avoid providing those numbers in your initial cover letter. You can usually say something like this: "I would be delighted to discuss the private details of my salary history with you in person."

Once you're at the interview, you must avoid even appearing *interested* in salary before you are offered the job. Make sure you've "sold" yourself before talking salary. First show you're the "best fit" for the employer and then you'll be in a stronger position from which to negotiate salary. **Never** bring up the subject of salary yourself. Employers say there's no way you can avoid looking greedy if you bring up the issue of salary and benefits before the company has identified you as its "best fit."

Don't appear excessively interested in salary and benefits at the interview.

Interviewers sometimes throw out a salary figure at the first interview to see if you'll accept it. You may not want to commit yourself if you think you will be able to negotiate a better deal later on. Get back to finding out more about the job. This lets the interviewer know you're interested primarily in the job and not the salary.

When the organization brings up salary, it may say something like this: "Well, Mary, we think you'd make a good candidate for this job. What kind of salary are we talking about?" You may not want to name a number here, either. Give the ball back to the interviewer. Act as though you hadn't given the subject of salary much thought and respond something like this: "Ah, Mr. Jones, I wonder if you'd be kind enough to tell me what salary you had in mind when you advertised the job?" Or ... "What is the range you have in mind?"

Don't worry, if the interviewer names a figure that you think is too low, you can say so without turning down the job or locking yourself into a rigid position. The point here is to negotiate for yourself as well as you can. You might reply to a number named by the interviewer that you think is low by saying something like this: "Well, Mr. Lee, the job interests me very much, and I think I'd certainly enjoy working with you. But, frankly, I was thinking of something a little higher than that." That leaves the ball in your interviewer's court again, and you haven't turned down the job either, in case it turns out that the interviewer can't increase the offer and you still want the job.

Salary negotiation can be tricky.

Last, send a follow-up letter.

Mail, e-mail, or fax a letter right after the interview telling your interviewer you enjoyed the meeting and are certain (if you are) that you are the "best fit" for the job. The people interviewing you will probably have an attitude described as either "professionally loyal" to their companies, or "maternal and proprietary" if the interviewer also owns the company. In either case, they are looking for people who want to work for *that* company in particular. The follow-up letter you send might be just the deciding factor in your favor if the employer is trying to choose between you and someone else. You will see an example of a follow-up letter on page 16.

A follow-up letter can help the employer choose between you and another qualified candidate.

A cover letter is an essential part of a job hunt or career change.

Many people are aware of the importance of having a great resume, but most people in a job hunt don't realize just how important a cover letter can be. The purpose of the cover letter, sometimes called a **"letter of interest,"** is to introduce your resume to prospective employers. The cover letter is often the critical ingredient in a job hunt because the cover letter allows you to say a lot of things that just don't "fit" on the resume. For example, you can emphasize your commitment to a new field and stress your related talents. The cover letter also gives you a chance to stress outstanding character and personal values. On the next two pages you will see examples of very effective cover letters.

A cover letter is an essential part of a career change.

Please do not attempt to implement a career change without a cover letter such as the ones you see in Part Two of this book. A cover letter is the first impression of you, and you can influence the way an employer views you by the language and style of your letter.

Special help for those in career change

We want to emphasize again that, especially in a career change, the cover letter is very important and can help you "build a bridge" to a new career. A creative and appealing cover letter can begin the process of encouraging the potential employer to imagine you in an industry other than the one in which you have worked.

As a special help to those in career change, there are resumes and cover letters included in this book which show valuable techniques and tips you should use when changing fields or industries. The resumes and cover letters of career changers are identified in the table of contents as "Career Change" and you will see the "Career Change" label on cover letters in Part Two where the individuals are changing careers.

Addressing the Cover Letter: Get the exact name of the person to whom you are writing. This makes your approach personal.

First Paragraph: This explains why you are writing.

Second Paragraph: You have a chance to talk about whatever you feel is your most distinguishing feature.

Third Paragraph: You bring up your next most distinguishing qualities and try to sell yourself.

Fourth Paragraph: Here you have another opportunity to reveal qualities or achievements which will impress your future employer.

Final Paragraph: She asks the employer to contact her. Make sure your reader knows what the "next step" is.

Alternate Final Paragraph: It's more aggressive (but not too aggressive) to let the employer know that you will be calling him or her. Don't be afraid to be persistent. Employers are looking for people who know what they want to do.

Date

Mr. James North
Forensic Supervisor
Major Crimes Division
San Marcos Police Department
4333 Marcosi Avenue
San Marcos, CA 99988

Dear Mr. North:

With the enclosed resume, I would like to formally express my interest in the full-time position of Forensic Technician with the San Marcos Police Department.

Criminal Justice education and hands-on experience as a Forensic Technician: As you will see from my resume, I maintained a perfect 4.0 GPA while earning an Associate of Science degree in Criminal Justice. I was subsequently one of eight individuals selected for the San Marcos Police Department's first Forensic Technician internship program, and I have excelled in my 350 hours of on-the-job training. In addition to skillfully performing all technical duties of a Forensic Technician, I have established cordial working relationships and have become very familiar with the organization and functions of other Police Department divisions.

Strong oral and written communication skills: One of my strongest assets is my ability to communicate effectively both orally and in writing. I refined my oral and written communication skills during my past eight years of employment with Hechts Department Stores. I began with Hechts as a Sales Associate, and then I advanced to Loss Prevention Associate. I became a Certified OSHA Inspector and learned to expertly operate electronic video surveillance as well as police radio and photographic equipment. As a Loss Prevention Associate with Hechts, I communicated extensively both orally and in writing, with duties ranging from preparing statistical and written reports, to training employees in OSHA procedures and shrinkage control.

Excellent analytical and problem-solving abilities: In my internship with the San Marcos Police Department, I have applied my analytical and problem-solving abilities as a Forensic Technician. Just as I excelled as a Loss Prevention Associate in recovering lost assets including stolen merchandise for Hechts, so too could I apply those same investigative and problem-solving abilities in responding to crime and accident scenes.

As my supervisor during my internship, you have had the opportunity to observe my dedicated hard work and commitment to top-quality results. I hope you will recommend me for the full-time position as Forensic Technician, as I am confident that I could become a valuable asset in that role to the San Marcos Police Department. I would truly be honored to serve the city and its citizens in that capacity.

Yours sincerely,

Katie Anne Doyle

Date

Exact Name of Person
Exact Title
Exact Name of Company
Address
City, State, Zip

Dear Exact Name of Person (or Dear Sir or Madam if answering a blind ad):

With the enclosed resume, I would like to make you aware of my education and experience related to law enforcement and human services. I offer a reputation as a compassionate, dedicated, and enthusiastic professional with a proven willingness to go the extra mile to achieve top-notch results.

Most recently I have served as a Juvenile Probation Officer for Dale County Youth Services in New York. In that position, I managed a caseload of over 100 active probationary juveniles, counseling them and their families and acting as liaison between my clients and local law enforcement, school systems, and other supporting agencies. I reported directly to the Chief Probation Officer, and I was being groomed to take over that position when my father passed away and I decided to return home to Arkansas to be with my mother.

With a Master's degree in Counseling and Psychology and a Bachelor of Science in Criminal Justice, I offer a solid educational background in addition to my years of experience. In previous positions, I have utilized my strong skills in youth counseling, patient evaluation and assessment, and substance abuse counseling. Though my main experience has been in providing crisis intervention, rehabilitation, and guidance to at-risk youth, I feel that my exceptional counseling skills and highly developed organizational, supervisory, and communication skills would be strong assets in any law enforcement environment.

If your organization can use the skills of an effective counselor and dedicated law enforcement professional, I hope you will contact me to suggest a time when we could meet to discuss your present and future needs and how I might serve them.

Sincerely,

Ebony Haigler

CC: Lorenzo McAlister

Semi-blocked Letter

Date
Three blank spaces

Address

Salutation
One blank space

Body

One blank space

Signature

cc: Indicates you are sending a copy of the letter to someone

Date

Exact Name of Person
Title or Position
Name of Company
Address (number and street)
Address (city, state, and zip)

Follow-up Letter

A great follow-up letter
can motivate the
employer
to make the job offer, and
the salary offer may be
influenced by the style
and tone of your follow-
up
letter, too!

Dear Exact Name:

I am writing to express my appreciation for the time you spent with me on 9 December, and I want to let you know that I am sincerely interested in the position of Corrections Officer which you described.

I feel confident that I could skillfully interact with your 60-person work force. I want you to know, too, that I would not consider relocating to Salt Lake City to be a hardship! It is certainly one of the most beautiful areas I have ever seen.

It would be a pleasure to work for a progressive prison system in a progressive state, and I feel I could contribute significantly to your organization not only through my corrections industry experience but also through my strong qualities of loyalty, reliability, and trustworthiness. I am confident that I could quickly become an asset to your prison system.

Yours sincerely,

Jacob Evangelisto

In this section, you will find resumes and cover letters of police, law enforcement, and security professionals—and of people who want to work in those fields. How do they differ from other job hunters? Why should there be a book dedicated to people seeking jobs in these areas? Based on more than 20 years of experience in working with job hunters, this editor is convinced that resumes and cover letters which "speak the lingo" of the field you wish to enter will communicate more effectively than language which is not industry specific. This book is designed to help people (1) who are seeking to prepare their own resumes and (2) who wish to use as models "real" resumes of individuals who have successfully launched careers in the police, law enforcement, or security field or who have advanced in the field. You will see a wide range of experience levels reflected in the resumes in this book. Some of the resumes and cover letters were used by individuals seeking to enter the field; others were used successfully by senior professionals to advance in the field.

Newcomers to an industry sometimes have advantages over more experienced professionals. In a job hunt, junior professionals can have an advantage over their more experienced counterparts. Prospective employers often view the less experienced workers as "more trainable" and "more coachable" than their seniors. This means that the mature professional who has already excelled in a first career can, with credibility, "change careers" and transfer skills to other industries.

Police, law enforcement, and security might be said to "talk funny." They talk in lingo specific to their field, and you will find helpful examples throughout this book.

Newcomers to the field may have disadvantages compared to their seniors. Almost by definition, the inexperienced professional—the young person who has recently earned a college degree, or the individual who has recently received certifications respected by the industry—is less tested and less experienced than senior managers, so the resume and cover letter of the inexperienced professional may often have to "sell" his or her potential to do something he or she has never done before. Lack of experience in the field she wants to enter can be a stumbling block to the junior manager, but remember that many employers believe that someone who has excelled in anything—academics, for example—can excel in many other fields.

Some advice to inexperienced professionals...
If senior professionals could give junior professionals a piece of advice about careers, here's what they would say: Manage your career and don't stumble from job to job in an incoherent pattern. Try to find work that interests you, and then identify prosperous industries which need work performed of the type you want to do. Learn early in your working life that a great resume and cover letter can blow doors open for you and help you maximize your salary.

Special help for career changers...
For those changing careers, you will find useful the resumes and cover letters marked "Career Change" on the following pages. Consult the Table of Contents for page numbers showing career changers.

Exact Name of Person
Title or Position
Name of Company
Address (no., street)
Address (city, state, zip)

**ADULT PAROLE SERVICES
CASE MANAGER**

Dear Exact Name of Person (or Dear Sir or Madam if answering a blind ad):

With the enclosed resume and this letter of introduction, I would like to begin the process of formally applying for the job you recently advertised as a program manager.

As I believe you will see from my resume, I offer the skills, experience, and personal qualities which you are seeking. Since graduating with my B.A. degree, I have excelled in what is generally considered one of the most high-stress jobs in the world: administering parole services. While handling a large caseload of 150 clients, I supervise a wide variety of parole conditions and assist people in finding employment, obtaining help for substance abuse problems, managing their personal affairs and finances, and generally reorganizing their lives in creative and productive ways. I believe my positive and cheerful attitude has been the key to my excelling in a profession known for its high "burnout" and turnover rate.

I have become skilled in finding creative solutions for difficult problems, and I can provide strong personal and professional references describing my character and professional abilities. Computer literate, I offer a reputation as a tactful and diplomatic communicator with excellent writing skills. I have become adept at working with law enforcement officials at all levels, from judges to police officers, while also performing liaison with attorneys, prison administrators, business managers and private sector employers, and federal/state assistance programs of every kind.

You would find me to be a warm and enthusiastic professional who offers an exceptionally creative approach to program/case management, office and operations administration, and law enforcement/community relations.

I hope you will write or call me soon to arrange a brief meeting at your convenience to discuss your current and future needs and how I might serve them. I feel certain I could become a valuable asset to your organization, and I would enjoy an opportunity to show you in person that I am the qualified individual you are seeking.

Yours sincerely,

Susan V. Runaround

SUSAN V. RUNAROUND

1110½ Hay Street, Fayetteville, NC 28305   •   preppub@aol.com   •   (910) 483-6611

OBJECTIVE   I want to contribute to an organization that can use an experienced administrator and program manager who offers proven decision-making and problem-solving skills along with a reputation as a resourceful, creative, well-organized professional with excellent written and oral communication skills.

EDUCATION   **Bachelor of Arts in Sociology** and **Business Administration**, Georgia State University, Mercer, GA, 1988. Have excelled in seminars and courses related to these and other areas:

case management	law enforcement administration
human resources administration	budget management
computer operations	effective counseling strategies
sexual harassment prevention	emergency first aid
management of sex offenders	alcohol and drug abuse prevention
adolescent counseling/crisis intervention	schizophrenia
impact of child abuse	advanced probation and parole
substance abuse counseling	family therapy/family counseling

Completed extensive training at the GA Justice Academy, Macon, GA.

EXPERIENCE   *Have become known for my ability to communicate well with others and to assist others in developing realistic strategies for solving their life problems, finding suitable employment, developing career goals, and becoming productive members of society:*

ADULT PAROLE SERVICES CASE MANAGER. Department of Corrections, Atlanta, GA (2000-present). Am extremely knowledgeable of how to network and "get things done" within the legal, law enforcement, business, and social services communities and apply that knowledge while managing a caseload of 150 clients comprised of offenders released from prison by the Parole Commission.

*   Assist parolees in all aspects of life management including seeking help for substance abuse problems, prospecting for and obtaining suitable employment, managing personal finances as well as personal relationships, and generally finding a "focus" in life that is meaningful and motivating.
*   Work with law enforcement officials at all levels, from judges to police officers, while also performing liaison with attorneys, prison administrators, business managers and employers in the private sector, and federal assistance programs of every kind.

ADULT PROBATION SERVICES CASE MANAGER. Department of Corrections, Macon, GA (1989-00). Became skilled in the counseling and supervision of offenders placed on probation by the court system; enforced conditions of parole.

*   Established an impressive track record of success in assisting dysfunctional people in becoming well adjusted, contributing members of society.

CERTIFICATIONS   Am Department of Corrections certified in unarmed self defense.
Am CPR certified. Certified in Arrest, Search, and Seizure.

SKILLS   Am computer literate and experienced in working with various types of software.
Am skilled in operating electronic house arrest equipment.

PERSONAL   Pride myself on my positive and cheerful attitude, and believe that a healthy mental attitude is the key to dealing with life's difficulties in a positive manner. Am respected for my ability to deal with emergencies in a prudent fashion. Excellent references.

CAREER CHANGE

Date

Exact Name of Person
Exact Title
Exact Name of Company
Address
City, State, Zip

**BICYCLE
PATROL OFFICER**

Dear Exact Name of Person (or Dear Sir or Madam if answering a blind ad):

With the enclosed resume, I would like to make you aware of my interest in exploring employment opportunities with your organization. I am particularly interested in your advertisement for a Claims Representative, as my background and skills seem tailor-made to your needs.

As you will see from my resume, I offer strong oral and written communication skills along with experience in solving problems in law enforcement environments. After graduating with a B.A. in Criminal Justice and Society, I worked for three years as a Real Estate Agent and made significant contributions to the profitability of a family-owned business which specialized in real estate sales, new home construction, and pre-owned car sales. In that position I became skilled at estimating property damage and negotiating costs of repairs and maintenance.

Subsequently I accepted a position in the District Attorney's Office as a Victim and Witness Legal Assistant. While excelling in that position, I went to school at night to complete my Law Enforcement Certificate. After becoming a certified law enforcement officer in the State of Vermont, I became a Patrol Officer with the Montpellier. I have established an outstanding reputation within the law enforcement community and court system, and I served with distinction as Chairperson of the Juvenile Crime Prevention Council. I was elected to that position by an organization comprised of judges, a police chief, representatives from the District Attorney's office, and other key organizations.

I am attracted to your organization because I feel that my strong analytical skills and problem-solving abilities would be a good fit with your needs. I offer highly refined negotiating skills along with a proven ability to work with disputing parties in order to form a consensus. I feel certain that I could enhance your organization through my versatile investigative and communication skills, and I can assure you that I can provide outstanding personal and professional references.

If my background and skills interest you, I hope you will contact me to suggest a time when we could meet in person to discuss your needs. Thank you.

Yours sincerely,

Cameron Dias

CAMERON DIAS

1110½ Hay Street, Fayetteville, VT 28305 • preppub@aol.com • (910) 483-6611

OBJECTIVE

I want to contribute to an organization that can use a versatile professional who offers strong analytical, investigative, negotiating, and problem-solving skills which have been refined through experience in the law enforcement community as well as in the private sector.

EDUCATION

Bachelor of Arts (B.A.) degree in Criminal Justice and Society, UVT at Montpellier, VT, 1994.
Earned Law Enforcement Certificate, Carson Community College, Carson, VT, 1997.
Completed this training at night while working full-time in the District Attorney's office.
Courses included:

Basic Law Enforcement Training	Evidence Collection & Chain of Custody
Domestic Violence Intervention	DMV Report Writing
Juvenile Justice Reform	Consent and Plain View Search
Interrogation Law and Techniques	Structured Sentencing
Report Writing for Patrol Personnel	Criminal Street Gangs
OC Pepper Spray Certification	

LICENSES & CERTIFICATIONS

Certified Law Enforcement officer in Vermont. Mobile Data Terminal Certified. VT State Bureau of Investigation Certified on Module 1-4.

HONORS

Elected **Chairperson,** Juvenile Crime Prevention Council, 2002-2003. This is a state-mandated council with 25 members who include district court judges, the city's police chief, representatives from the District Attorney's office, and other organizations.
Served as **Security Chairperson,** American Cancer Society fundraiser, 2002.

EXPERIENCE

BICYCLE PATROL OFFICER. City of Montpellier, Montpellier, VT (2001-present). Enforced state laws and city ordinances while also serving warrants and other court papers, testifying in court, and working with a wide range of community groups and human services organizations.

- Continuously maintained surveillance related to gang violence and possible criminal behavior; played a role in reducing gang violence. Was involved in drug intervention.
- At numerous crime scenes, collected evidence and assisted crime victims.
- Have become skilled at communicating with people at all socio-economic levels, and have learned the "art" of effectively integrating into any group; have learned how to blend in and communicate effectively in drug-infested neighborhoods, and am equally comfortable dealing with business executives and operating in formal situations.

VICTIM & WITNESS LEGAL ASSISTANT. State of Vermont, District Attorney's Office, Montpellier, VT (1997-00). Became knowledgeable of how the court system operates, and established strong working relationships with law enforcement officials throughout the state of Vermont.

- Assisted Assistant District Attorneys by preparing Superior Court files.
- Refined my research and analytical skills while preparing criminal histories.
- Computed structured sentencing for District and Superior court judges.

REAL ESTATE AGENT. ReMax Real Estate of Vermont, Montpellier, VT (1994-97). Refined my skills in working with the public while working for a diversified company involved in selling residential real estate, building new homes, and selling used cars.

PERSONAL

Excellent references on request. Computer skills include Word and Excel.

Date

Mr. David Frizelle
Personnel Director
City of Monterey
City Square, Suite 110
Monterey, CA 87098

**CAPTAIN, PATROL
SUPPORT DIVISION**

Dear Mr. Frizelle:

With the enclosed resume, I would like to formally initiate the process of becoming considered for the job of Chief of Police for the City of Monterey.

As you will see from my resume, I am currently serving the Los Angeles Police Department as a Police Captain in charge of one of the city's Patrol Divisions. As one of the department's Captains, I have transformed the city's newest Patrol Division into a highly respected and productive operating unit known for the high morale and productivity of its 192 personnel.

In previous jobs with the City of Los Angeles, I performed with distinction as Lieutenant in charge of both the Major Crimes Investigative Division and Emergency Operations. I began working for the City of Los Angeles as a Patrol Officer in 1978 after serving my country briefly in the U.S. Army as a Military Policeman. I have enjoyed a track record of promotion because of my hard work and common sense, my outstanding police work in all functional areas, as well as my excellent administrative skills and ability to deal articulately and tactfully with everyone, from employees to citizens' groups.

I can provide outstanding references at the appropriate time, and I can assure you that you would find me to be an individual who is known as a gifted strategic thinker, powerful motivator, and fair supervisor.

Please contact me if you would like me to make myself available for a personal interview at your convenience. Although I am held in high regard within the Los Angeles Police Department, I have a strong interest in exploring ways in which my leadership ability and extensive experience in all aspects of police work could be put to use for the City of Monterey as its Chief of Police.

Sincerely,

Daniel W. Miller

DANIEL W. MILLER

1110½ Hay Street, Fayetteville, NC 28305 • preppub@aol.com • (910) 483-6611

OBJECTIVE   I want to contribute to your city as its Chief of Police through my experience in all aspects of police operations as well as through my outstanding community relations skills, administrative abilities, and highly respected personal and professional style.

EXPERIENCE   *Have excelled in this track record of promotion to increasing responsibilities within the Los Angeles Police Department, Los Angeles, CA:*
POLICE CAPTAIN, PATROL SUPPORT DIVISION. (July 2000-present). In July 2000, was assigned to command the Patrol Support Division and the Police Sub-Station.
- In addition to motivating, supervising and evaluating a 192-person division comprised of Lieutenants, Sergeants, and Officers, skillfully handle a wide range of administrative responsibilities ranging from strategic planning to statistical analysis.
- Develop the overall budget for the Division and Sub-Station.
- Have made vast improvements in all areas under my management including the Traffic Section, Neighborhood Improvement Team, Housing Officers (Safe Streets Program), School Resource Officers, Mounted Police Unit, and Park Unit.

POLICE CAPTAIN, PATROL. (1996-2000). In 1996, was promoted to the rank of Captain and became one of the six Captains in this 420-person police department; was placed in charge of the newly formed 3rd Patrol Division and transformed the division's employees into a highly respected and productive operating unit.
- Motivated, supervised, and evaluated a 62-person division comprised of Lieutenants, Sergeants, and Officers.
- Developed portions of the overall annual budget and controlled budgeted expenses.

LIEUTENANT, MAJOR CRIMES INVESTIGATIVE DIVISION. (1995-96). While still serving in 1995 as Lieutenant in charge of Emergency Operations, was selected to take over as Lieutenant of the Major Crimes Investigative Division with nine Officers and one Sergeant.
- Provided leadership to a division in charge of investigating robberies and homicides; we had 100% clearance in homicides and an 84% clearance in robbery cases.

LIEUTENANT, EMERGENCY OPERATIONS. (1993-95). Commanded operations of the department's S.W.A.T. Team and Narcotic Vice Task Force; earned widespread respect for my work in revitalizing this area of police operations; took over a team which had made 200 felony arrests in 1993; led the team to make 365 felony arrests in only four months in 1994.

Highlights of other experience within the Los Angeles Police Department:
- **Unit Supervisor, Major Crimes Investigative Division.** (1990-92). As Sergeant of Police, supervised nine Investigators assigned to Crimes Against Persons and Property and was credited with producing an unusually high arrest rate.
- **Platoon Sergeant, Patrol Division.** (1985-90). Supervised 15 Officers while assigning patrol cases, evaluating effectiveness of divisional operations, and acting as Patrol Supervisor.
- **Sergeant of Police, Street Crimes Unit.** (1984-85). Planned and coordinated unit operations while supervising five Officers; also worked on active investigations.
- **Investigator, Street Crimes Unit.** (1982-84). Handled a wide range of duties as an Investigator related to vice, narcotics, drug operations, and intelligence gathering.
- **Field Training Officer.** (1980-82). Handled general patrol work as well as the training of newly appointed Police Officers; acted as supervisor in the absence of the Shift Supervisor.
- **Patrol Officer.** (1978-80). Performed with distinction all duties of a Patrol Officer.

EDUCATION   **B.S. degree in Political Science**, Los Angeles State University, LA, CA, 1985.
A.S. degree in Criminal Justice, Monterey Community College, Monterey, CA, 1983.
Hold Advanced, Intermediate, and Basic Law Enforcement Certificates.

Date

Exact Name of Person
Exact Title
Exact Name of Company
Address
City, State, Zip

CHIEF OF POLICE   Dear Exact Name of Person (or Dear Sir or Madam if answering a blind ad):

With the enclosed resume, I would like to make you aware of my interest in exploring employment opportunities with your organization.

As you will see from my enclosed resume, I am currently excelling as Chief of Police with a 450,000-person community near Chicago, IL. I have advanced to the Chief job in a track record of promotion which has included serving with distinction as a Patrol Officer, Detective, Special Agent, Detective Division Sergeant, Patrol Division Watch Commander, and then Deputy Chief of Police. I am held in the highest regard in the community and within the law enforcement community. I have served as President of the District Chiefs of Police Association, and I have been elected to community leadership roles which include serving on the executive board of the city's computer dispatching center that serves multiple fire departments and police departments. While managing a $2 million budget and 68 individuals, I have written grants that obtained $3 million in funds for modernizing the department, and I have provided leadership in developing new programs for teens, seniors, and others.

Although I am held in the highest regard in my current position, I am ready for a new challenge, and I am selectively exploring opportunities with organizations which can utilize a resourceful leader with strong programming skills as well as international project management experience.

If you feel you could use my creative programming ability, leadership skills, and expertise related to security and law enforcement, please contact me to suggest a time when we might meet in person to discuss your needs. I am available for worldwide relocation and/or extensive travel as your needs require.

Sincerely,

Kevin Q. Jackson

KEVIN Q. JACKSON

1110½ Hay Street, Fayetteville, NC 28305   •   preppub@aol.com   •   (910) 483-6611

OBJECTIVE To contribute to an organization that can use a seasoned law enforcement executive with strong public relations, program development, management, and communication skills.

EDUCATION **Bachelor of Science (B.S.) degree in Criminal Justice,** Chicago University, 1988. Extensive police and law enforcement training sponsored by the University of Illinois, University of Louisville, Northwestern University, U.S. Dept. of Justice, the International Association of Chiefs of Police, and others.
Training related to management, hazardous materials handling, narcotics, criminal investigation, successful grant writing, counterterrorism, and personnel supervision.

HONORS & AWARDS Humanitarian Service Award, 2002
Presidential Award from President of U.S., 2002
Elected President, 8th District Chiefs of Police Association, 1999
Special Community Service Award, Chamber of Commerce, 1999
Kuwait Liberation Medal, Bronze Star, Southwest Asia Medal, 1995 and 1994, for service
    during Desert Storm/Desert Shield, 1995
FBI Commendations for arrests in kidnapping and hostage situations, 1993
Named Officer of the Year, 1985
Numerous letters of commendation and Police Commendations for law enforcement skill
Numerous badges, medals, and ribbons recognizing distinguished military service

EXPERIENCE **CHIEF OF POLICE.** City of Rutledge, IL (1992-present). Began as Deputy Chief of Police in 1992 and was promoted to Chief in 1995; have gained a reputation as an innovator and articulate advocate of programs designed to enhance efficiency and meet the needs of various segments of the population in this 450,000-person community.
*   **Departmental management and leadership:** Manage a $2 million budget and a 68-person police force; provided the leadership needed to modernize the department—computerized operations and developed a system for wireless computers in squad cars which allows officers to prepare reports and obtain data in their cars.
*   **Communication and negotiation:** Negotiated with the Illinois House of Representatives for $3 million in funding used for modernization; wrote several successful federal and state grants for improvements to police equipment.
*   **Program development:** Developed new programs including a Senior Citizens Program.
*   **Community leadership:** Was elected to serve on the executive board of the city's computerized Dispatching Center which serves 10 police departments and 10 fire departments as well as a population of one-quarter million people.

Prior positions in the City of Rutledge:
PATROL DIVISION WATCH COMMANDER. Managed uniformed patrol functions on various shifts.
DETECTIVE DIVISION SERGEANT. Supervised four detectives and one police psychologist.
SPECIAL AGENT & UNDERCOVER NARCOTICS AGENT. Investigated the sale of controlled substances, the infiltration of motorcycle gangs, and underworld criminal organizations engaged in the sale of large quantities of narcotics.
DETECTIVE. Investigated crimes, controlled crime scenes, initiated crime prevention programs, acted as body guard, and participated in stakeouts.

PERSONAL Highly motivated individual with outstanding character. Excellent references on request.

Exact Name of Person
Title or Position
Name of Company
Address (number and street)
Address (city, state, and zip)

CID INVESTIGATOR

Dear Exact Name of Person (or Sir or Madam if answering a blind ad):

I would appreciate an opportunity to talk with you soon about how I could contribute to your organization through my versatile experience in law enforcement and security operations as well as my technical electronics skills.

With an eye for detail and ability to quickly learn, absorb, and apply new ideas and concepts, I offer a reputation as a professional who can be depended on for personal integrity, resourcefulness, and dedication to excellence in everything I attempt.

You will see on my enclosed resume a track record of accomplishments in positions including criminal investigation, technical communications, police work, and as a member of the elite U.S. Marine embassy guards. I have consistently been described as an intelligent, articulate professional with a talent for responsiveness to change, the ability to handle pressure and deadlines, and the adaptability to fit into any situation that arises.

My background has allowed me opportunities to work in international settings where sound judgment and common sense were necessary to handle dangerous situations in high-visibility settings such as while providing security for the 1988 Olympics in Seoul, Korea, and in American embassies in Pakistan and Guatemala.

During my career in the U.S. Marine Corps I have been recognized with numerous certificates of achievement and certificates of accomplishment as well as with an Army Achievement Medal for my contributions to a mobile maintenance team in Haiti and two Meritorious Unit Commendations.

I hope you will welcome my call soon to arrange a brief meeting to discuss your current and future needs and how I might serve them. Thank you in advance for your time.

Sincerely,

Bruce M. Allstone

Alternate last paragraph:
I hope you will call or write me soon to suggest a time convenient for us to meet and discuss your current and future needs and how I might serve them. Thank you in advance for your time.

BRUCE M. ALLSTONE

1110½ Hay Street, Fayetteville, NC 28305   •   preppub@aol.com   •   (910) 483-6611

OBJECTIVE   To offer my versatile experience in law enforcement and security as well as technical electronics operations to an organization that can use a talented and articulate leader.

EXPERIENCE   **CID INVESTIGATOR.** U.S. Government, locations throughout the U.S. (2000-present). Utilized my law enforcement training and experience while conducting criminal investigations in an on-the-job training program for Special Agents in all 50 states.
- Earned a certificate of appreciation for assisting in a hostage rescue situation.

POLICE OFFICER. Richmond County, VA (1995-2000). Worked independently while patrolling one of seven districts in the department's jurisdiction.
- Mastered the use of a number of standard weapons and was selected to assist in training other police officers in their use and safety procedures.
- Displayed maturity, analytical skills, and common sense needed in this volatile law enforcement situation where decisions had to be made regarding the use of deadly force.
- Was handpicked for this critical career path from among a large number of volunteers and survived a rigorous screening and training process.

EMBASSY GUARD. U.S. Marines, Islamabad, Pakistan; and Guatemala City, Guatemala (1990-94). Earned a reputation as a responsible professional with a high degree of personal initiative and respect for others in these high-visibility positions which called for tact and sound judgment while protecting American government personnel and property as well as the security of classified material dealing with national security issues.
- Contributed time and efforts controlling and maintaining 11 vehicles and a large inventory of communications-electronics equipment and repair parts.
- Worked long hours as a member of a mobile maintenance team repairing and maintaining this equipment in support of engineering activities in Haiti.
- Was singled out for recognition for my technical skills, attention to detail, and leadership which allowed the unit to earn high ratings in an external evaluation.
- Cited for my responsiveness to changing circumstances, maintained tight perimeter security and force protection during an annual evaluation.

CLEARANCE   Entrusted with a Top Secret security clearance as a Marine Embassy Guard.

SPECIAL SKILLS   Offer specialized skills and knowledge which includes the following:
communications electronics: troubleshoot and repair to the component level computer systems and electromechanical devices with analog and digital circuitry systems include KY-57/58, KG-84, and KG-94/94A
security and law enforcement: counterterrorism, reconnaissance, surveillance, VIP protection, and industrial security
weapons: Smith and Wesson .357 magnum revolver, Remington 870 shotgun, Uzi 9mm submachine gun, and Ruger Mini-14 5.56 rifle
other: self defense, riot control, and PR-24 nightstick

EDUCATION   Completed 93 credit hours, Virginia Western Community College, Roanoke, VA.
& TRAINING   Received U.S. Marine Corps training in communications center operations, radio fundamentals, professional leadership development, the Marine Security Guard School, drill/ ceremonies/inspections/customs/courtesy, administrative planning, instructions techniques.

PERSONAL   Versatile and adaptable individual. Reputation for being able to get along well with others.

Date

Exact Name of Person
Title or Position
Name of Company
Address (number and street)
Address (city, state, and ZIP)

COAST GUARD MANAGER

Dear Exact Name of Person (or Dear Sir or Madam if answering a blind ad):

I would appreciate an opportunity to talk with you soon about how I could contribute to your organization through my versatile background gained while serving in the U.S. Coast Guard where I have earned a reputation as a total professional who can be counted on to accomplish the job no matter how difficult or hazardous.

As you will see from my enclosed resume, I possess a vast amount of experience in managing a variety of activities in the marine transportation field. With close to 20 years of experience I of course am accustomed to doing tasks at sea or around water and can work harmoniously in jobs requiring frequent contact with Coast Guard personnel. I am qualified as a Master for 500 GT near-coastal vessels and as an able-bodied seaman and lifeboatman.

With my law enforcement background and extensive experience in teaching law enforcement and boarding procedures to people of 31 different foreign countries, I am confident of my ability to communicate with people of other nations. I have earned a reputation as a tactful and diplomatic professional who approaches every assignment with enthusiasm and the determination to succeed.

I am a very dedicated hard-working professional who can be counted on to find ways to ensure that equipment is available when needed, personnel trained and performing at high levels of competence, and that multitasked operations are coordinated smoothly.

I hope you will call or write me soon to suggest a time convenient for us to meet and discuss your current and future needs and how I might serve them. Thank you in advance for your time.

Sincerely yours,

Clive B. Avalon

Alternate last paragraph:
I hope you will welcome my call soon to suggest a time convenient for us to meet and discuss your current and future needs and how I might serve them. Thank you in advance for your time.

CLIVE B. AVALON

1110½ Hay Street, Fayetteville, NC 28305 • preppub@aol.com • (910) 483-6611

OBJECTIVE

To offer my expertise related to marine operations to an organization that can benefit from my knowledge of navigation, security and law enforcement, and resource management as well as my superior communication skills and experience in international settings.

EXPERIENCE

Earned a reputation as a talented and diplomatic professional while building a track record of success in training, instructional, and managerial roles with the U.S. Coast Guard:

GENERAL MANAGER. Yankeetown, FL (2000-present). Direct all activities in a remote location conducting approximately 300 search-and-rescue operations and 400 law enforcement boardings annually along a 170-mile coastline.
- Manage a four-boat facility with millions of dollars worth of land and buildings, an $80,000 annual operating budget, and an average strength of 26 people.
- Trained and integrated approximately 400 Coast Guard Auxiliary members into activities.
- Deal directly with federal, state, and local law enforcement, hazardous waste, and public relations personnel as senior Coast Guard representative.

LAW ENFORCEMENT INSTRUCTOR. Yorktown, VA (1993-00). Received numerous medals and commendations for my expertise: assigned as a resident instructor, after one year transferred to international operations and traveled extensively in South and Central America to provide training for foreign naval, police, and customs personnel.
- Led teams during overseas assignments including two high-risk trips to El Salvador.
- Graduated more than 1,800 foreign students in 31 countries; represented the Coast Guard during the first multiagency law enforcement training in Chile in over 20 years.
- Provided training on hidden compartments which led to six narcotics seizures.
- Earned praise from high-level officials for expertise in instructing 23 Navy boarding teams which significantly contributed to the embargo of Iraq during the Middle East war.

MAINTENANCE SUPERVISOR. Rockaway, NY (1991-93). As third-in-command of a New York Harbor-area facility, directed station and maintenance activities while conducting search-and-rescue and law enforcement training.
- Refined supervisory and managerial abilities as well as navigational skills.

STATION MANAGER. San Diego, CA (1985-90). Honored with a commendation award for accomplishments in my first assignment managing a station, supervised six people who achieved outstanding results and increased morale despite being in an isolated facility.
- Was handpicked for special assignments in the Caribbean on the basis of my Spanish-speaking skills and experience as a law enforcement boarding officer.

EDUCATION

A.A. in Spanish, California State College, San Diego, CA, 1990.
Completed the U.S. Coast Guard Senior Enlisted Academy, Petaluma, CA, 1994.

SKILLS

Through training and experience, have become knowledgeable and qualified in these areas:
Master for 500 GT near-coastal vessels   federal law enforcement officer
able-bodied seaman and lifeboatman   classified materials handler
supervisor for law enforcement planning, operations, and logistics support
FBI use-of-force policies: application and training others OIC of multimission stations
law enforcement instructor for international and domestic procedures
weapons: M-60 machine gun, M-16 rifle, riot shotgun, 9 mm pistol, and .45 caliber pistol

PERSONAL

Currently hold a Secret security clearance. Fluent in Spanish, speak some Portuguese.

Exact Name of Person
Exact Title
Exact Name of Company
Address
City, State, Zip

CORRECTIONAL OFFICER

Dear Exact Name of Person (or Dear Sir or Madam if answering a blind ad):

With the enclosed resume, I would like to make you aware of my exceptional supervisory, communication, and organizational skills, as well as my background in corrections, automation security, and personal and property accountability.

As a Corrections Officer for Hoke Correctional Institution, I am responsible for the security and supervision of 140 inmates. I conduct visual, audio, and video surveillance of the facility and search all vehicles entering and leaving the facility to ensure that no personnel, weapons, drugs, or other contraband are smuggled into or out of the institution.

In my previous position as Customer Service Representative for TASCOR (IBM), I handled all drug screenings for IBM personnel worldwide, coordinating with drug-screening agencies to schedule testing and verifying that all personnel have taken the prescribed tests. As Postal Operations Manager in Korea, I worked with Korean customs agents to detect illegal shipments of drugs, weapons, ammunition, and other contraband coming into and out of the country.

While serving at Fort Stewart as Information Systems Operations Supervisor, I completed the rigorous U.S. Army Logistics Security course and established and trained a reaction force to meet the growing threat of terrorism. In addition, I served as Automated Data Processing Systems Security Officer, and have excelled in numerous military training programs having to do with security procedures, criminal investigation methods, special operations, and other security-related issues.

If you can use an experienced and self-motivated security and corrections professional, I look forward to hearing from you soon to arrange a time when we might meet to discuss your present and future needs, and how I might meet them. I assure you that I have an excellent reputation, and would quickly become an asset to your organization.

Sincerely,

Matthew Frinak

MATTHEW FRINAK

1110½ Hay Street, Fayetteville, NC 28305   •   preppub@aol.com   •   (910) 483-6611

OBJECTIVE

To offer expertise in human and material resources management to an organization that can use a skilled professional with a proven background of success in the areas of personnel and property accountability as well as automation security, budgeting, office management, and data processing operations.

EDUCATION

Attended Hillsborough Technical Community College, Hillsborough, AL, in a Digital Electronic Repair Technician program.

Completed college-level studies in Human Resources Management and Business Administration.

EXPERIENCE

CORRECTIONAL OFFICER. Hoke Correctional Institution, Raeford, AL (2001-present). Provide security and inmate control in this busy prison environment. Responsible for the security and supervision of 140 inmates.

- Operate security towers, conducting visual surveillance and searching all vehicles and personnel entering and leaving the premises to ensure that no personnel, weapons, drugs, or other contraband are smuggled into or out of the facility.
- Proficient in techniques of unarmed self-defense and defensive shooting. Familiar with prison security functions and procedures, as well as the operation of audio and visual security devices.
- Transport prisoners to and from the center in authorized prison vehicles.
- Search prisoners and prison property for contraband, using various search techniques.
- Wrote incident reports for detailing all actions involving altercations or problems with inmates. Certified in adult CPR.

CUSTOMER SERVICE REPRESENTATIVE (ADMIN). TASCOR (IBM), Morrisville, AL (1997-2001). Handled all drug screenings for IBM personnel worldwide, including coordinating with drug testing agencies to schedule testing and verifying that all personnel have taken the proper prescribed tests.

- Ensure proper documentation is received with specimens that appear to be inaccurate in order to properly perform final analysis to clear personnel for drug screenings.
- Determine inconsistencies between proclaimed drug intake and formal drug screening reports to make recommendations to medical staff or human resources department.
- Perform a variety of administrative functions including data entry to create or update medical files, file and post medical records, and correspond through e-mail.

Highlights of military experience: was consistently selected for positions normally held by higher-ranking personnel including commissioned officers as a First Sergeant, U.S. Army:
PERSONNEL AND ADMINISTRATION CENTER SUPERVISOR. Hunter AFB, GA; Saudi Arabia; and Ft. Benning, GA (1994-96). Supervised a 15-person staff during a period of severe change and stress due to the war in the Middle East: consolidated my center's activities with those of another similar center to provide support in preparation for war and the period of readjustment afterwards.

SUPERVISOR, INFORMATION SYSTEMS OPERATIONS. Ft. Stewart, GA (1989-94). Supervised 40 employees who controlled the flow of data for personnel strength accounting and maintained the data base and systems which supported this constant flow of information.

- Established and trained a reaction force to meet the growing threat of terrorism.

PERSONAL

Am accustomed to working long hours under tight time constraints.

Date

Exact Name of Person
Exact Title
Exact Name of Company
Address
City, State, Zip

CORRECTIONAL OFFICER   Dear Exact Name of Person (or Dear Sir or Madam if answering a blind ad):

With the enclosed resume, I would like to make you aware of my skills related to law enforcement, management, and computer operations. I would also like to express my interest in exploring employment opportunities with your organization.

Prior to my current position as a Correctional Officer, I excelled as a Police Officer with the U.S. Army and as a Police Cadet with the City of Montgomery. I hold an Associate's degree in Criminal Justice and have completed numerous training programs related to weapons use, anti-terrorism, and other areas. I am certified in CPR and First Aid.

My management and communication skills have been refined in several positions which I have held. In one job as a Police Officer, I supervised and trained ten personnel. You will notice that I offer strong computer skills. I am proficient with Windows and I am knowledgeable of Excel, Access, and Microsoft Word. I type 60 wpm.

If you can use a versatile hard worker who can provide excellent personal and professional references, I hope you will contact me to suggest a time when we might meet to discuss your needs.

Sincerely,

Gabriel Reece

GABRIEL REECE

1110½ Hay Street, Fayetteville, NC 28305   •   preppub@aol.com   •   (910) 483-6611

OBJECTIVE

I want to contribute to an organization that can use a dedicated and versatile professional with extensive knowledge related to criminal justice, law enforcement, and corrections as well as management, public relations, and customer service.

EDUCATION

Completing **Bachelor of Science** degree in Criminal Justice, Montgomery State University (a campus of the University of Alabama), Montgomery, AL.
*   Completed additional courses in Psychology and Business at other colleges.

Received **Associate of Science** in Criminal Justice, Cape Fear Community College, Montgomery, AL, 1991.
*   Earned this degree in my spare time while working full-time as a Police Cadet.

As a police officer, completed courses and training programs including these:

Street survival seminar	Terrorist and gang awareness training
Hand and arm combat	Weapons qualification: 9mm, M16, M60, 50cal
Stress management	Driver's testing including weather training
Combat driving	Anti-mine awareness training

Received **Expert Marksmanship Badge** (Rifle M-16 and 9mm); certified in CPR, First Aid.

COMPUTERS

Proficient with Windows, NT, Lotus 1-2-3, Word Perfect, Microsoft Word, Excel, Access; type 60 wpm.

EXPERIENCE

CORRECTIONAL OFFICER. Alabama Department of Corrections, facilities in Whiteville and Hoke County, AL (2001-present). Ensured security of employees and staff in this facility housing 125 inmates; performed rounds, on foot and during vehicular patrols; utilized radios for communication, and manipulated various chemical munitions, weapons, and equipment.

POLICE OFFICER. U.S. Army, Germany (1998-2000). Supervised and trained 10 people while enforcing laws established by the U.S. Army; assisted the public and wrote reports documenting incidents; counseled military professionals and their families.
*   In my leisure time, worked part-time as a **MARTIAL ARTS INSTRUCTOR** and **AEROBICS INSTRUCTOR.** Instructed students in performing basic and proper stretches, steps, and other aerobic movements; established creative class formats, choreographed aerobic routines, and taught dieting.

POLICE OFFICER. U.S. Army, Ft. Lewis, WA (1996-1998). Supervised two personnel while performing law enforcement duties such as routine patrols, investigations, interviews, and interrogations; wrote reports and maintained records.

POLICE OFFICER. U.S. Army, Ft. Ord, CA (1992-1995). Supervised and trained four personnel in Joint Security Intrusion Detection System for Post Installation; provided computer training, maintained criminal records, and performed law enforcement duties.

POLICE CADET. Montgomery, AL (1990-91). Assisted the public in obtaining information, and assisted police officers in CID with mug shots and photo album upkeep.
*   Resigned from this position in order to attend college full-time to complete my degree.

PERSONAL

Secret Clearance. Excellent communication, problem-solving, and decision-making skills. Received nine medals and ribbons for exceptional performance in military service.

MARSHALL ARTS

1110½ Hay Street, Fayetteville, NC 28305   •   preppub@aol.com   •   (910) 483-6611

CORRECTIONS OFFICER

Here's an example of a two-page resume. The cover letter that accompanied this resume was similar to the cover letters on the preceding pages.

OBJECTIVE

To offer my well-developed skills in planning and implementing projects, communicating with and motivating others, and my special skills in law enforcement and security to an organization that can benefit from my weapons expertise and instructional abilities.

SPECIAL SKILLS

Am certified as a *Firearms Training Officer* by the Rhode Island Department of Corrections, and offer skills and knowledge related to activities, equipment, and systems including the following:
Qualified as Expert with the M-4 and M-16 rifle as well as the .45 and .38 caliber pistols and 9 mm pistol
Providing instruction in weapons handling, deployment, proper care, and maintenance, Counterterrorism, reconnaissance, surveillance, direct actions, counterdrug, VIP protection, foreign internal defense, and the establishment of police forces in other countries
Recruiting, training, organizing, advising, and supervising indigenous forces in the use of communications equipment as well as heavy, light, and special weapons and tactics
Installing, operating, and maintaining AM, FM, UHF, and SHF satellite communications equipment
Transmitting and receiving radio messages in voice, CW, and burst on a wide variety of radio frequencies to include secure and remote equipment
Languages: Speak, read, and write French; speak and comprehend German
Clearance: Hold a Secret security clearance with NSA

EXPERIENCE

CORRECTIONS OFFICER. Department of Corrections, Cranston, RI (2001-present). Refined the ability to develop mutual respect and deal with violent and disturbed people; ensured the security, custody, and control of a 500-person inmate population while personally supervising from two to 99 inmates.
- Became adept at surviving in an environment which required the ability to react quickly, make sound decisions, and remain in control under often hostile conditions.

Earned a reputation as a natural leader and skilled supervisor in the Special Forces community with the U.S. Army, Ft. Campbell, KY:
WEAPONS AND COMMUNICATIONS SPECIALIST/TEAM LEADER. (1999-2001). Handled often-simultaneous responsibilities in roles including the following:

WEAPONS AND TACTICS SPECIALIST. (1998-99). Recognized as a subject matter expert, advised a Special Forces "A" Team commander on weapons placement/tactics while refining my talents as an instructor.

COMMUNICATIONS SPECIALIST. (1996-98). Advised an "A" Team commander on the use of high-tech radio equipment and on how it could be used most effectively in a given area of operations; used Morse code to send and receive messages.

TEAM LEADER. (1995). Supervised the performance and training of a 12-person Special Forces team involved in unconventional real-world activities.
- Increased leadership skills by deciding when to take charge and when to delegate.

MILITARY POLICE OFFICER. Providence, RI (1988-94). As a team leader, supported military combat operations as well as supervising employees involved in providing security and law enforcement support for facilities as well as human and material resources.
- Was singled out for my compassion and professionalism while assisting at an area Mental Health and Retardation Center during a strike by center employees.

SUPERVISOR & TEAM LEADER. Ft. Bragg, NC (1987-88). Trained and supervised a four-person reconnaissance vehicle (Sheridan tank) crew who consistently earned the highest possible scores in evaluations of their professional skills.
- Was selected as **"1987 Regimental Non-Commissioned Officer of the Year."**

Highlights of earlier experience: Was the recipient of two Army Achievement Medals in recognition of my determination to excel and my enthusiastic approach which directly impacted on my unit's ability to pass important inspections and earn distinctions.

TRAINING   Studied Law, Criminal Justice, and Business at the college level.
Completed extensive military training in military police procedures as well as in Special Forces communications and weapons systems.
Attended Rhode Island Department of Corrections training including the Firearms Instructor Course on teaching people to use firearms safely and an instruction techniques course.

PERSONAL   Am confident of my abilities and talents. Can handle pressure and tough situations. Enjoy teaching others to safely use and maintain firearms. Will provide excellent references.

SUSAN MCDOUGAL

1110½ Hay Street, Fayetteville, NC 28305 • preppub@aol.com • (910) 483-6611

CORRECTIONS OFFICER

Here is another example of a two-page resume. Be assured that this individual used a cover letter similar to the ones on the preceding pages which accompanied the resumes of other corrections officers.

OBJECTIVE

To benefit an organization that can use an educated and experienced security professional with outstanding technical skills, a Master's degree in Security Management, along with practical experience as a corrections officer known for excellent judgment and the ability to make decisions under pressure.

EDUCATION

Master's degree in Security Management, Webster University. Pope AFB Campus, 2002.
Performed a Risk Analysis of a local business which was voted on by the Board of Directors and incorporated into the company's security policy; received an "A" on the assignment.
Bachelor of Science degree in Business Administration, with a concentration in Accounting, Hawaii Pacific University, Honolulu, HI, 1998.

CERTIFICATIONS

Earned a Disturbance Control Instructor certification through the Federal Law Enforcement Training Center, 2001.
Certified by Mace Laboratory, Inc. in the use of Oleoresin Capsicum (Pepper Spray).

CLEARANCE

Top Secret security clearance; background investigation by OPM.

TRAINING

Completed the Correctional Officer Academy, San Jose City College, San Jose, CA, 1993.
Weapons: Qualified on M-16, .38 revolver, .9 mm, 12-gauge shotgun.
Self-Defense: Koga and Aikido; 80 hours of training completed.
Crime Scene Investigations: Completed training with Santa Clara County Correctional Academy.
Evidence Procedures/Protection/Collection: Completed three semester hours of training.
Law Enforcement: Completed 9 weeks of training for the Santa Clara County Department of Corrections and three weeks of training at the Federal Law Enforcement Training Center.
Computers: Experienced in operating Windows 95; Microsoft Word, Excel, and PowerPoint; Corel WordPerfect; and Lotus 1-2-3; am knowledgeable of computer authentication of passwords, pass codes, and security identification badges.
Radio-Communications: Utilize portable radios and control base radios.
Prison Procedures: Trained in riot control, CS gas, baton use, defensive tactical assault maneuvers, and other similar procedures.

EXPERIENCE

SENIOR OFFICER SPECIALIST and **CONTROL CENTER OFFICER.** Federal Bureau of Prisons, FCI Boulder, Boulder, CO (1998-present). Immediately after my probationary period was completed, was assigned to one of the most critical posts in this institution which provides care and custody of medium-security male inmates; serve as Escort Officer for inmates on commercial airline flights.

- Monitor the Control Center, issuing equipment to incoming personnel, greeting and processing official visitors, and accounting for all institution keys.
- Direct perimeter fence alarm and zone alarm testing to ensure institution security.
- Operate base radio to transmit all emergency information to portable radios throughout facility; ensure all staff have working radios and emergency body alarms through frequent inspections and testing.
- Initiate emergency contingency plans including notification of outside hospitals, emergency vehicles, and outside law enforcement assistance.
- Maintain inmate census logs and document official institutional counts of inmate population through housing units, work details, and hospital-bound inmates.
- Conduct random searches of inmates, their quarters, and personal property; strip search female inmates and transport them to other institutions.
- Supervise inmate work details; oversee meal rotations; escort inmates to hospitals and medical appointments and transport federal inmates to airports and relinquish them to Federal Marshals.
- Respond to medical emergencies including suicides, fights, seizures, sports injuries.
- Initiate random urinalysis and breath analysis as I deem necessary.

COLLEGE STUDENT. (1995-98). Earned a Bachelor of Science in Business Administration with a concentration in Accounting.

CORRECTIONS OFFICER. Santa Clara County Department of Corrections, San Jose, CA (1993-94). Guarded inmates in a municipal jail and routinely conducted searches for drugs, valuables, or narcotics; investigated disturbances and investigated causes of assaults, fights, theft, and suicide attempts.

- Questioned prisoners to obtain information used in solving crimes.
- Prepared written reports; documented arrest information; handled fingerprinting.

PERSONAL   Am known for my tactful and diplomatic communication skills. Known for integrity.

Dear Sir or Madam:

I would appreciate an opportunity to talk with you soon about how I could contribute to your organization through my experience and personal qualities.

As you will see from my enclosed resume, I am currently serving my country as a Special Agent with the Department of Defense and I have earned widespread respect for my knowledge of the intelligence and counterintelligence field. I have relocated back to Boise because I have family in the area, and I am interested in exploring opportunities within your organization.

While serving my country, I held one of the nation's highest security clearances and received prestigious medals because of my technical expertise and administrative skills. I offer extensive computer knowledge along with in-depth experience in performing research, writing reports, interviewing people, and finding ways to improve internal productivity.

If you can use a versatile young professional with unlimited initiative, excellent administrative and communication skills, and a "track record" of excelling in anything I take on, I would enjoy the opportunity to meet you in person. I can provide excellent personal and professional references, and I will make myself available for an interview at your convenience.

Sincerely yours,

Renee L. Lullaby

RENEE L. LULLABY

1110½ Hay Street, Fayetteville, NC 28305   •   preppub@aol.com   •   (910) 483-6611

OBJECTIVE

I want to contribute to an organization that can use a dedicated young professional who has refined my analytical, problem-solving, and communication skills while proudly serving my country in a demanding career path which requires the highest level of integrity.

CLEARANCE

Hold one of the nation's highest security clearances: Top Secret with SBI

COMPUTERS

Proficient with highly specialized software used in the intelligence/counterintelligence field.

EXPERIENCE

SPECIAL AGENT/COUNTERINTELLIGENCE AGENT. Department of Defense, Washington, DC (2000-present). Received numerous certificates of appreciation while serving my country with distinction in the intelligence and counterintelligence field; have developed highly refined skills related to developing and implementing plans to safeguard people, property, documents, and equipment.

- As a Special Agent, investigate threats of espionage, sabotage, subversion, and terrorism. Perform as a security consultant; conduct threat vulnerability assessments on units and government installations.
- Authored and delivered briefings about how to identify and report suspicious activities which might involve espionage, subversion, and terrorism; briefed them on what to do if approached by a foreign intelligence service.
- Planned and conducted counterintelligence operations to include analyzing, selecting, exploiting, and neutralizing targets of a counterintelligence interest.
- Gathered information of a counterintelligence nature through various sources.
- Conducted liaison with local law enforcement authorities.
- Conducted background investigations on Department of Defense personnel requiring a Top Secret security clearance. Controlled classified documents.

Highlights of special projects performed for the Department of Defense:
COUNTERINTELLIGENCE TEAM LEADER (1999): Received a prestigious medal for my exemplary performance as manager of a counterintelligence team consisting of two counterintelligence agents and two linguists working in support of U.N. missions worldwide.

- Was praised in writing for my timely collection and reporting of critical information.
- Planned and implemented more than 110 successful intelligence missions.
- Authored detailed intelligence reports which were classified in nature.

SPECIAL AGENT/COUNTERINTELLIGENCE MANAGER (1998). At classified locations in Asia, became very familiar with Japanese customs and protocol while handling a wide range of responsibilities related to supervising the conduct of background investigations, the preparation of intelligence reports, and assessments of security weaknesses.

COUNTERINTELLIGENCE AGENT. (1997). At locations in the Middle East, analyzed security deficiencies and developed plans to thwart terrorism.

EDUCATION & TRAINING

Excelled in the six-month Counterintelligence Agent's Course, Ft. Huachuca, AZ.
Completed Combat Lifesaver's Course; am certified in CPR.
Completed advanced training in interviewing and interrogation through attending the five-day intensive Reid Seminar on Interviewing and Interrogation.

PERSONAL

Can provide outstanding personal and professional references. Known as a hard worker.

LARRY THOMAS GIDEON

1110½ Hay Street, Fayetteville, NC 28305   •   preppub@aol.com   •
(910) 483-6611

OBJECTIVE

To offer my experience related to investigative and security operations to an organization that can use a persistent and skilled young professional who can provide a background of extensive intelligence gathering and protective services.

EXPERTISE

- Through training and experience, have become skilled in counter-surveillance, surveillance, counterterrorism, industrial security, photography, evaluating locks/safes/locking systems, surreptitious entry techniques, and basic electronics.
- Operate mainstream computer equipment and software, photo lab equipment, electronic tracking transmitters, direction finders, RF transmitters, and optical systems including 35mm cameras, video, pinhole installations, and telephone intercept equipment.
- Was entrusted with a Top Secret/SCI security clearance with SSBI.

EXPERIENCE

Earned a reputation as a skilled instructor, investigator, and security professional while serving as a Counterintelligence Special Agent, U.S. Department of Defense:

SPECIAL AGENT. Washington, DC (2000-present) Supervise two people involved in a variety of security procedures including processing security clearances, checking local records, and acting as couriers for classified materials.

- Refined skills in areas such as supervising employees and prioritizing the work flow.

COUNTERINTELLIGENCE AGENT. Central Intelligence Agency, Washington, DC (1999). Provided assistance to foreign military teams while analyzing intelligence data and making determinations on the seriousness and probability of hostile enemy threats while producing counterintelligence products.

- Participated in activities such as debriefing personnel after the completion of their assignments and preparing detailed reports.
- Oversaw the programs which provided the company with security for information, physical, and personnel security.
- Learned the proper procedures for processing requests for visas including the special requirements for the Latin American countries that allowed for quick processing in case of rapid deployments.
- Became familiar with the ways to process courier orders and security clearances.
- Selected for a two-week special project with a Seattle, WA, military intelligence organization: gained familiarity and refined skills in advanced foot surveillance in an urban environment, team leadership, and interrogation.
- Handpicked as a member of a tactical analysis team, analyzed and assessed drug organizations in a project to help support

counternarcotics missions based at the U.S. Embassy in Mexico City, Mexico.
- Refined managerial skills controlling an $85,000 operating budget and preparing . detailed, error-free reports.
- Operated and maintained complex computer and communications electronics equipment while analyzing message traffic.

COUNTERINTELLIGENCE AGENT. Central Intelligence Agency, locations in Central America (1993-98). Developed and enhanced skills in areas such as determining hostile threats, developing counterintelligence products, debriefing personnel, preparing detailed reports following debriefings, providing security for human and materials assets, and providing support in the areas of mapping as well as passport and visa processing for elements in preparation for overseas deployment.
- Selected for a project at Ft. Polk, LA, worked closely with security/law enforcement personnel while planning security for personnel and assets during a training exercise.
- Set up a photography section capable of developing intelligence photos in an hour.
- Was taught the specialized art of sweeping for surreptitious listening devices and ensuring that an area was clear.

COUNTERINTELLIGENCE AGENT. Central Intelligence Agency, locations in South America (1991-93). Polished my interviewing techniques and learned to write concise but thorough reports while debriefing Special Forces personnel after they returned from missions.
- Gained knowledge in functional areas including planning and carrying out exercises designed to locate weaknesses in physical security at key facilities.
- Made recommendations of countermeasures which would help make personnel and physical assets safe from terrorist actions.

EDUCATION & TRAINING

Attend Liberty University, Lynchburg, VA, in an external degree program.
Excelled in training programs emphasizing the following: methods for handling and safeguarding classified materials, alcohol and drug program coordination, basic electronics and technical surveillance, and computer intelligence systems.

PERSONAL

Received honors including a Joint Services Achievement Medal for my contribution in Venezuela and commendation and achievement medals for professionalism and dedication.

Exact Name of Person
Exact Name of College
Address
City, state zip

COUNTY JAILER   Dear Exact Name of Person (or Dear Sir or Madam if answering a blind ad):

With the enclosed resume, I would like to make you aware of my interest in exploring employment opportunities with your institution. I believe my background and credentials are well suited to your needs.

As you will see from my resume, I am currently directing educational programs and course registration for the inmates in the Newton County jail. In addition to supervising other instructors, I also teach the GED Course and act as registrar for all students enrolling in classes.

Previously as a member of the Defense Intelligence Agency, I excelled in numerous top-level assignments which required outstanding consulting, administrative, and advising skills. For example, I was selected as the Special Advisor on the Middle East and was the trusted advisor to the U.S. Ambassador. I also advised the Department of Defense and the intelligence community on matters related to sensitive subjects. In another assignment as a United Nations Observer, I was in daily contact with Egyptian military officials as well as ambassadorial-level Egyptian government authorities as I briefed and counseled them. In another assignment, I was the Desk Officer for the Africa Division and earned widespread respect for my strong communication and consulting skills. I am confident that I could be of valuable assistance to students in their need for resourceful insights and strategic problem-solving related to their curriculum and careers.

I hold a Master's degree in National Security Affairs with a concentration in Middle East Studies, and I also hold a Bachelor of Science degree in Education with a minor in Political Science.

Although I am held in the highest regard in my current position and can provide outstanding references at the appropriate time, I would ask that you not contact my current employer until after we talk. My wife and I are in the process of relocating to your area, and I am interested in using my proven administrative, strategic planning, and communication skills for the benefit of your institution.

I hope you will contact me to suggest a time when we could meet in person to discuss your needs. Thank you in advance for your time.

Yours sincerely,

Ryan Wilson

RYAN WILSON

1110½ Hay Street, Fayetteville, NC 28305 • preppub@aol.com • (910) 483-6611

OBJECTIVE   To benefit an academic institution that can use a highly educated and experienced individual who offers a proven ability to counsel and motivate others while providing quality academic services and optimizing the use of scarce financial resources.

EDUCATION   **Master of Arts Degree, National Security Affairs major with concentration in Middle East Studies,** North Dakota University, Selma, ND, 2001.
Completed the two-year graduate-level Command and General Staff Course; also completed these courses sponsored by the Defense Intelligence Agency:

Military Operations Training Course	Military Attache Training Course
Psychological Operations Course	Foreign Area Officer Course
Special Forces Officer Course	Military Intelligence Officer Course

Bachelor of Science, Education major with concentration in Political Science, Monterey State University, Arkadelphia, AR, 1987.
Completed other training courses related to law enforcement and policing, Hostage Situations and Pressure Point Control Tactics, OSHA, CPR, and other subjects.

CLEARANCE   Top Secret (SBI/SCI) security clearance
- Have undergone both CI and Lifestyle Polygraphs.

LANGUAGE   Speak, read, and write Arabic

EXPERIENCE   **EDUCATIONAL ADMINISTRATOR/INSTRUCTOR & COUNTY JAILER.** Newton County Sheriff's Department, Selma, ND (2000-present). Have expanded the educational opportunities available to inmates since assuming this position.
- Administer three classes and manage two other instructors; coordinate with colleagues from Selma Technical Community College.
- Expanded the number of courses offered from one to three.
- Prepare, analyze, and implement instructional program recommendations.
- Teach GED classes; oversee all testing in GED classes.
- During the course of a term, register 60 people for Adult Basic Education classes.
- In my capacity as County Jailer, perform highly physical and strenuous activities in a job which requires constant alertness and independent judgement.

AFRICA DIVISION, DESK OFFICER. Defense Intelligence Agency, Washington, DC (1997-99). Was selected for a top-level position which involved determining the appropriate utilization of human intelligence resources; supervised the planning and development of projects and programs which affected thousands of people worldwide.
- Played a key role in the planning, programming, and budgeting process.

SPECIAL ADVISOR, MIDDLE EAST. Defense Intelligence Agency, Washington, DC (1994-97). Excelled in a job in which I functioned as an international diplomat and trusted advisor to an ambassador; applied my vast knowledge of the Middle East while advising and counseling the U.S. Ambassador on political and military affairs.

OBSERVER, UNITED NATIONS. United National Security Organization, Palestine (1989-93). Maintained daily contact with and provided briefings to Egyptian military officials as well as ambassadorial-level Egyptian government authorities.

PERSONAL   Extensive knowledge of Middle East and Northern Africa. Excellent references.

Date

The Honorable Tad Brown
Congressman
Second District of Arizona
25580 Rayburn House Office Building
Washington, DC 20515

Dear Congressman Rose:

With the enclosed resume I am formally indicating my interest in the job of United States Marshal for the Western District of Arizona, and I am requesting that you support me for this position. I can tell you that you would be backing a respected professional with an unblemished record of service to my country along with a thorough knowledge of what is required of the U.S. Marshal.

As you will see from my resume, I have worked for the United States Marshals Service (USMS) as a Court Security Officer and, during that time, I have established excellent working relationships with individuals from the USMS, other law enforcement agencies, U.S. attorneys, and the judiciary. Previously I worked for the Arizona Wildlife Commission, advancing into a supervisory position which involved training and managing other wildlife officers while enforcing state and federal laws related to hunting, fishing, and boating.

I strongly believe that the U.S. Marshal can make a difference in the Western District, and I believe he will make a difference not by sitting behind a desk but by a "hands-on" approach to working with, helping, and motivating deputies. An energetic "hands-on" professional with a "walk around" management style, I know all the deputies, judicial officials, and most of the law enforcement officers in the district and could count on their 100% support.

Please support me for this position, and let me hear from you if you need any other supporting documentation from me. Thank you very much.

Sincerely yours,

Arthur C. Bisque

ARTHUR C. BISQUE

1110½ Hay Street, Fayetteville, NC 28305   •   preppub@aol.com   •   (910) 483-6611

OBJECTIVE

To serve as the United States Marshal for the Western District of Arizona.

EXPERIENCE

COURT SECURITY OFFICER. United States Marshals Service (USMS), Tempe, AZ (2000-present). Have developed excellent working relationships with individuals from the Marshals Service, law enforcement agencies, U.S. attorneys, and the judiciary while involved in a wide range of activities related to providing security and protection.
- *entrance control*: Operate and enforce a system of personal identification which includes checking handbags, packages, and other items to detect weapons and contraband.
- *roving patrol*: Conduct roving patrols of the court area in accordance with schedules.
- *fixed post*: Maintain a fixed, stationary position outside and inside the chambers of courtroom judges and jury rooms in order to prevent unauthorized entrance.
- *personal escort*: Provide a personal escort for judges, court personnel, attorneys, jurors, and witnesses when directed to do so in order to assure their personal safety.
- *law and order*: Am responsible for the detection and detention of any person(s) seeking to gain unauthorized access to court proceedings.

AREA SERGEANT. Arizona Wildlife Commission, Tempe, AZ (1990-00). Refined my leadership ability and problem-solving skills while supervising and directing several wildlife officers in a geographical area in the enforcement of AZ and federal laws related to hunting, fishing, other game activities, and boating.
- *employee training/supervision*: Trained numerous officers in the wildlife field; evaluated their performance.
- *organizing/scheduling/coordinating*: Set up work details to handle wildlife activities; worked with state and federal law enforcement agencies; assisted in search and rescue missions.
- *inventory control*: Procured new equipment and monitored its maintenance and care.
- *budgeting and finance*: Planned and administered budgets of varying sizes.

WILDLIFE ENFORCEMENT OFFICER. Arizona. Wildlife Commission, Tempe, AZ (1985-90). Enforced game, fish, and boating laws in an assigned area and assisted other officers in high violation locations; maintained equipment in top condition.

EDUCATION & TRAINING

Court Security Officer School (law enforcement training), 2000.
Institute of Government (in-service training), Tempe, AZ, 1998.
Arizona Justice Academy (NC Criminal Code), Salemburg, AZ, 1995.
Riot and Crowd Control, Tempe, AZ, 1990.
Institute of Government (leadership training), Tempe, AZ, 1989.
Coast Guard Boarding School, San Diego, CA, 1988.
Basic, Intermediate, and Advanced Law Enforcement Courses, 1985-present.

DISTINCTIONS & HONORS

- Received letters of commendation from a federal judge for outstanding work
- Received letter of commendation for exceptional performance from U.S. Attorneys Office
- Was the recipient of numerous awards from clubs and civic organizations
- Received the State Conservation Award
- Was named Officer of the Month

PERSONAL

Have a strong desire to strengthen law enforcement in the Western District of Arizona. Can pass the most rigorous security background check; background is free of obscurities.

Date

Exact Name of Person
Title or Position
Name of Company
Address (no., street)
Address (city, state, zip)

CRIME ANALYST   Dear Exact Name of Person (or Dear Sir or Madam if answering a blind ad):

I would appreciate an opportunity to talk with you soon about how I could contribute to your organization through my experience as an intelligence analyst along with my background of success in security management.

As you will see from my resume, I am a Crime Analyst with the Crime Analysis and Career Criminal Apprehension Program of the New Orleans Sheriff's Department in Louisiana. Like many places in the world, this county has seen a tremendous increase in crime over the past four to five years. Since joining the department in this capacity, I have been able to increase the registration of known sex offenders to 90% from the previous rate of only 14%. Upon assuming this position, I trained more than 100 people in utilizing AS400 hardware with Crimes Management System software, which transformed manual operations into computerized activities. The sheriff depends on my strategic analysis for long-range planning and my tactical analysis for specific problem areas. I prepare a wide range of statistical analyses and reports, including the annual report used by the sheriff to justify new personnel and capital expenditures.

While serving with distinction in the U.S. Army, I advanced as an Intelligence Analyst and Security Manager at locations including Korea and the Middle East. Often singled out for special assignments, I handled such activities as assessing the effect of the exodus to the U.S. by refugees, studying and making recommendations on policy changes, and researching the impact on displaced persons in the Middle East.

I believe I offer the experience, skills, and expertise as an intelligence analyst and the experience in security management that would allow me to make important contributions to your organization.

I hope you will welcome my call soon to arrange a brief meeting at your convenience to discuss your current and future needs and how I might serve them. Thank you in advance for your time.

Sincerely yours,

Vern D. Grape

VERN D. GRAPE

1110½ Hay Street, Fayetteville, NC 28305   •   preppub@aol.com   •   (910) 483-6611

OBJECTIVE   To offer my expertise as an intelligence analyst and security professional to an organization that can use my research and analytical skills along with my communication, leadership, and managerial abilities.

EXPERIENCE   **CRIME ANALYST** and **SUPERVISOR, CRIME ANALYSIS UNIT.** New Orleans Sheriff's Department, New Orleans, LA (2000-present). As supervisor of the Crime Analysis Unit in a county of approximately 250,550 people, have successfully completely automated the department's operations while single-handedly analyzing, preparing, and disseminating information concerning actual and anticipated criminal activity.

- Upon assuming this job, trained more than 100 people in utilizing AS400 hardware with Crimes Management System software; apply my software knowledge in creating computer graphics presentations to present crime trends and to visually show statistical analyses and forecasts I have prepared.
- As liaison with the California Department of Justice Sexual Habitual Offender Program, monitored the collection of information on high-risk, violent individuals.
- Increased the registration of known sex offenders to above 90% from the previous 14% by using computer applications and GIS tracking (automated map plotting).
- Correlated crime scene information and suspect's MOs (modus operandi) in order to help with the apprehension of suspects.
- Prepared the annual report used by the sheriff to report on past trends and offer predictions; my analyses/forecasts are used to justify new personnel and capital expenditures.
- Applied my intelligence background in modifying internal forms to better capture the data needed to conduct analyses, develop tactical plans, and identify problem areas.

Built a strong reputation as a perceptive analyst and security professional, U.S. Army:
INTELLIGENCE ANALYST/SECURITY MANAGER. Ft. Dix, LA (1995-00). Often singled out to advise managers on community and assets security, recognized and evaluated indicators which affected foreign government operations or organizations while managing information and personnel security with a flawless record of "no reported violations."

- Was selected for a special assignment assessing effects of refugee exodus to U.S. territories.
- Prepared and conducted briefings and debriefings for personnel assigned to terrorist and hostile intelligence service activities.

STRATEGIC INTELLIGENCE ANALYST. Korea (1991-94). Prepared analyses and assessments of strategic enemy capabilities for senior-level U.S. government officials including the Secretary of Defense.

EDUCATION   B.A., **Criminal Justice,** Louisiana State University, New Orleans, LA, 1990.

SPECIAL TRAINING & PROFESSIONAL AFFILIATIONS
Completed extensive special training programs including the following:
    Crime Analysis Extended Applications Course, Louisiana Department of Justice, 2000.
    Sensitive Compartmented Information Course, Defense Intelligence College, 1991
    Intelligence issues for African and Caribbean countries, Special Operations School, 1991
    Individual Terrorist Awareness Course, Special Forces, 1990

PERSONAL   Lead by example is my management style. Am relied on by others for astute judgments and analytical assessments. Have a Top Secret security clearance with SBI and SCI access.

CRIME SCENE INVESTIGATOR

Dear Mr. Smith:

Enclosed please find a copy of my resume. I would appreciate your consideration for the position of Identification Officer with the Chicago Police Department.

I do meet the qualifications for this position based on my experience as a crime scene investigator with the Sheriff's Department in Phoenix, AZ. My background includes almost three years in investigation, collection and interpretation of fingerprints, photography, and other technical police work.

I completed the Basic Law Enforcement Training Program after earning an A.A.S. degree in **Criminal Justice-Protective Services Technology** from Phoenix Technical Community College. As detailed on my enclosed resume, I have also received specialized training in such specific areas as crime scene preservation, infectious control and handling of hazardous materials, reporting procedures, and law enforcement photography.

With a reputation as a thorough, detail-oriented young professional, I feel that I offer the training and experience your department needs to fill this important position. I hope you will call or write me soon to suggest a time convenient for us to meet and discuss your current and future needs and how I might serve them. Thank you in advance for your time.

Sincerely yours,

Alex Pate

ALEX PATE

1110½ Hay Street, Fayetteville, NC 28305 • preppub@aol.com • (910) 483-6611

OBJECTIVE
To offer a reputation as a confident, articulate, and detail-oriented law enforcement professional with special emphasis in the areas of crime scene investigation and the technical aspects of police work.

EXPERIENCE
DEPUTY SHERIFF and **CRIME SCENE TECHNICIAN.** The Phoenix County Sheriff's Department, Phoenix, AZ (1997-present). Rapidly earned a reputation as a self-motivated professional who could be counted on to ensure that crime scene evidence was thoroughly collected, investigated, and documented according to regulations and so that the chain of custody remained intact.

- Have a 100% conviction rate for the few occasions when my cases have gone to trial and have proven myself a reliable and credible witness—however, the bulk of my cases are settled by plea bargains and never go to trial.
- Received a Letter of Commendation for singlehandedly locating and detaining two suspects upon responding to an attempted armed robbery.
- Respond to the full range of crimes: burglary, felony larceny, recovered stolen vehicles, armed robbery, sexual assaults, and child abuse as well as shootings, stabbings, homicides, officer-involved shootings, suicides, and auto or fire fatalities.
- Provide support by processing crime scenes for all of the separate police departments in the state and handled a wide range of duties including the following:
  processed the scene to *collect and preserve* latent prints
  photographed scene for preservation and evidence which could not be removed
  prepared sketches and diagrams
  collected items of evidence to be submitted to the SBI lab for processing
  prepared evidence for use in court and *testified* when required
  responded to identification calls from other agencies
  performed clerical tasks dealing with reports, evidence, and identification
  maintained detailed files and ensured the proper control of records
  researched files for suspects
  arrested suspects at the crime scene and held them

EDUCATION, TRAINING, & CERTIFICATIONS
Completed 500-hour Basic Law Enforcement Training (BLET) program certification. Excelled in studies which included weapons, self-defense, civil law, and criminal law. Earned an Associate of Applied Science (A.A.S.) degree in **Criminal Justice-Protective Services Technology**, Phoenix Technical Community College (PTCC), AZ, 1994.
- Maintained a 3.5 GPA.

Completed PTCC and department-sponsored specialized training including the following:

crime scene preservation	juvenile laws
dealing with victims and witnesses	domestic violence
patrol techniques and OSHA standards	reporting procedures
involuntary commitment use of force	pursuit driving
infectious control and the handling of hazardous materials	

TECHNICAL EXPERTISE
- Use different powders and chemicals to develop latent fingerprints: graphic powder, "super-glue," am iodine fuming.
- Am experienced in using plaster casting to make tire and shoe impressions.
- Offer state certification with the .45 caliber and .380 caliber Sig Sauer pistols.

PERSONAL
Am confident of my ability to produce high-quality results. Easily relate to members of the public as well as my peers and co-workers.

Date

Exact Name of Person
Exact Title
Exact Name of Company
Address
City, State, Zip

**CRIMINAL
INVESTIGATOR**

Dear Exact Name of Person (or Dear Sir or Madam if answering a blind ad):

With the enclosed resume, I would like to make you aware of my background related to fraud investigations.

In my current job as a Special Agent with the Criminal Investigation Division (CID), I have specialized in general crimes including auto theft, criminal background checks and information, as well as various fraud investigations. I routinely account for an inventory of equipment which includes burglary kits, visual ID kits, various types of fingerprint kits, body armor, hostage negotiation crisis telephones, cameras, and other devices.

After completing the Army's CID Special Agent Course, I was assigned to Ft. Rucker, AL. A successful federally sworn agent with a high level of skill in dealing with people, I have testified before the grand jury and local magistrates in all types of courts martial. I have also obtained arrest and search warrants/authorization before federal magistrates and local authorities. I hold a Top Secret security clearance with SBI.

I was selected for advanced training and career opportunities on the basis of my effectiveness as an investigator and assistant to Army CID Special Agents in Italy. I have qualified "Expert" with the M16 rifle, 9mm pistol, shotgun and am familiar with the processing and protection of crime scene physical evidence.

If you can use a well-trained, thorough, and knowledgeable professional who is highly articulate, cool under pressure, and able to easily adapt to pressure and change, please contact me to suggest a time when we might meet to discuss your needs. I am sincerely interested in a career in your industry, and I can assure you in advance that I could rapidly become an asset to your organization.

Sincerely,

Jonathon Sweeney

JONATHON SWEENEY

1110½ Hay Street, Fayetteville, NC 28305 • preppub@aol.com • (910) 483-6611

OBJECTIVE   To offer my expertise related to specialized fraud investigations, interviewing and interrogation, and crime scene processing to an organization that could benefit from my creativity, understanding of human nature, and personal reputation for integrity and honesty.

EDUCATION   Completed 72 college credit hours including Law Enforcement courses at Central Texas
& TRAINING   University; computer courses at University of Maryland; currently enrolling in Penn State's Administration of Justice Program.

Completed the 15-week Apprentice **CID Special Agent Course**, U.S. Army Military Police School, Ft. McClellan, AL, with an emphasis on the following areas:

crime scene processing	investigative photography	testimonial evidence
crimes against persons	crimes against property	physical evidence
special investigations	drug investigations	protective services
investigative reports	crisis management	fraud and waste

Attended additional training programs in ground surveillance systems operations, street gangs, hate crimes training, advanced fraud, combat lifesaving, alcohol and drug abuse, and traffic safety as well as earlier training as a welder.

SPECIAL SKILLS   *Computers:* Windows; Microsoft Word, Excel, PowerPoint, Works, and Outlook; ACIRS
Weapons: M16 rifle, 9 mm pistol, shotgun, pepper spray, baton, and hand grenade
Other equipment and procedures: ground sensor/infrared intrusion devices, UAV (Unmanned Air Vehicle) surveillance, electrostatic print lifter, and taking cast impressions
Security clearance: Top Secret with SBI

EXPERIENCE   *Am earning a reputation as a thorough and top-notch professional, U.S. Army:*
SPECIAL AGENT – CID (CRIMINAL INVESTIGATION DIVISION). Ft. Rucker, AL (2000-present). Have become known for my ability to achieve positive results and set an example of professionalism and dedication while conducting criminal investigations—interview victims and witnesses, interrogate suspects for testimonial evidence, prepare investigative reports, testify in court, and examine and process physical evidence.
- Identified a team of thieves, secured their confessions, and solved a series of construction-site larcenies.
- While specializing in fraud investigations, have accounted for thousands of dollars in equipment including burglary kits, visual ID kits, various types of fingerprint kits, body

CRIMINAL INVESTIGATOR. Italy (1997-99). Was selected for training as a Special Agent on the basis of my performance assisting Special Agents in conducting felony investigations.
- Became skilled in recruiting and utilizing confidential sources of information while earning a reputation as one who could be counted on to accomplish the mission.

INVESTIGATOR AND TEAM LEADER. Berlin, Germany (1990-97). Provided the leadership which allowed my team to complete more than 20 safe and successful border surveillance missions during a one-year period in support of international peacekeeping operations in the Former Yugoslav Republic of Macedonia.
- Was chosen to provide training in ground surveillance techniques to personnel from other UN-member countries.

PERSONAL   Highly skilled professional who has conducted and assisted in excess of 300 felony investigations. Have obtained arrest and search warrants/authorizations from federal magistrates.

Date

Exact Name of Person
Exact Title
Exact Name of Company
Address
City, State, Zip

CRIMINAL INVESTIGATOR

Dear Exact Name of Person (or Dear Sir or Madam if answering a blind ad):

With the enclosed resume, I would like to make you aware of my experience in managing criminal investigation, law enforcement, and protective service operations and to acquaint you with the leadership, training, and motivational skills that I could put to work for your organization.

As you will see from my resume, I have recently excelled as the Operations Manager of a Criminal Investigation unit, supervising 19 investigators including eight junior managers servicing a community with a population of more than 100,000 military and civilian personnel. In addition to performing liaison with federal and civilian law enforcement agencies, social services, and other organizations, I oversee the juvenile, special operations, and Armed Forces Disciplinary Control Board (AFDCB) investigative teams and direct the investigation of general crimes.

In an earlier position as a Security Consultant, I was praised by both my superiors and by foreign dignitaries for my professionalism in conducting more than 300 hours of protective service missions with zero incidents. While serving as Lead Investigative Officer, I demonstrated my exceptional communication and training skills while teaching a gang awareness course to more than 500 military executives and senior managers.

I have earned nearly two years of college credit towards a Bachelor of Science in Criminal Justice, and I have consistently been singled out to receive advanced instruction. While training to become a Special Agent with the Criminal Investigative Division (CID) and in later law enforcement positions, I have been trained in areas ranging from Advanced Narcotics Investigation, to Countering Domestic & International Terrorism, to Advanced Interviews & Interrogations.

Although I am highly regarded by my present employer and am being groomed for further promotion into positions of increased responsibility, I have decided to explore other career opportunities within the civilian law enforcement community. If you can use a skilled investigator, trainer, and leader whose management and investigative skills have been proven in a variety of challenging environments, I hope you will welcome my call soon when I try to arrange a brief meeting to discuss your goals and how my background might serve your needs. I can provide outstanding references at the appropriate time.

Yours sincerely,

Kerri Moore

KERRI MOORE

1110½ Hay Street, Fayetteville, NC 28305 • preppub@aol.com • (910) 483-6611

OBJECTIVE

To benefit an organization that can use a skilled investigator with the proven ability to lead, motivate, and train personnel who offers a background of excellence in the management of criminal investigation, protective services, and physical security operations.

EDUCATION

Finished nearly two years of college course work towards a B.S. degree in Criminal Justice. Completed numerous military training courses in management and law enforcement, including:
Leadership and Management: Primary Leadership and Development Course and Basic Non-Commissioned Officers Course
Law Enforcement: Criminal Investigation Division Apprentice Special Agent course, Protective Services Training, Advanced Narcotic Investigation, Countering Domestic & International Terrorism, Advanced Interviews & Interrogating, Advanced Surveillance & Counter-Surveillance, Intrusion Detection System (CCTV) operation and others.

EXPERIENCE

Advanced to positions of responsibility and selected for specialized training, while excelling in the following "track record" of accomplishments, U.S. Army 1990-present:
2002-present: **CRIMINAL INVESTIGATION OPERATIONS MANAGER.** Ft. Gordon, GA. Oversee the operation of a 19-person police investigation section serving an installation of more than 100,000 civilian and military personnel; perform liaison with federal and civilian law enforcement agencies, social services, and other relevant organizations.
- Directly supervise eight junior managers in the investigation of general crimes while overseeing the juvenile, special operations, and AFDCB investigative teams.
- Recognized for my attention to detail and careful preparation which resulted in a substantial increase in the percentage of cases solved by the section.
- A gifted instructor, was lauded for my "uncanny" teaching ability.
- Manage protective security operations for visiting dignitaries and high-risk personnel; hold final responsibility for more than $100,000 worth of equipment and supplies.

2001: **INVESTIGATOR** and **SECURITY CONSULTANT.** Saudi Arabia. Provided expert advice from my extensive knowledge, performing physical security and vulnerability assessments for various sites as well as coordinating with officials from other agencies on matters related to crimes outside my area of authority.
- Trained Security Force and Task Force members in protective service operations.

2000: **LEAD INVESTIGATIVE OFFICER.** Fort Gordon, GA. As leader of the Gang Investigations unit, taught gang awareness courses to more than 500 military executives and senior managers; supervised all school resource officers, coordinated the Think Smart program, and served as a member of the Juvenile Rehabilitation Board.
- Cited for my excellent street knowledge related to gangs as well as my sound judgment.

1995-99: **POLICE SUPERVISOR.** Korea. Provided supervisory oversight and training to a 14-person law enforcement and security team; maintained 100% accountability for the Physical Security Enhancement Program System valued at more than $1 million.

Highlights of earlier military experience: Described by my senior manager as "one of the finest Military Police Investigators I've ever served with."

PERSONAL

Received prestigious awards, including four Army Commendation, three Army Achievement, and four Good Conduct Medals. Top Secret (SCI) clearance. Excellent references.

CAREER CHANGE

Date

FASC
310 Green St.
Suite 110
Nashua, NH 28301

CRIMINAL JUSTICE AIDE

How do you launch a
career in a new field? With
a great resume and cover
letter, that's how!

Dear Sir or Madam:

I was so happy to read your advertisement for a CASE DEVELOPER in the *Nashua Observer-Times*. With the enclosed resume describing my background in the criminal justice field as well as my strong counseling and management skills, I would like to formally request that you consider me for the position.

As you will see from my resume, I hold a B.A. degree in Criminal Justice and have completed some work towards my M.A. degree in Counseling. Since earning my degree, I have excelled in some jobs related to the criminal justice and social services field. For example, I was a Criminal Justice Administrative Aide through an internship with the Tinker House in New York City. In that halfway house for men and women let out of prison, I performed a wide variety of tasks vital to ensuring secure and efficient operations.

In all my jobs, including my experience unrelated to the criminal justice field, I have excelled through my strong counseling, management, and communication skills. I offer a proven ability to work well under pressure, and I can provide outstanding personal and professional references. Although my current job is certainly well paid and satisfying in many respects since I enjoy dealing with people, I am sincerely interested in making contributions to society through the criminal justice and social services field, for which I have been extensively educated. I can assure you that you would find me to be a congenial and reliable professional who always strives to do my best and to help others.

I hope you will write or call me soon to suggest a time when we could meet to discuss your current and future needs and how I might serve them. Thank you in advance for your time.

Sincerely yours,

Violet Rae Mahoghany

VIOLET RAE MAHOGHANY

1110½ Hay Street, Fayetteville, NC 28305   •   preppub@aol.com   •   (910) 483-6611

OBJECTIVE

To offer my background in criminal justice and my desire to work in the human services field to an organization that can use my excellent written/oral communication skills, my knowledge of community resources, and my ability to establish outstanding working relationships.

EDUCATION

Pursuing **Master of Arts** (M.A.) degree in **Counseling**, New Hampshire University, Nashua, NH.
- During a course in correctional counseling and treatment, gained interviewing and investigative reporting skills.

Earned a **Bachelor of Arts** (B.A.) degree in **Criminal Justice**, New Hampshire Central University, Nashua, NH, 1986.
- Member, Criminal Justice Club, New Hampshire University.
- Excelled in course work related to these and other areas:

Strategies for Dealing with Adult Offenders	Correctional Counseling
Prison Procedures and Policies	Juvenile Justice
Criminal Procedures	Criminal Law Personnel
Fundamentals of Substance Abuse Counseling	Psychology
Computer Applications to Public Administration	Sociology

RELATED EXPERIENCE

Hands-on experience in the criminal justice field through an internship includes:
CRIMINAL JUSTICE ADMINISTRATIVE AIDE. Tinker House, New York City. In this halfway house for men and women released from penal institutions on work programs, performed a variety of tasks vital to secure and efficient operations.
- Controlled access of inmates to and from the halfway house.
- Became intimately knowledgeable of inmates' personal and confidential files.
- Briefed inmates on rules and regulations of the halfway house.
- Developed knowledge of group counseling procedures.
- Gained valuable knowledge about halfway houses and penal institutions.
- Refined my skills in listening to and communicating with people.

OTHER EXPERIENCE

Have excelled in positions requiring excellent counseling, communication, people, and management skills:
COSMETOLOGIST. Regal Plaza, Nashua, NH (2000-present). Have developed a loyal clientele of customers who appreciate my interpersonal skills and tactful style of dealing with public; manage all finance and accounting as well as all matters related to tax preparation.
- Although I enjoy this field and find it lucrative, I strongly desire to contribute to my fellow human beings through involvement in the criminal justice and social services field, for which I have educated myself extensively.

HOMEMAKER. London, England (1995-00). Enjoyed the opportunity to learn about Europe and gain experience dealing with people from various cultural backgrounds while living in Germany with my military spouse.

CLERK-TYPIST. Internal Revenue Service, Nashua, NH (1990-94). Worked closely with eight Revenue officers in a Collection Division Group and provided a wide range of administrative support; prepared and math-verified travel vouchers, maintained group timekeeping records, and maintained a filing system.

PERSONAL

Am a highly motivated individual who enjoys helping others. Known for my common sense and good judgment as well as my ability to make sensible decisions under pressure.

CAREER CHANGE

Date

Human Resources Office
Fayetteville Technical Community College
PO Box 35236
Fayetteville, NC 28303

**CRIMINAL JUSTICE
INSTRUCTOR**

This individual seeks to
make a career change into
an academic environment.

Dear Sir or Madam:

With the enclosed resume, I would like to express my interest in exploring employment opportunities with your organization. I am applying for the position as **Criminal Justice Instructor, Basic Law Enforcement.** With a Top Secret security clearance, I hold degrees in Criminal Justice and General Education and offer a background which includes distinguished service as a Police Officer with the Chesapeake, VA, Police Department, and as a Consultant with one of the country's leading defense contractors. I offer extensive experience as an Instructor.

As you will see from the resume, I offer a background of accomplishments and track record of success in environments where the emphasis has been on the development and training of personnel and building of teams who work together to achieve outstanding results. I have been singled out for tough jobs in high-visibility settings where technical expertise, managerial abilities, and skills in developing and instructing personnel have been of prime importance.

I have earned the respect of my superiors, peers, and subordinates for my calm and deliberate manner and true concern for others. Cited as a top-notch planner and administrator, I have a reputation as one who can be counted on to find ways to improve procedures and integrate changes into existing programs with quality results. My ability to manage time and resources has also been displayed while pursuing my college education and simultaneously excelling in demanding jobs within the unique and time-sensitive Special Forces community with its immediate response to worldwide missions.

I have also been recognized for my skills in planning and conducting effective training activities, maximizing human and material resources, and dealing with people at all levels with fairness.

If you can use a mature management professional who is highly self-motivated and thrives on pressure and deadlines, I hope you will contact me soon to suggest a time we might meet to discuss how I could contribute to your organization. I will provide excellent professional and personal references at the appropriate time. Thank you for your time and consideration.

Sincerely,

Drake F. Robinson

DRAKE F. ROBINSON

1110½ Hay Street, Fayetteville, NC 28305 • preppub@aol.com • (910) 483-6611

OBJECTIVE

To contribute to an organization that can use a seasoned management professional with strong technical, training and instructional, and program development expertise.

EDUCATION & TRAINING

Bachelor of Science (B.S.) degree in Criminal Justice, Seattle University, Seattle, WA, 1998.
- Graduated *cum laude* with a 3.3 GPA.

Associate of Arts degree (A.A.) in General Education degree, Seattle Technical Community College, Seattle, WA, 1986.

Completed extensive law enforcement, management, and technical training which included programs in the following areas:

Airdrop Technician Warrant Officer Basic, RAM Air Parachute System, Free Fall Auto Rip Assembly, Jungle Warfare, Defense Hazardous Material Packing and Handling, Free Fall Parachutist and Jumpmaster, Jumpmaster, and Airdrop Load Inspector courses.

Received 40 hours of on-the-job training with Bantam Place, a halfway house for the federal prison system.

EXPERIENCE

AIRDROP CONSULTANT and **GENERAL MANAGER.** Marcusi Contractor Services, Combat Applications Group, Ft. Bragg, NC (2000-present). Plan, provide technical guidance for, and personally participate in special air delivery training and operations while supervising state-of-the-art developmental systems which include aerial delivery rigging, packing, maintenance, and life-support breathing.
- Have trained 300 inexperienced personnel to become skilled parachute riggers.
- Manage a $5 million annual repair parts, equipment, and training budget.
- Officially evaluated as "the best" manager in this unit's history, was described as a "visionary" with a special talent for anticipating requirements and maximizing advances in technology for enhanced training and ultimate success.
- Handpicked as the Army's liaison for joint training and transitioning within all branches of the military to a new automatic ripcord release system, also established a program to reduce the weight of shipping containers, which allowed user units greater flexibility.

MANAGER OF AIRDROP RIGGING SERVICES/AIRDROP SYSTEMS TECHNICIAN. Marcusi Contractor Services, Ft. Campbell, KY (1992-00). Known as an extremely articulate and adaptable manager, trainer, and technical expert, supervised a 30-person work force of parachute riggers and support personnel. Directed maintenance and storage activities in support of a $20 million inventory of parachutes and air drop equipment.

Highlights of prior experience:
Police Officer. Chesapeake Police Department, Chesapeake, VA. Built a wide range of skills and gained familiarity with law enforcement activities ranging from patrolling, to the lock up and fingerprinting of apprehended personnel, to search and seizure. Was a Police Search and Recovery SCUBA Diver.
Warrant Officer. Advanced to the rank of Warrant Officer in the U.S. Army.

AWARDS

Recipient of numerous medals, badges, and awards for exemplary performance.

CLEARANCE

Was entrusted with a **Top Secret** security clearance.

PERSONAL

Highly motivated individual with outstanding character. Excellent references on request.

CAREER CHANGE

Date

Exact Name of Person
Exact Title
Exact Name of Company
Address
City, State, Zip

Dear Exact Name of Person (or Dear Sir or Madam if answering a blind ad):

With the enclosed resume, I would like to make you aware of my interest in offering my education in criminal justice and experience as a paralegal to an organization in need of a bright, articulate, and adaptable young professional.

As you will see from my resume, I earned my bachelor's degree in Criminal Justice from Louisville State University, Louisville, KY. I was a member of the university Criminal Justice Club and an award-winning student athlete who was named as an All-Conference football player in 2000 for my accomplishments as a leader both on and off the playing field.

While attending college, I completed an eight-month internship as a Paralegal. This gave me a valuable opportunity to take knowledge gained in the classroom in the Criminal Justice curriculum and apply it on a day-to-day basis in the environment of a busy law practice with three partners. I carried out research, analyzed material, utilized computers, and dealt with clients. My interpersonal relations and communication skills were applied as I worked closely with the police department while scheduling officers for court appearances, related to the attorneys and other legal professionals, and kept clients informed of court dates and case dispositions.

I am confident that through my blend of education, practical experience, and training, I offer a mature and professional manner which would allow me to quickly become a valuable addition to any team of law enforcement, corrections, or legal professionals in need of an individual with my abilities and knowledge. Proficient with computers, I have continually gained new skills and refined my ability to manage time and resources most effectively. A physically and mentally tough individual, I enjoy meeting challenges head on and applying my considerable problem-solving, decision-making, and creative skills.

If you can use an excellent communicator with high degrees of enthusiasm, energy, and drive, I hope you will contact me soon to suggest a time we might meet to discuss how I could contribute to your organization. I can provide excellent professional and personal references at the appropriate time. Thank you for your time and consideration.

Sincerely,

James Q. Jenkins

JAMES Q. JENKINS

1110½ Hay Street, Fayetteville, NC 28305 • preppub@aol.com • (910) 483-6611

OBJECTIVE To offer an education in criminal justice and a versatile background where managerial, communication, and human relations skills have produced excellent results to an organization that can use a physically and mentally tough young professional.

EDUCATION Received a **B.S. in Criminal Justice,** Louisville State University, Louisville, KY, 2002.
- Played varsity football; was named All-CIAA Conference in 2001; played offensive guard.
- Member, Criminal Justice Club.
- Member, Groove Phi, a social/fellowship club.

Graduated from Louisville High School, Louisville, KY, 1996.
- Played football and was a member of the **wrestling** and **track** teams.
- Was named **All-State** and **All-Conference** in **football,** junior and senior years.
- In my junior year, came in second place in the state in wrestling.
- In track, was named **All-District** and **All-Conference.**
- Member, Spanish Club and Key Club.

COMPUTERS Familiar with Word, WordPerfect, and Excel, offer excellent skills with personal computers; completed courses in project management, graphics, spreadsheets, and database management.

EXPERIENCE **Am building a reputation as an articulate, resourceful, and bottom line-oriented young management professional who can be counted on to find ways to increase sales, profits, and the level of productivity while adapting to change and growth.**
TELEPHONE SALES REPRESENTATIVE. Telespectrum, Louisville, KY (2003-present). Originally hired as a temporary employee, was quickly offered full-time permanent employment. Have been strongly encouraged to enter the company's management training program.

ADMINISTRATIVE ASSISTANT. The Kansas City Club, Kansas City, MO (2002-03). Handled a wide range of clerical and office administration duties in this oldest of the city's social clubs which catered to a membership consisting primarily of physicians and attorneys.
- Refined computer skills and applied my attention to detail while verifying, proofreading, and typing or entering data into automated systems: materials including correspondence, bills, statements, receipts, checks, and other related documents.
- Compiled and maintained records and forms relating to business transactions.
- Excelled in customer service activities while dealing with a wide range of professional and community leaders as well as sales personnel and other employees.

PARALEGAL INTERN. Folsom Law Firm, Louisville, KY (2001). Gained a broad introduction into the day-to-day working of a law firm with three partners while refining my research, analytical, and human relations skills.
- Carried out research activities and analysis of factual information for accuracy, completeness, and compliance with applicable law.
- Utilized statutes, recorded judicial decisions, legal briefs and documents, and other sources to gather and verify information for attorneys.
- Dealt with clients tactfully and professionally in order to keep them informed of new court dates and the disposition of their cases.
- Worked closely with the police department while scheduling police officers for court appearances. Filed motions; used a computer on a daily basis while making court dates.

PERSONAL Available for relocation. Am certified by the American Red Cross as a Lifeguard. In excellent physical condition, am a skilled weightlifter.

November 6, 2002

Major Smith
Wyett County Sheriff's Office
131 Dick Street
Wyett, WY 28301

Dear Major Smith:

I would appreciate an opportunity to talk with you soon about how I could contribute to the Sheriff's Office as a DCI Operator for the fugitive/warrant section.

As you will see from my enclosed resume, I am presently a DCI Operator for the Wyett Police Department and completed the SBI certification program for DCI Operators. I have become familiar with using this system for retrieving, maintaining, and entering data for all categories of local, state, and national activities as well as with typing and filing reports and court documents.

Prior experience includes loss prevention with the Wyett Belk department store and industrial security with an Army and Air Force Exchange System (AAFES) retail store in Germany. In addition to my clerical skills and knowledge of office operations, I am trained in OSHA safety requirements, the use of electronic video surveillance systems, and asset protection.

I am a dedicated young professional who can work independently or with others to achieve team goals and objectives. I possess a high level of self-motivation along with the ability to motivate others.

I hope you will welcome my call soon to arrange a brief meeting to discuss your current and future needs and how I might serve them. Thank you in advance for your time.

Sincerely,

Ruby D. Tokay

RUBY D. TOKAY

1110½ Hay Street, Fayetteville, NC 28305 • preppub@aol.com • (910) 483-6611

OBJECTIVE   To offer my experience in office operations and clerical procedures to an organization that can use a detail-oriented young professional with a strong customer service orientation and ability to work well with others as part of a team or on my own.

SPECIAL SKILLS   Knowledgeable of accepted professional office operations and procedures along with experience in using standard office equipment such as computers, typewriters, and phone systems.

EXPERIENCE   **DIVISION OF CRIMINAL INFORMATION (DCI) OPERATOR & RECORDS CLERK.** The Wyett Police Department, Wyett, WY (2000-present). Became skilled in using a specialized information management system (the Division of Criminal Information system) while entering, maintaining, and retrieving information on all classes of police inquiries and record keeping.
- Completed a training program in May 2000 which resulted in certification by the State Bureau of Investigation (SBI) as a DCI Operator.
- Typed and filed police reports; ran criminal history and driving history checks.
- Accessed the computer records of the administrative office of the courts to retrieve information used to maintain criminal court records.
- Generated documents used by local law enforcement personnel for court cases.
- Entered, maintained, and cleared information on local, state, and national level categories including the following:

stolen or recovered property	juvenile runaways
wanted, missing, or unidentified individuals	firearm permits
employment criminal history checks	driving history inquiries

- Sent confirmation requests and responses on matches from stolen or wanted files.

ADMINISTRATIVE ASSISTANT. Belk, Wyett, WY (1995-99). In addition to handling loss prevention responsibilities, completed accident and incident reports and daily merchandise inventories.
- Maintained up-to-date records and files used to complete case files for court; represented the store by testifying in court cases.
- Received a letter of commendation for "actions above and beyond the call of duty" for staying after hours with a customer having car trouble until her husband came.

INDUSTRIAL SECURITY SPECIALIST. AAFES Europe, Germany (1994-95). Worked closely with military police and CID (Criminal Investigation Division) personnel in order to safeguard government property from theft, fraud, and vandalism in a large retail shopping location. Earned certification and conducted OSHA inspections.
- Operated electronic video surveillance systems and planned new procedures which were put into place to protect property.
- Received a monetary award and letter of appreciation for my professionalism.

CERTIFIED NURSE'S AIDE. Home Health Services of Flint County, Inc., Flint, MI (1990-93). Provided personalized private duty nursing care for terminally ill, diabetic, and other seriously ill patients.
- Maintained detailed, up-to-date, and thorough charts and records on each patient.

EDUCATION   Completed the Medical Assistant Program, Ross Medical Education Center, Flint, MI, 1989.

PERSONAL   Excellent human relations and customer service skills. Skilled in motivating others.

DEPUTY SHERIFF   Dear Police Commissioners:

With the enclosed resume, I would make you aware of my interest in the job of Chief of Police of Cheyenne.

As you will see from my resume, I offer 12 years of experience in law enforcement and served with distinction on the Layton Police Force. I have shouldered extensive responsibilities for training, supervising, and evaluating other police officers, and I have been involved in these and other aspects of community police work and police department administration:

Emergency Operations	Investigations	Field Training
Street Crimes	Community Relations	Neighborhood Watch
S.W.A.T. Operations	K-9 Patrol	Budgeting, Grants, Proposals
Police Department Accreditation		

You will see from my resume that I have completed training in most aspects of police work, and I am radar certified, intoxilizer certified, and certified as a Field Training Specialist. While serving with the Layton Police Force, I was involved in the departmental accreditation process, and I also made significant contributions to grants and proposals which were effective in obtaining state and federal money for personnel and equipment.

Although I offer in-depth experience in most aspects of police work, I believe my greatest contributions to the Layton community would be my commitment to quality police work and quality law enforcement. I am well known for my ability to work cordially and effectively with community groups and civic leaders in order to tactfully resolve problems and initiate programs such as Community Watch. As an experienced Patrol Officer of some of Layton's most high-crime areas, I have seen the deadly results of drug traffic, and I am a strong believer in the need for police departments to form strong relationships with youth groups and school systems in order to educate youth about the perils of narcotics. As a relatively young professional (I am 33 years old), I am known for my effective style in relating to young people.

I can provide outstanding personal and professional references, and I would welcome the opportunity to relocate to the Cheyenne community in order to serve as Chief of Police. I hope you will give me the opportunity to show you in person that I am the qualified law enforcement professional and strong leader you are seeking.

Yours sincerely,

Jorge Salvatore

JORGE SALVATORE

1110½ Hay Street, Fayetteville, NC 28305   •   preppub@aol.com   •   (910) 483-6611

OBJECTIVE

I would like to contribute to the city of Roseboro as its Chief of Police through my twelve years of experience in police work which included supervisory and administrative responsibilities, extensive interaction with community groups and civic leaders, and involvement in investigations, emergency operations, and other police activities.

EDUCATION

Basic Law Enforcement Training, Layton Technical Community College, Layton, NV, 1990. Completed training programs on numerous aspects of **police management**:

Budgeting and Budget Proposals	Personnel Management
Field Training Management	Liability Issues for Police Supervisors
Emergency Response Management	

Nevada Justice Academy: Completed 80 hours of training, 1996.

Other Professional Training:

Traffic Accident Investigations	Weapons Training
Special Operations Training	Narcotics Task Force Operations
Covert Investigations	Intelligence Enforcement Training
Street Survival Training	Criminal Investigations
Narcotics Investigations	First Responder Training
Arrest, Search, and Seizure	Serving High-Risk Warrants
Multi-Agency Response Training Related to Violent Crimes	

Radar Certified, Intoxilizer Certified, and certified as a Field Training Officer.

EXPERIENCE

DEPUTY SHERIFF & POLICE OFFICER. Layton Police Department, Layton, NV (1990-present). Began with the department in 1990 and, in 1996, was specially selected for the position of Police Specialist because of my 98% score on a comprehensive exam; was promoted to Deputy Sheriff in 1999.

- **Emergency Operations:** Supervised eight Police Officers while assuring that the Emergency Operations Team was poised at all times to engage in high-risk surveillance, high-risk entries, decoy operations, hostage situations, and tactical operations.
- **Field Training:** As Field Training Officer, handled general patrol work as well as the training of newly appointed Police Officers; trained approximately 70 new police recruits and acted as supervisor in the absence of the Shift Supervisor; prepared employee evaluations, counseled employees, and prepared recommendations.
- **S.W.A.T.:** As Assistant Team Leader, provided leadership to the department's S.W.A.T. Team and Narcotic Vice Task Force.
- **Investigations:** Maintained 100% clearance on the robberies/ homicides investigated.
- **Training and Supervision:** As a Police Specialist assigned to the Patrol Division, trained and supervised other patrol officers while assigning patrol cases and evaluating employee performance.
- **Street Crimes Unit:** Gained experience in patrolling some of Layton's most dangerous areas while handling a wide variety of investigations related to vice, narcotics, drug operations, and intelligence gathering.
- **Community Relations:** Worked with community groups and civic leaders, and became known as a tactful individual known for integrity, common sense, and articulate communication skills.
- **Neighborhood Watch:** Worked with citizens groups to expand Community Watch.
- **K-9 Patrol:** Became skilled in all aspects of K-9 operations.
- **Grants and Proposals:** Assisted in writing grant proposals for the department.

PERSONAL

Offer a proven ability to successfully manage a small law enforcement operation.

CAREER CHANGE

Date

Ms. Rose Smith
Program Analyst
BICS Region #3
Falls Church, VA 22043

**DETECTIVE,
INTERNAL AFFAIRS**

Dear Ms. Smith:

I would appreciate an opportunity to talk with you soon about how I could contribute to the FBI through my expertise related to conducting background investigations and preparing investigative reports. I am skilled in conducting security, background, criminal, and other types of Federal investigations.

As you will see from my enclosed resume, I have excelled in jobs as a Deputy U.S. Marshal and as a detective in an internal affairs section and in a fugitive section. As a detective, I routinely interview prospective employees for the Sheriff's Department and conduct background investigations, which includes developing the plan for the investigation and preparing written and oral reports presenting my findings in a clear and concise manner. I offer a reputation as an articulate communicator and am known for my sound judgement and common sense as well as for my ingenuity and resourcefulness in developing plans for difficult investigations.

While in the U.S. Marshals Service I also conducted background investigations for applicants and prepared investigative reports which I submitted to the Director of the U.S. Marshals Service. I am known for my ability to think logically and objectively in order to arrive at sound conclusions when analyzing facts and evidence.

In prior military service, I held a Top Secret security clearance and received numerous medals and decorations including two Purple Hearts and the Bronze Star with "V" Device. I can provide outstanding personal and professional references which will attest to my high level of physical stamina as well as my keen intellect, integrity, and ability to work well with people at all levels, from governors and senators to prisoners and children.

I possess a valid FL driver's license and will obtain the required investigators insurance. I have access to a facsimile machine and will purchase one if necessary.

I hope you will write or call me soon to suggest a time when we might meet in person to discuss your current and future needs and how I might put my expertise to work for you. Thank you in advance for your time.

Sincerely yours,

Franklin Blintz

FRANKLIN BLINTZ

1110½ Hay Street, Fayetteville, NC 28305   •   preppub@aol.com   •   (910) 483-6611

OBJECTIVE   To serve as a Special Investigator for FBI Background Investigative Contract Service.

EXPERIENCE   *Norvelle County Sheriff's Department*. Norvelle, FL (2000-present).
DETECTIVE, INTERNAL AFFAIRS. Investigate noncriminal citizen or intra-departmental complaints against Sheriff's Department personnel, gathering and evaluating all relevant evidence to determine if violations of policies occurred and reporting directly to the Sheriff.
- Open investigations; interview complainants, department employees, and witnesses; gather background information; complete and file reports.
- Carefully cultivate an unbiased approach in making difficult and objective decisions on character and reliability based on a thorough weighing of all evidence.
- Through observation and past experience drawn from working as a Deputy U.S. Marshal, am able to make recommendations to improve many areas within the department, including jail security, courtroom security, and training.
- Provide guidance and counseling to help departmental operations and morale; have been recognized by employees as instrumental in improving working relationships.
- Interview all prospective employment applicants, run background investigations, and prepare investigative reports for the Sheriff and the FL Sheriff Standards Division.

DETECTIVE, FUGITIVE SECTION. In this first position with the Sheriff's Department, tracked and traced fugitive criminal violators; located and apprehended the suspects in order to return them to the Department's jurisdiction to stand trial.
- In one instance, successfully traced a suspect having 39 warrants through five counties before crafting a plan that led to apprehension.

United States Marshals Service (USMS). Tampa and Miami, FL (1990-00).
DEPUTY U.S. MARSHAL. Started my Marshals Service career in the Miami Office; was selected in 1992 to open and serve as the **Deputy in Charge** of the new Tampa Sub-Office, establishing operational systems, procuring office equipment, and recruiting and then supervising, training, and counseling my staff consisting of two Deputy U.S. Marshals and two Court Security Officers; supervised the Tampa Sub-Office until 2000, earning promotions to **Criminal Investigator** and **Senior Criminal Investigator** during my tenure.
- Frequently served as **Acting Supervisor** and **Chief Deputy U.S Marshal**, supervising the Central District headquarters in Middle and four sub-offices, communicating and coordinating with the Director of the U.S. Marshals Service and his staff in Washington, DC; visited Washington on several occasions representing the Marshals Service.
- Enforced all court orders issued by U.S. District Courts.
- Provided security/protective service for judges, foreign dignitaries, government officials, courtrooms, sequestered juries, and government witnesses.
- Conducting investigations, locating, and arresting federal fugitives.
- Planning and coordinating major asset seizures in drug cases.
- Conducted background investigations of applicants seeking USMS employment; prepare investigative reports and submitted them to the Director, U.S. Marshals Service.
- Prepared and submitted to Washington complex operations plans for high-risk trials.
- Promoted the U.S. Marshals Service by developing and maintaining excellent communication, liaison, and working relationships with other USMS districts, other law enforcement agencies, U.S. Attorneys, and the judiciary.

TRAINING   United States Marshals Service: Completed training in specialized law enforcement, court security, supervisory skills, and street survival.

CAREER CHANGE

Date

Special Agent Wanda Johnson
Federal Bureau of Investigations

DETECTIVE

This talented military officer is changing careers. She hopes to become a Detective with a state law enforcement organization or a Special Agent with the FBI.

Dear Special Agent Johnson:

The purpose of this letter is to initiate the process of being considered for an appointment as a Detective or Special Agent with the FBI.

I presently serve my country as a U.S. Army officer. With a background in Military Intelligence, I have proven that I possess strong abilities in analyzing and tracking real-world activities, combining attention to detail with excellent planning and organizational skills. Since my first days as an officer, I have quickly earned the respect of my superiors for my physical and mental toughness. I have been described as an individual who will find a way to get the job done whether I am providing training, supervising intelligence gathering activities, planning and carrying out exercise and crisis response actions throughout the world, or controlling multimillion-dollar inventories of equipment.

Since joining the military, I have met the challenges of working with a vast array of people from newly assigned technical personnel, to supervisors and managers, to senior executives. I have earned the reputation as an articulate, self-motivated professional with exceptional communication and motivational skills. I am a proactive manager and an aggressive, result-oriented professional who possesses sound judgment, keen analytical ability, and persuasive speaking skills.

I am confident that the qualities which helped me excel as a military officer would easily translate to success with the Federal Bureau of Investigation. From my experience in deploying the Common Ground Station with the Joint Surveillance Target Attack Radar System and preparing units to deal with U.S contingency operations in Bosnia and Panama, to my ability to converse in English, Spanish and Mandarin Chinese, I believe my background will prove to be a tremendous asset to the Federal Bureau of Investigation. I appreciate the opportunity to meet and discuss the Bureau's requirements, needs and goals and will provide outstanding references at the appropriate time.

Sincerely,

Sandy W. Davis

SANDY W. DAVIS

1110½ Hay Street, Fayetteville, NC 28305   •   preppub@aol.com   •   (910) 483-6611

OBJECTIVE   To obtain a position as a Special Agent with the FBI.

EDUCATION   **B.S. in Chemistry,** University of Michigan, Ann Arbor, MI, 1994.

CLEARANCE   **Top Secret/SCI** security clearance

EXPERIENCE   **COMPANY EXECUTIVE OFFICER.** Ft. Polk, LA (2000-present). Was handpicked for
this job as "second in command" of a 95-person company which must be ready to respond to
crisis situations and carry out operations throughout the world.
- Commended for the success of the All Service Combat Identification and Evaluation
  Team 2002/Limited User Test by the Chief of Military Intelligence.
- Oversee the individual and group training for personnel in 21 different job specialties.
- Ensure the company is ready to respond with no notice and carry out JSTARS (Joint
  Surveillance Target Attack Radar System) support missions.
- Accountable for the readiness of 53 vehicles which include two Common Ground Stations
  (CGS), and ensure the quality of training, welfare, and readiness of imagery specialists
  operating and maintaining the CGS System. Oversee administrative and logistics support
  for 20 people operating $15 million worth of imagery and intelligence equipment.

PLATOON LEADER. Ft. Polk, LA (1997-00). Officially evaluated as "an aggressive young
officer who excels under pressure . . .clearly head and shoulders above her peers," was
selected for advancement to a higher managerial level based on my performance as supervisor
of one of the U.S. Army's only airborne CGS units which supported the 18th Airborne Corps
in its short-notice worldwide response mission.
- Deployed 13 soldiers to five different command posts throughout Europe to support U.S.
  efforts in Kosovo, "Operation Allied Force."
- Tailored the type and level of support needed in JSTARS contingency missions to
  supported units in response to the operation's status as deliberate or crisis action.
- Controlled two CGS systems as well as vehicles and generators with a total value in
  excess of $15 million while supervising 20 people.
- Deactivated a company in just three weeks: turned in or transferred 131 lines of excess
  equipment worth over $10 million. De-fielded five outdated Medium Ground Station
  Modules and turned in 74 lines of excess equipment with a value of $28 million.

INTELLIGENCE OFFICER. Ft. Polk, LA (1995-97). As Intelligence Officer for the Army's
only Airborne Military Police battalion, prepared, analyzed, and assimilated tailored intelligence products to the Battalion Commander to ensure all necessary information was available for sound decision-making. Controlled a $35 million inventory.
- Earned a reputation as a "truly outstanding officer ... who continues to excel in every
  area" and as one who made "immeasurable contributions."
- Advised the battalion commander, subordinate company commanders, and staff members
  on issues related to physical security, personnel, information, and information systems
  security as well as on security management and crime prevention.

TRAINING   **Jumpmaster School,** inspecting/approving equipment for airborne operations
Airborne School, how to exit and land from a high-performance Air Force aircraft
Security Manager's Course, providing security for physical assets and information systems
Motor Officer Course, procedures for managing vehicle maintenance operations.
Military Intelligence Officer's Course, military decision-making process

Date

Exact Name of Person
Exact Title of Person
Exact Company Name
Exact Address
City, state zip

DISPATCHER   Dear Exact Name:

With this letter and the enclosed resume, I would like to initiate the process of formally applying for the position of Dispatcher with the Newton Grove Police Department.

As you will see from my resume, I have excelled in employment with the Department of Defense as well as with civilian contractors and private firms. In one position, I controlled access to an area which housed multimillion-dollar aircraft. I also played a key role in securing U.S. President George W. Bush during his visit to Chicago in 2001. In other assignments I have provided protection for business assets, VIPs, nuclear facilities, and government buildings.

You will also see from my resume that I am aggressive in pursuit of training related to security and law enforcement. With a reputation a highly motivated individual, I seek out opportunities to refine my knowledge in areas including weapons operation, surveillance systems, and counterterrorism. On my own initiative, I have earned numerous certifications and credentials related to security and law enforcement.

My communication skills are highly refined, and I am confident that I could excel in the Dispatcher position which you have advertised. I can provide outstanding references at the appropriate time, and I hope you will contact me to suggest a time when we might meet in person to discuss the position.

Yours sincerely,

Andrew J. Eliot

ANDREW J. ELIOT

1110½ Hay Street, Fayetteville, NC 28305 • preppub@aol.com • (910) 483-6611

OBJECTIVE

I want to contribute to an organization that can use a versatile professional with a background related to security, law enforcement, and protective services along with professional credentials and licenses as a driver and vehicle/equipment operator.

EDUCATION

Completed one year of General Studies, Prince William Community College, IL, 1993-94.

SECURITY SKILLS

Security: Received Certificate of Training from six-month **Security and Law Enforcement Procedures Training Program**, Chicago, IL, 1996.
Through experience and training, am knowledgeable of the following:

Confinement Operations	Law Enforcement/Security Procedures
Dispatcher Operations	VIP Protection
Physical Restraint Skills	Building/Vehicle Searches
Antiterrorism	Surveillance

• Knowledgeable of the following weapons, security, and alarm systems and devices: Pepper sprays, 9 MM, 40 cal., M16A2 rifle, 50 cal. machine gun, lidar/radar devices, Venticator alarm surveillance system, surveillance thermal imager, annunciator systems
Hold Secret security clearance

DRIVING SKILLS

Licenses and Certifications: Class A CDL, State of Illinois, 1998.
Forklift License, Center for Employment Education (CEE); **Hazardous Materials Certified**, Department of Defense, 1997, and CEE, 1998.
• Completed **Professional Truck Driving Course**, Center for Employment Education (CEE), Chicago, IL, 1999.
• Offer the ability to repair minor problems on tractors and various trailers to include oil changes, brake adjustments, tire changes; capable of operating manual/13-speed tractor with doubles, triples, tanker, flatbeds, lowboys, forklifts, hazardous material endorsements; experienced in driving Kenworth 9 speed or M 2.5 ton military vehicle.

EXPERIENCE

SECURITY POLICEMAN & DISPATCHER. Department of Defense, Chicago, IL (2001-present). Monitor alarms to nuclear weapons while protecting assets and personnel; dispatch fire teams to alarmed areas.

SECURITY POLICEMAN. Private Security Services, Chicago, IL (2000-01). Controlled entry to restricted areas which involved maintaining security of $3 billion in aircraft and support equipment; ensured proper authorized entry into 13 restricted areas, and monitored alarms which secured priority resources.
• Personally averted a breach of security by three unauthorized people in a restricted area.
• Played a key role in securing U.S. President George Bush during his visit to Illinois.

Other experience: Worked in the security field in these positions:
1996-99: **SECURITY GUARD.** International Security, VA. Provided security for local businesses and stores; monitored locked doors, helped evacuate buildings during alarms, and checked IDs.
1994-95: **SECURITY GUARD.** Guardsmark Security, Chicago, IL. Protected the Court House Building, scanned individuals for weapons, checked personal items, secured personal items, and secured entry to building; learned to use X-ray machines and metal detectors and learned to detect bombs, guns, and hidden weapons.

PERSONAL

Outstanding references. Dedicated worker known for integrity who strives for excellence.

Date

Exact Name of Person
Exact Title
Exact Name of Company
Address
City, State, Zip

EMERGENCY MANAGEMENT

Dear Exact Name of Person (or Dear Sir or Madam if answering a blind ad):

With the enclosed resume, I would like to express my interest in exploring employment opportunities with your organization.

As you will see from my resume, I have more than 15 years of successful program management experience. I am especially adept at researching, organizing, and presenting technically complex information in support of senior decision makers. I have excelled in providing guidance and advice on nuclear, biological, and chemical (NBC) defense matters, emergency management/disaster preparedness operations and exercises, and developing defense measures against terrorist attacks.

In my present assignment on the Department of Defense staff, I manage the planning and implementation of the Chemical Weapons Treaty. In prior jobs, I served as the senior government representative during politically sensitive, international arms control inspections, and I supervised the inspection team escorts. I have been the primary staff advisor on NBC matters at three separate organizational levels and additionally on a medical center staff. As an environmental engineering project officer, I managed multimillion-dollar, multi-year contracts to investigate explosives and heavy metal contamination at several government facilities. During an earlier assignment, I represented the U.S. Army as its technical expert in NBC decontamination policy and procedures during a visit to the British Self-Defense Forces to share NBC information.

Widely recognized for my technical expertise and problem-solving abilities, I possess a strong work ethic and reputation as a team builder who sets high standards. In addition to the diversity of positions held and accomplishments mentioned on my resume, I would like to point out that I authored the U.S. Army's field manual on de-mining operations.

If you can use a versatile and mature management professional, I hope you will contact me soon to suggest a time we might meet to discuss how I could contribute to your organization. I can provide excellent professional and personal references at the appropriate time. Thank you for your time and consideration.

Sincerely,

Creighton Flowers

CREIGHTON FLOWERS

1110½ Hay Street, Fayetteville, NC 28305   •   preppub@aol.com   •   (910) 483-6611

OBJECTIVE

To benefit a company that can use a senior military officer experienced in program management with expertise related to the chemical weapons treaty, disaster preparedness, and weapons of mass destruction.

EDUCATION & TRAINING

Earned an **M.S. in Chemistry** and **B.A. in Biology**, State University of New York (SUNY). Received advanced training for military executives, including programs for chemical officers and graduate-level training in leadership and staff management.

EXPERIENCE

Advanced to hold national-level program management roles, Department of Defense:
PROGRAM IMPLEMENTATION MANAGER. Washington, DC (2000-present). Managed the policy planning and implementation of DoD agencies to ensure compliance with the Chemical Weapons Treaty. Oversaw 29 inspections of chemical weapons facilities.

DEPARTMENT CHIEF, ARMS CONTROL INSPECTION AGENCY. Washington, DC (1998-2000). Supervised 33 people. Led, trained, and deployed a 10-person multi-disciplined team for international inspections to U.S. facilities. Served as the U.S. representative and team leader on seven inspections to U.S. chemical weapons facilities.

ADVISOR/PROGRAM MANAGER. Germany (1994-97). Subject matter expert on NBC (nuclear, biological, chemical) defense for an Army division. Supervised a 13-person operations, training, and logistics section. Oversaw mission readiness of a 120-person chemical company.
- Designed a hazardous response capability and trained and equipped the teams to provide support to deployed U.S. forces in the Middle East.
- Managed an annual million-dollar budget of NBC defense equipment.
- Molded a diverse group of people into a successful team and established a forward node in Bosnia coordinating air, rail, and road movement of 800 people and 100 vehicles.

DEPUTY OPERATIONS AND SECURITY MANAGER. Germany (1992-93). Primary advisor on NBC defense and security matters for a 1600-person regional medical center, including eight outlying clinics.
- Developed and coordinated the emergency preparedness plans in support of the chemical and nuclear weapons retrograde operations from Europe.
- Initiated major physical and procedural security measures at the medical center during the Gulf War, yielding zero security incidents and a public relations success story.
- Designed a hazardous response capability and trained and equipped the teams to provide support to deployed U.S. forces in the Middle East.
- Managed an annual million-dollar budget of NBC defense equipment.
- Molded a diverse group of people into a successful team and established a forward node in Hungary coordinating air, rail, and road movement of 800 people and 100 vehicles.

COMMUNITY MANAGER. Germany (1990-92). Directed base operations support and quality-of-life issues for an 1800-person community on three different installations.
- Instituted cost savings initiative to relocate facility engineering workers, which improved remote site support and avoided costly labor relations suits.
- Despite base closure actions, identified methods and executed facility upgrade programs which significantly improved the quality of life for community residents.

PERSONAL

Excellent references on request.

Date

Orlando Police Department Recruiting Officer
Orlando Police Department
P.O. Box 913
Orlando, FL 32802-0913

**EMERGENCY
OPERATIONS MANAGER**

Dear Sir or Madam:

I would appreciate an opportunity to talk to you soon about how I could contribute to the Orlando Police Department as an Emergency Operations Manager through my skills, knowledge, and abilities as well as through my strong interest in relocating to your area to work in this capacity.

As you will see from my enclosed resume, I am presently a First Lieutenant in the U.S. Army stationed with the 82nd Airborne Division at Ft. Sill, OK. As a junior military officer I have excelled through my strong leadership, personnel management, and motivational skills. In my current role as the Administrative and Training Manager for a medical support company I have been involved in developing plans and overseeing the operation of an 18-person ambulance platoon which is a part of the rapid deployment forces which are responsible for responding immediately to "real-world" trouble spots.

I earned a bachelor's degree in Criminal Justice prior to entering the U.S. Army. I was selected for leadership roles and singled out for my dedication, professionalism, and supervisory skills. As an ROTC (Reserve Officers Training Corps) cadet commander I was honored as the Distinguished Military Graduate of my class, was elected president of the Alpha Phi Sigma National Criminal Justice Honor Society, and was Valedictorian of my baccalaureate class with a 3.9 GPA.

While serving in the Army as a commissioned officer, I excelled in jobs requiring expertise in managing human and material resources. I feel that through the combination of my education in Criminal Justice, natural intelligence and leadership skills, and success while serving my country as a military officer, I can offer your department a strong base of professionalism and dedication.

I hope you will welcome my call soon to arrange a brief meeting at your convenience to discuss your current and future needs and how I might serve them. Thank you in advance for your time.

Sincerely yours,

Beth Nilson Smith

BETH NILSON SMITH

1110½ Hay Street, Fayetteville, NC 28305 • preppub@aol.com • (910) 483-6611

OBJECTIVE   To offer my education in criminal justice and strong interest in this field to an organization that can use a talented and intelligent young professional who has excelled as a junior military officer with a reputation for superior leadership, analytical, and troubleshooting skills.

EXPERIENCE   *Became known as a very dedicated, self-motivated, and goal-oriented individual who could be counted on to provide leadership as well as problem-solving abilities, U.S. Army:*
ADMINISTRATIVE AND TRAINING MANAGER. Ft. Sill, OK (2000-present). Ensured that an 18-person airborne ambulance platoon was at all times ready to deploy worldwide on short notice: oversaw the maintenance and readiness of more than $450,000 worth of items and supplies including medical equipment.

- Developed plans and the standard operating procedures (SOPs) for safety which were adopted for use and became the model for the parent organization.
- Earned ratings above 90% in all areas of responsibilities during numerous inspections.
- Coordinated the evacuation of 900 casualties by land and air during a joint service training exercise: achieved some of the highest statistics ever for a project of this scope.
- Was officially described as highly flexible and enthusiastic, quick to react to rapidly changing priorities, and intensely loyal although not afraid to voice an opinion.
- Used my educational background and knowledge while managing the organization's physical security and NBC (nuclear/biological/chemical) programs.

OPERATIONS MANAGER. Republic of Korea (1997-00). As second-in-command of training, staffing, and logistics activities, supported these areas for two health clinics and their headquarters centers which provided medical care to a population of 8,500 people.

- Controlled a $2 million inventory of medical supplies and equipment in a 105-employee organization with an annual operating budget of $331,500.
- Coordinated the Republic of Korea Army's first-ever Combat Lifesavers Course, modeled after the U.S. Army program.
- Applied my knowledge and communication skills while developing and publishing standard operating procedures (SOPs) in 12 separate areas of company activities.
- Established and supervised the organization's improved physical security program.
- Combined two clinics into one and created the standard operating procedures (SOPs) as well as conducting regular assistance visits.

TRAINING PROGRAM PLANNER AND MANAGER. OK National Guard, Maysville, OK (1993-96). Developed training plans for areas including range operations and command post operations as well as procedures for loading/transporting personnel and equipment.
- Set the standard for physical conditioning and health awareness by achieving the maximum possible score of 300 on the Army Physical Fitness Test.

COLLEGE STUDENT. Oklahoma State University, Tulsa, OK (1991-93) and Tulsa Community College, Tulsa, OK (1989-91). Graduated with honors in two degree programs.

EDUCATION   B.A., **Criminal Justice**, Tulsa State University, Tulsa, OK, 1993.
- Graduated Valedictorian.

Date

Exact Name of Person
Exact Title
Exact Name of Company
Address
City, State, Zip

**EMERGENCY
TELECOMMUNICATOR**

Dear Exact Name of Person (or Dear Sir or Madam if answering a blind ad):

With the enclosed resume, I would like to express my interest in exploring employment opportunities with your organization.

As you will see from my resume, I am currently excelling as an Emergency Telecommunicator with the City of Harrisburg. In that capacity, I supervise nine emergency telecommunicators as I assist in the planning and implementation of department goals. I have been commended on numerous occasions for my strong written and oral communication skills as I discharged my responsibility of performing liaison with numerous city and county departments.

Although I am held in high regard in my current position, I am selectively exploring opportunities in other cities which might use my services. I hope you will contact me if you feel that my technical expertise and management skills could be of value to you.

Sincerely,

Crystal Gale

CRYSTAL GALE

1110½ Hay Street, Fayetteville, NC 28305 • preppub@aol.com • (910) 483-6611

OBJECTIVE   To benefit an organization that can use an experienced telecommunications manager with exceptional communication and organizational skills who offers a track record of success in managing a staff handling a large volume of inbound calls in high-pressure situations.

COMPUTERS   Familiar with many of the most popular computer operating systems and software, including Windows, Microsoft Word and Excel, Corel WordPerfect, and others. Have quickly mastered new systems, including proprietary programs used for computer-aided dispatch, auditing, and accounting.

CERTIFICATIONS   Have completed certification courses in training, supervision, and telecommunications through the APCO Institute, including:
- Training Officer certification course.
- Pennsylvania Division of Criminal Information, SBI certification.
- Basic Telecommunicator course.
- Supervisory Skills course, City of Harrisburg and Pennsylvania Sheriff's Association.

EXPERIENCE   *With the City of Harrisburg, started as an Emergency Telecommunicator and advanced to positions of increasing responsibility:*
2000-present: ASSISTANT SUPERVISOR, EMERGENCY TELECOMMUNICATIONS SERVICES. Harrisburg, PA. Provide supervisory oversight and plan, prioritize, assign, and review the work of a shift crew of emergency telecommunicators taking calls and dispatching emergency services for the 911 system.
- Supervise nine emergency telecommunicators, monitoring their performance to ensure that information is taken and services dispatched in a timely and accurate manner.
- Interview, hire, and train new employees; conduct performance appraisals for personnel under my supervision to evaluate and improve organizational efficiency.
- Assist in the planning and implementation of emergency communications goals.
- Evaluate the overall operations and activities of personnel assigned to the shift, recommending improvements and modifications to existing policies and procedures.
- Oversee the operation of the computer-aided dispatch and radio systems to ensure that all calls are dispatched in accordance with established policies and procedures.
- Prepare monthly employee schedules and shift assignments; ensure that employees perform their duties in compliance with federal, state, and local regulations.
- Serve as liaison for the Communications Department with other city and county departments, as well as with other divisions, outside agencies, and the general public.

1993-00: EMERGENCY TELECOMMUNICATOR. Harrisburg, PA. Operated a variety of communications equipment, including wide-band radios, telephones, computer consoles and systems, and dictaphones to coordinate emergency calls and relay requests for information and assistance involving emergency services and law enforcement agencies.
- Monitored radio broadcast frequencies of police, fire, and rescue units, dispatching the appropriate service to answer 911 calls. Managed tense situations requiring diplomacy.

ACCOUNTING AUDITOR. Sears, Roebuck, & Company, Harrisburg, PA and Lawton, OK (1989-1993). Performed a wide variety of sales, bookkeeping, and accounting functions while serving as an auditor in two different locations for this large national retailer.

PERSONAL   Excellent personal and professional references are available upon request.

CAREER CHANGE

Date

Exact Name of Person
Title or Position
Name of Company
Address (no., street)
Address (city, state, zip)

EVALUATOR & SECURITY INSPECTOR

This distinguished young law enforcement professional has a good idea of what he wants to do next: he wants to supervise a small security team in a casino. Usually the objective in a resume is not this specific, but in this case it makes sense to have at least one version of his resume with a very focused objective.

Dear Exact Name of Person (or Dear Sir or Madam if answering a blind ad):

I would appreciate an opportunity to talk with you soon about how I could apply my expertise related to industrial security, resource protection, and security operations and planning for the benefit of your organization.

As you will see from my resume, I offer a "track record" of successful performance. In my present position as Training Manager and Evaluator, I am the U.S. Army's liaison with the Maryland Army National Guard. During my short time in this position I have played a positive role in gaining acceptance for this program which was mandated by law and, in its early stages, was meeting resistance from people who did not feel the concept would work. I ensure that military police personnel in 11 separate units are trained and ready to respond when called on during international situations.

Throughout my years of service to my country in the military, I earned a reputation for my expertise in the areas of resource protection, VIP protection, and antiterrorism operations while earning a reputation for unquestioned leadership skills and personal integrity.

Known for my ability to "always get the job done" no matter how difficult it may be, I have been recognized for "meritorious service" with five commendation medals. I am proud of my efforts while working with a German Army organization, resulting in my earning the German Army "Efficiency Badge" in silver for my abilities as a soldier.

I hope you will welcome my call to ensure you received my resume and arrange a brief meeting to discuss your current and future needs and how I might serve them. Thank you in advance for your time.

Sincerely yours,

Elias H. Johnson

ELIAS H. JOHNSON

1110½ Hay Street, Fayetteville, NC 28305   •   preppub@aol.com   •   (910) 483-6611

OBJECTIVE
To supervise a small security team in the casino industry.

SECURITY SKILLS & COMPUTER KNOWLEDGE
- Hold a **Top Secret** security clearance with **Special Background Investigation**.
- Graduate of MP Supervisor's Development Course with Honors.
- Use the IBM-compatible computer with MS-DOS 5.0 operating system; familiar with a variety of software including Word and PowerPoint.

EXPERIENCE
SECURITY INSPECTOR. U.S. Army, Ft. Meade, MD (2000-present). As the liaison with the Army National Guard, train and evaluate military police units; ensure that 11 units are trained to participate as "rapid deployment forces" in international crises.
- Strengthened coordination among staff sections while improving resource management.

SUPERVISORY MILITARY POLICEMAN (MP). U.S. Army, Ft. Ord, CA (1997-00). Improved vehicle capabilities by 70% while overseeing training and work performance of personnel in an organization providing security and law enforcement support for an infantry division. Received an award for excellence.

SECURITY SUPERVISOR. U.S. Army, Germany (1993-96). Trained, inspected, supervised, and evaluated 50 people involved in guarding a NATO nuclear weapons storage site for the protection of millions of dollars worth of assets.
- Won an Army-wide "MP Company of Excellence Award" and two quarterly awards.

SECURITY ADMINISTRATOR. U.S. Army, Ft. Dix, NJ (1990-92). Promoted from Security Supervisor and Instructor, was chosen to direct large-scale security operations while coordinating logistical and administrative support for 158 specialists protecting a 20,000-person facility; coordinated disaster relief and civil disturbance functions.
- Administered a $300,000 annual operating budget and $800,000 in equipment.
- Planned and scheduled the training and operations of a 200-person rapid deployment/combat military police organization with an extremely tight budget.
- Received an award for superior duty performance.

VIP SECURITY COORDINATOR/EXECUTIVE AIDE. U.S. Army, Korea (1988-90). As the ranking representative of the Provost Marshal, directed 14 patrols, a security office, and a 14-person multinational police force handling responsibilities ranging from aircraft crash investigation to VIP protection.

Highlights of Earlier Experience
Communication: Refined my communication skills prospecting for U.S. Army recruits.
Employee training and supervision: Earned a reputation as an outstanding leader while training, scheduling, and supervising 50 security specialists performing police work.
Security and counterterrorism expertise: As a Facility Security Supervisor/Desk Sergeant, became thoroughly familiar with alarm system management while supervising 14 personnel securing a 2,000-acre ammunition storage site in a country with a high level of terrorist activity.
VIP protection: Handpicked to plan/coordinate security for VIP's including the President and the Army Chief of Staff, increased security when a jet fighter crashed during Mr. Bush's visit; supervised 20 law enforcement personnel securing restricted areas.

EDUCATION TRAINING
Have completed 60 credit hours toward a degree in Criminal Justice.
Received extensive training in counterterrorism, physical security, and S.W.A.T. tactics.

Exact Name of Person
Title or Position
Name of Company
Address (no., street)
Address (city, state, zip)

FEDERAL AGENT   Dear Exact Name of Person (or Dear Sir or Madam if answering a blind ad):

I would appreciate an opportunity to talk with you soon about how I could contribute to your organization through my exceptional analytical, decision-making, and managerial abilities refined through my accomplishments in security, protection, investigation, and law enforcement.

Currently I am a Federal Agent assigned to the Los Angeles Office of Special Investigations, designing and conducting investigations and protection plans for Top Secret defense plants located in California, Hawaii, and the Southwest. I liaise with top-level governmental and law enforcement officials on the development of counter-measures against terrorism, narcotics smuggling, and gang-related activities.

I have attended courses and seminars and studied on my own to remain knowledgeable of counterterrorism, counternarcotics, VIP protection, weapons training, evidence collection, and gang investigation. My technical knowledge also extends to intercepting voice communications and surveillance as well as hiring, training, and supervising both large and small armed guard forces with recent exposure to economic espionage and terrorism. My enthusiastic and thorough speaking and briefing skills are utilized on a routine basis while working in close coordination with senior officials at the national level.

My unique combination of creativity and vision, practical technical knowledge, and extensive experience are transferable to many situations where I could make important contributions.

I hope you will welcome my call soon to arrange a brief meeting at your convenience to discuss your current and future needs and how I might serve them. Thank you in advance for your time.

Sincerely yours,

Jared Y. Lego

Alternate last paragraph:
I hope you will call or write me soon to suggest a time convenient for us to meet and discuss your current and future needs and how I might serve them. Thank you in advance for your time.

JARED Y. LEGO

1110½ Hay Street, Fayetteville, NC 28305   •   preppub@aol.com   •   (910) 483-6611

OBJECTIVE   To offer a broad range of analytical, policy and decision-making, and problem-solving abilities to an organization that can benefit from my years of accomplishments as an expert in the areas of security, protection, investigation, and law enforcement.

EDUCATION   Attended over 400 hours of college-level training courses, including classes in gang investigation, quality management process, HAZMAT response, VIP protection skills, weapons training, supervisory/management skills, safety training, and Office of Special Investigations (OSI) training; ranked second in the graduating class of the U.S.A.F. OSI School. Completed 60 credit hours in the **Bachelor of Science in Criminal Justice** degree program, Community College of the Air Force, Maxwell AFB, AL.

SKILLS   Tactical and protective operation planning and execution, surveillance, loss prevention & work place safety, industrial security, violent crime, fraud, narcotics, counterintelligence and counterterrorism investigative program development, physical security, evidence collection, and evasive & aggressive driving techniques; proficient with semiautomatic weapons.

EXPERIENCE   **FEDERAL AGENT**. Department of Defense, Los Angeles, CA (2002-present). Develop, plan, conduct, and supervise major criminal counterintelligence and fraud investigations for California-based space and missiles systems center, Los Angeles Airport, and 14 major defense plant security offices located throughout Hawaii and the Southwest; brief senior intelligence and security officials on gang and narcotic related issues, including DEA, NSA, FBI, Department of State, and Department of the Army personnel.
- Act as Point of Contact for all area narcotic, gang, and environmental crime issues; cultivate and supervise covert information sources, while also serving as Lead Agent for the Protective Services Operation Team, which provides high-level personal security for VIPs located in southern California; train, supervise, and evaluate 38 civilian law enforcement personnel and 18 federal agents.
- Developed and now direct the Department of Defense antismuggling task force based at Los Angeles International Airport; researched, coordinated, and conducted covert narcotics programs within various agencies.
- Designed and implemented a $120,000 secure-voice radio system, significantly increasing agent safety and operations communications. Trained Federal and local law enforcement personnel on handling both gang activity and narcotics smuggling.

FEDERAL AGENT. Department of Defense, Harrison, MS (1991-02). Refined technical and investigative procedures while planning, coordinating, and conducting criminal, fraud, counterintelligence, and felony investigations within a tri-state area, in addition to providing support to military training centers.
- Coordinated security support and child abuse investigations with local, state, and Federal agencies. Convicted over 100 drug dealers while working undercover.

DEPUTY SHERIFF. Harrison County, MS (1987-90). Gained valuable "street-level" law enforcement experience while serving as a reserve deputy patrolling up to 100 hours a month responding to violent crimes and medical emergencies.
* Worked in undercover operations with a multi-agency narcotic task force.
* Handled crowd control at concerts, sporting and special events, and night clubs.

LICENSURES   Hold Federal Agent Status with the Department of Defense and OSHA/Hazardous Materials First Responder and an American Red Cross Basic Life Support/CPR Instructor certification.

Date

Exact Name of Person
Title or Position
Name of Company
Address (no., street)
Address (city, state, zip)

**FIRE FIGHTER &
EMERGENCY
MEDICAL TECHNICIAN**

Dear Exact Name of Person (or Dear Sir or Madam if answering a blind ad):

I would appreciate an opportunity to talk with you soon about how I could contribute to your organization through my background as a Fire Fighter and Emergency Medical Technician.

You will see from my resume that I am currently serving the city of LaRue, Maine, as a Fire Fighter and EMT. I am excelling in all aspects of my job and can provide outstanding references at the appropriate time.

My wife has just completed a master's degree program in Gerontology and we are in the process of relocating to Syracuse, NY, where she has accepted a management position with a private practice. Naturally I am seeking to relocate along with her, and I feel confident that I could benefit a fire department through my extensive experience and attractive personal qualities which include initiative and integrity.

I hope you will welcome my call soon to arrange a brief meeting at your convenience to discuss your current and future needs and how I might serve them. Thank you in advance for your time.

Sincerely yours,

Adrian C. Reason

ADRIAN C. REASON

1110½ Hay Street, Fayetteville, NC 28305　•　preppub@aol.com　•　(910) 483-6611

OBJECTIVE　　To offer my strong working knowledge of emergency services to an organization that can benefit from my abilities related to administration and supervision of emergency services operations through my well-developed communication skills.

CERTIFICATIONS　Completed training programs leading to certification in the following areas:

ME Fire Fighter Level I	ME Fire Fighter Level II
ME Level II Fire Service Instructor	ME Fire Fighter Level III
ME Emergency Medical Technician (EMT)	Basic Vehicle Extraction
ME Hazardous Materials Operation Level I	Basic Trauma Life Support

EDUCATION　　Attend continuing education courses in **Fire/Emergency Services,** LaRue Technical Community College (LTCC), ME.

Am knowledgeable of a wide range of fire fighting activities including:

Hazardous material control	Scene evaluation building inspection
Advanced rescue techniques	Incident command system

EXPERIENCE　　*Have developed the ability to manage my time for maximum productivity while holding multiple jobs and volunteer roles simultaneously:*

FIRE FIGHTER and **EMERGENCY MEDICAL TECHNICIAN.** LaRue Fire Department, LaRue, ME (2000-present). Have developed a working knowledge of PROBER Chief and WordPerfect software and how to use these computer programs for record keeping and preparing reports.

INSTRUCTOR. Clinton Community College, Clinton, ME (1997-00). Served as the Lead Instructor for the Fire Academy portion of the school's curriculum.

FIRE FIGHTER. LaRue Fire Department, LaRue, ME (1994-97). Made important contributions to this station's operations including doing extensive public relations work and was promoted to hold a captain's slot.
* Developed and implemented a HAZCOM policy in accordance with ME General Statutes 95-173-95-218 of the Hazardous Chemicals Right-to-Know Act — also included information from OSHA and SARA regulations.
* Implemented a fire prevention program after developing information geared to hold the interest of elementary school children.
* Presented fire prevention programs to nursing homes serviced by this station.

VOLUNTEER FIRE FIGHTER. LaRue Fire Department, LaRue, ME (1989-95).

SQUAD SERGEANT. LaRue County Rescue Squad, LaRue, ME (1988). Supervised a six-person squad at substation #60, Bryson Creek Road.

AFFILIATIONS　　Hold membership in the following professional organizations:
ME Fire Fighters Association
ME Fire Instructors Association
ME Association of Rescue Squads

PERSONAL　　Am highly self-motivated. Offer outstanding communication skills. Am very effective in calming people and dealing with people of all ages under difficult and dangerous conditions.

Date

Exact Name of Person
Title or Position
Name of Company
Address (no., street)
Address (city, state, zip)

FIRE FIGHTER & E.M.T.

Dear Exact Name of Person (or Dear Sir or Madam if answering a blind ad):

I would appreciate an opportunity to talk with you soon about how I could contribute to your organization through my background as a Fire Fighter and Emergency Medical Technician.

I offer strong credentials as an EMT and Fire Fighter. I was placed on the *National Registry of Emergency Medical Technicians in* 2000 as a Basic EMT and I subsequently earned *Intermediate EMT* certification which is valid until 2008. I also became certified as a *Hazardous Materials Responder Level I* (the Operations Level) .

In my current position as an Emergency Medical Technician with the Columbus County Emergency Medical Service, I work on a part-time basis while still serving on active duty with the U.S. Army. I have completed the county protocol and megacode tests, and I only need to respond to 12 calls with a preceptor to observe to be fully certified by Columbus County. It is my desire to become employed with Columbus County full time when I leave military service.

I hope you will welcome my call soon to arrange a brief meeting at your convenience to discuss your current and future needs and how I might serve them. Thank you in advance for your time.

Sincerely yours,

Oliver G. Lorgnette

OLIVER C. LORGNETTE

1110½ Hay Street, Fayetteville, NC 28305   •   preppub@aol.com   •   (910) 483-6611

OBJECTIVE   To offer my experience and strong interest in emergency services to an organization that can use a certified fire fighter and emergency medical technician who is known for possessing a high level of self motivation and a pleasant and concerned personality.

TRAINING &   Have completed approximately 1,200 hours of continuing education credit hours which led
CERTIFICATION   to *National Fire Protection Association Fire Fighter Professional Qualifications for Fire Fighter I and II,* Columbus Technical Community College, GA. Specific courses included:

sprinklers	overhaul	ropes
foam fire streams	ventilation	safety
portable extinguishers	fire control	rescue
emergency medical care	water supplies	ladders
CPR instructor training	forcible entry	salvage
fire department organization	fire behavior	streams
fire alarms and communication	building construction	trench rescue
fire hose appliances and streams	personal protective equipment	
fire prevention education and cause determination		

- Was placed on the *National Registry of Emergency Medical Technicians,* December 15, 2000, as a Basic EMT.
- Earned *Intermediate EMT* certification which is valid until October 31, 2008
- Was certified as a *Hazardous Materials Responder Level I* (the Operations Level) by the State of Georgia Fire and Rescue Commission.
- Was certified as a *Level II Fire Fighter* by the Georgia Fire and Rescue Commission.

EXPERIENCE   *Am expanding my knowledge base and gaining skills with fire and rescue squads in the Columbus, GA, area:*
EMERGENCY MEDICAL TECHNICIAN. Columbus County Emergency Medical Service, Columbus, GA (August 2000-present). Hired on a part-time basis while still serving on active duty with the U.S. Army, am called on to work an average of 40 hours a week.
- Completed the county protocol and megacode tests; only need to respond to 12 calls with a preceptor to observe to be fully certified by Columbus County.

VOLUNTEER FIRE FIGHTER. Landsome Fire Department, Landsome, GA (July 1996-present). Assist in responding to approximately 15 or 20 calls a month in a small rural volunteer fire department.

VOLUNTEER FIRE FIGHTER. Manchester VFD, Columbus, GA (February to July 1997). Assisted in responding to as many as 30 to 45 calls a month in this rural area department.

Other experience: **ADMINISTRATIVE SPECIALIST.** U.S. Army, Ft. Benning, GA (1990-1997). Earned numerous awards and certificates for my accomplishments and service in office management and stock control after earlier gaining experience as a vehicle mechanic.
- Based on my skills and abilities, was selected to attend training which resulted in qualifications in the specialized field of chemical equipment repair: learned to troubleshoot, repair, and maintain a wide range of equipment.

PERSONAL   Am a soft-spoken and pleasant person who gets along well with others. Work effectively and productively either independently or as a contributor to team efforts.

Date

Exact Name of Person
Title or Position
Name of Company
Address (number and street)
Address (city, state, and zip)

FIREFIGHTER   Dear Exact Name of Person (or Sir or Madam if answering a blind ad):

I would appreciate an opportunity to talk with you soon about how I could contribute to your organization through my background in firefighting, emergency response, and hazardous material response and education.

As you will see from my resume, I have completed training leading to certification by the State of South Carolina in the following career specialties: Emergency Medical Technician-B, Fire Driver/Operator, Confined Space Rescue Instructor, Firefighter III, Instructor — Level II, and Hazardous Materials Specialist — Level III. I also attended courses at the National Fire Academy in Emmittsburg, MD, in HazMat Site Operating Practices, Chemistry of Hazardous Materials, and Incident Command as well as Radiological Response.

Through my simultaneous jobs as a Firefighter with the City of Macon and as a volunteer with the Mercer Fire Department in Mercer, GA, I have become adept at handling multiple simultaneous tasks and projects, coordinating activities between various agencies, and dealing extensively with the public. Respected as an instructor, I am frequently requested by name to teach members of civic organizations, firefighting professionals, and local businesses in HazMat, firefighting, and emergency response.

Throughout my career I have become familiar with other aspects of administration and operations including writing policy statements, developing standard operating procedures, and using automated systems to maintain records and information as well as with budgeting and purchasing.

If you are in need of an energetic, enthusiastic quick learner with excellent problem-solving skills, I hope you will welcome my call soon to arrange a brief meeting to discuss your current and future needs and how I might serve them. Thank you in advance for your time.

Sincerely,

Leland Ray Camembert

Alternate last paragraph:
I hope you will call or write me soon to suggest a time convenient for us to meet and discuss your current and future needs and how I might serve them. Thank you in advance for your time.

LELAND RAY CAMEMBERT

1110½ Hay Street, Fayetteville, NC 28305   •   preppub@aol.com   •   (910) 483-6611

OBJECTIVE   To contribute my extensive experience as a firefighter and recognized subject matter expert in the specialized area of emergency management and hazardous material handling to an organization that can benefit from my planning, human relations, and communication skills.

CERTIFICATIONS   Excelled in training programs which led to certification by the State of Georgia.

Emergency Medial Technician-B	Firefighter III
Fire Department Driver/Operator	Instructor — Level II
Confined Space Rescue Instructor	Hazardous Material Specialist — Level III

EXPERIENCE   *Have become adept at handling multiple simultaneous tasks and projects, coordinating activities between various agencies, and dealing with co-workers and the public:*

FIREFIGHTER. Macon Fire Department, Macon, GA (2000-present). Have become widely recognized as thoroughly knowledgeable in the highly sensitive area of hazardous material emergency response, equipment maintenance, planning, and follow-up report writing procedures and am often called on to provide education and instruction.

- Represented the department to the public while responding to fire, rescue, and hazardous material incidents and became known as an informative teacher with a clear, concise manner of providing instruction to civic groups, professionals, or the public.
- Frequently requested as an instructor by agencies throughout the state, have taught HazMat for organizations including the Department of Insurance, Fire & Rescue Division as well as for area companies such as Monsanto, ICI, and DuPont.
- Applied my analytical skills and technical knowledge while preparing risk assessments.
- Provided assistance in establishing specifications and purchasing new equipment.
- Gained understanding of EPA, OSHA, and local policies for toxic release reporting.
- Assisted in establishing operating procedures for several related areas of activities as well as maintaining detailed, accurate records and providing regular reports.
- Wrote policy statements on subjects including EMS response, carbon monoxide detector alarm response, and air monitoring equipment calibration and maintenance.
- Achieved familiarity with computer equipment used to input, review, and access information and records; used industry-specific software including TOMES and Cameo.
- Served on the Hazardous Materials Regional Response Team #3 which covers 16 surrounding counties.
- Expanded my knowledge of environmental and occupational compliance.

OPERATIONS CAPTAIN and **VOLUNTEER FIREFIGHTER.** The Mercer Fire Department, Mercer, GA (1990-2000). Selected in 1994 for this supervisory role after several years as a part-time employee, oversee daily operations, participate in routine report writing, budgeting, purchasing, and personnel supervision as well as emergency planning.

- Played an important role in developing a fire prevention program that was accepted for use throughout the county.
- Served as chairman of a committee which helped develop uniform promotion standards.

EDUCATION & TRAINING   Studied Criminal Justice at Macon Technical Community College, GA.
Attended National Fire Academy (Emmittsburg, MD) courses in Hazardous Material Site Operating Practices, Chemistry of Hazardous Materials, and Incident Command as well as in Radiological Response.

PERSONAL   Am an enthusiastic, energetic, and self-motivated individual. Have excellent problem-solving skills and the ability to learn new concepts and equipment quickly.

Date

Exact Name of Person
Exact Title
Exact Name of Company
Address
City, State, Zip

FIREFIGHTER Dear Exact Name of Person (or Dear Sir or Madam if answering a blind ad):

With the enclosed resume, I would like to make you aware of my interest in exploring employment opportunities with your organization. My wife and I are in the process of permanently relocating back to the Midwest, where we grew up and where our extended families still live.

As you will see from my resume, I recently completed six years of distinguished service to my country while serving in the U.S. Army. While excelling in full-time jobs in the supply management field, I pursued training through a respected community college in order to obtain my firefighting certification. In addition to receiving my Firefighter Certification in Georgia, I worked as a Volunteer Firefighter for the Red Springs Emergency Service. I am interested in pursuing professional employment opportunities which can utilize my background related to firefighting and law enforcement.

As a military professional, I gained extensive knowledge related to law enforcement. After completing professional driver's training sponsored by the U.S. Army, I received my Driver Badge. Entrusted with a Secret security clearance, I was specially selected to attend Primary Leadership Development Course, the Army's course designed to refine the management skills and leadership ability of middle managers. My law enforcement training also included Airborne School, Unit Armorer School, Alcohol and Drug Abuse Prevention training, as well as extensive training in supply management. I was promoted ahead of my peers to supervisory positions and became known for my strong personal initiative and problem-solving skills. In my most recent position, I trained and managed six individuals while controlling $2 million in equipment and supplies.

I hope you will contact me to suggest a time when we could meet in person to discuss your needs. I can provide excellent personal and professional references. Thank you.

Yours sincerely,

Andy Frank

ANDY FRANK

1110½ Hay Street, Fayetteville, NC 28305 • preppub@aol.com • (910) 483-6611

OBJECTIVE To contribute to an organization that can use an accomplished young professional who offers strong computer operations skills along with a versatile background related to firefighting and law enforcement as well as supply system management and inventory control.

EDUCATION *College:* Completed more than one year of college courses, Presidio Technical Community College, Presidio, GA.
Supply Management: Graduated from the Army's Supply Management Course, Quartermaster School, Ft. Lee, VA, 1999; Supply Specialist Courses, Army Institute for Professional Development, Ft. Eustis, VA, 2002; Sanitation Course, Ft. Campbell, KY, 2003.
Leadership Development and Executive Training: Completed the Army's Primary Development Course for mid-level managers, Noncommissioned Officer Academy, 2002.
Technical Training: Graduated from Airborne School, Unit Armorer Course, Serbo/Croatian Language Training, and the Alcohol and Drug Abuse Prevention Course.
Driver's Training: Gained professional driving certifications; completed Bus Driver Training, 2000; awarded my Driver Badge.

FIREFIGHTING **Certified Firefighter;** completed Fire Department Orientation/Safety I & II, Cape Fear Community College.

CERTIFICATION Completed Personal Protective Equipment Course, Foxhall Community College and Southeast Fire/Rescue College, 2002. Courses taken include:

Portable Extinguishers	Fire Hose, Appl. And Streams	Ladders I & II
Emergency Medical Care	Salvage — Level I & II	Fire Prevention
Sprinklers	Rescue — Level I & II	Fire Alarms
Fire Control	Hazardous Materials	Structural Burn
Ropes	Building Construction I & II	Fire Behavior
Safety	Forcible Entry I & II	Water Supplies
Wildland Fire Suppression	Incident Command Systems	

COMPUTERS Completed formal training in Excel, Windows NT, Access, Windows, Word; have used automated systems for supply management.

EXPERIENCE **VOLUNTEER FIREFIGHTER.** Red Springs Emergency Service, Cameron, GA (2002-present). While earning my state Firefighter Certification, performed all the duties of a firefighter as a volunteer.

SUPPLY MANAGER. U.S. Army, Ft. Stewart, GA (2000-present). At the nation's largest U.S. military base, was promoted to train and manage six supply technicians while tracking and maintaining more than $2 million in equipment and supplies; was authorized to utilize a military credit card for supply purchases; held a Secret security clearance.
• Led employees to earn "excellent" rating during a major inspection of supply operations.

PROPERTY CONTROL CUSTODIAN & SUPPLY TECHNICIAN. U.S. Army, Ft. Campbell, KY (1998-00). Excelled in a succession of assignments and received nearly 10 medals, including the Joint Service Commendation Medal; was recognized as a highly motivated young professional and recommended for rapid promotion ahead of my peers.

PERSONAL Highly motivated individual who constantly seeks to improve skills and increase knowledge.

Date

Mr. James North, Forensic Supervisor
Forensic Supervisor
Major Crimes Division
San Marcos Police Department
4333 Marcosi Avenue
San Marcos, CA 99988

FORENSIC
TECHNICIAN

Dear Mr. North:

With the enclosed resume, I would like to formally express my interest in the full-time position of Forensic Technician with the San Marcos Police Department.

Criminal Justice education and hands-on experience as a Forensic Technician: As you will see from my resume, I maintained a perfect 4.0 GPA while earning an Associate of Science degree in Criminal Justice. I was subsequently one of eight individuals selected for the San Marcos Police Department's first Forensic Technician internship program, and I have excelled in my 350 hours of on-the-job training. In addition to skillfully performing all technical duties of a Forensic Technician, I have established cordial working relationships and have become very familiar with the organization and functions of other Police Department divisions.

Strong oral and written communication skills: One of my strongest assets is my ability to communicate effectively both orally and in writing. I refined my oral and written communication skills during my past eight years of employment with Hechts Department Stores. I began with Hechts in 1993 as a Sales Associate, and then I advanced to Loss Prevention Associate. I became a Certified OSHA Inspector and learned to expertly operate electronic video surveillance as well as police radio and photographic equipment. As a Loss Prevention Associate with Hechts, I communicated extensively both orally and in writing, with duties ranging from preparing statistical and written reports, to training employees in OSHA procedures and shrinkage control.

Excellent analytical and problem-solving abilities: In my internship with the San Marcos Police Department, I have applied my analytical and problem-solving abilities as a Forensic Technician. Just as I excelled as a Loss Prevention Associate in recovering lost assets including stolen merchandise for Hechts, so too could I apply those same investigative and problem-solving abilities in responding to crime and accident scenes.

As my supervisor during my internship, you have had the opportunity to observe my dedicated hard work and commitment to top-quality results. I hope you will recommend me for the full-time position as Forensic Technician, as I am confident that I could become a valuable asset in that role to the San Marcos Police Department. I would truly be honored to serve the city and its citizens in that capacity.

Yours sincerely,

Katie Anne Doyle

KATIE ANNE DOYLE

1110½ Hay Street, Fayetteville, NC 28305   •   preppub@aol.com   •   (910) 483-6611

OBJECTIVE
To benefit the San Marcos Police Department as a Forensic Technician in the Forensic Unit.

EDUCATION
Associate of Science (A.A.S.) degree, Criminal Justice, San Marcos Technical Community College, San Marcos, NC, 2002. Excelled academically with a **perfect 4.0 GPA.**
• Named to the President's List every semester and selected as a Graduation Marshal.
Certified OSHA Inspector; certification obtained in 1999 is valid through 2010.
Completed extensive training in Safety, Customer Service and Sales, Keyboarding and Computer Operations, Communication, and other areas, sponsored by AAFES.

PHOTO SKILLS
Operate electronic video surveillance equipment, police radio, and photographic equipment.

EXPERIENCE
FORENSIC TECHNICIAN INTERN. San Marcos Police Department, San Marcos, CA (2002-present). Was one of eight individuals selected for the San Marcos Police Department's first internship program; have excelled in all aspects of my on-the-job training as a Forensic Technician while establishing strong working relationships within the police department and in other organizations. Perform analyses and physical comparisons to assist in crime detection; identify fingerprints, and prepare detailed technical reports of findings.
Tasks, activities, and responsibilities:
• Responded to crime and accident scenes; recorded physical descriptions of scenes while gathering and photographing evidence. Interviewed personnel to obtain accounts of events.
• Examined surfaces and dust for prints and other latent traces of evidence including hair, blood, paint, toolmarks, and other matter; collected and preserved evidence. **For example:** obtained one latent print from a drink bottle in a 93 Toyota in 2002 which subsequently led to the apprehension of a suspect.
• Collected, processed, and logged film taken at crime and accident scenes as well as other department photographs; developed black and white and color film; printed black and white and color negatives; filed negatives and dry mounted photos.
• Operated basic photographic and developing equipment. Photographed the victim of a crime. Processed special requests for fingerprints and related information; examined, analyzed, evaluated, and processed physical evidence gathered at crime scenes.
• Prepared reports required of a Forensics Technician; documented findings; forwarded results to appropriate agencies. Maintained logs, inventory, and work sheets.
• Prepared sketches for death investigations and suicides; learned to construct composites.
Highlights of knowledge gained and applied during this time:
• Have become knowledgeable of the N.C. Criminal law including the Penal Code, Code of Criminal Procedure, and Family Code. Knowledgeable of investigative resources, procedures.
• Am very familiar with the organization and functions of other Police Department divisions.

LOSS PREVENTION ASSOCIATE (previously SALES ASSOCIATE).. Hechts Department Store, locations throughout CA (1993-2002). Performed OSHA inspections, operated electronic video surveillance systems, and applied my strong analytical and problem-solving skills while recovering lost assets including stolen merchandise. Detected employee fraud, waste, and abuse.
• Assisted in training new employees in OSHA procedures as well as shrinkage control.

PERSONAL
Can pass the most rigorous background investigation and would welcome polygraph testing. Offer the ability to obtain fingerprint classification certification from the FBI.

RILEY H. LIFE

1110½ Hay Street, Fayetteville, NC 28305 • preppub@aol.com •
(910) 483-6611

**HIGHWAY SAFETY
SPECIALIST**

OBJECTIVE

To serve the National Highway Traffic Safety Administration as a Highway Safety Specialist through my demonstrated knowledge of criminal justice systems and traffic law enforcement as well as through my vast experience in developing, evaluating, and administering highway safety programs, vehicle safety systems, and other safety programs.

PUBLICATIONS

Currently responsible for the development, evaluation, revision, and marketing of the following publications:

The Specialized Driver Training Instructors' Manual
RADAR Operator Manual
Time-Distance Operator Manual
Law Enforcement Driver Training Curriculum

**SUMMARY OF
EXPERIENCE**

In the following track record of career advancement, have earned a reputation as a leading expert in South Carolina in program administration work concerned with highway, traffic, motor vehicle safety, accident/injury prevention, and public safety programs related to both the criminal justice system and the traffic law enforcement system; daily utilize my written and oral communication skills as well as my ability to plan, budget for, implement, and administer criminal justice or traffic enforcement operational programs.

- At national levels, am widely regarded as an expert in the development and administration of community highway or related safety programs, especially as pertaining to the licensing and training of motor vehicle operators.

EXPERIENCE

LAW ENFORCEMENT TRAINING COORDINATOR. South Carolina Department of Justice, Attorney General's Office, Columbia, SC (2000-present). Am responsible for program development and implementation of programs related to the criminal justice system and traffic law enforcement and handle key responsibilities in these and other areas:

Technical Assistance: Ensure that technical assistance is accurate and conforms to currently accepted practices; keep the South Carolina Justice Academy, Criminal Justice Training Standards and Sheriffs' Standards Divisions and their staff informed on issues which have impact on the speed enforcement and driver training.

Course Coordination: Ensure that training is appropriately organized and that students' training needs are appropriately facilitated while coordinating the following courses:

Specialized Driver Training Instructor Course
RADAR Instructor Training Course
Criminal Justice TD/SMI Instructor Training Course
Re-Certification Training for RADAR Instructors
Re-Certification Training for TD/SMI Instructors
Driver Training Modules

Development: Ensure that curricula are job-related and applicable, reflect current information and practices, employ appropriate training methodology, and accurately measure student achievement while developing or redeveloping courses including: RADAR Instructor Training, Criminal Justice TD/SMI Instructor Training Course, and In-Service Driver Training Course; assess additional RADAR TD/SMI and law enforcement driver training needs and resources.

Teaching: Ensure that materials are applicable and job-related while instructing in: Specialized Driver Training Instructor Course, RADAR Instructor Training Course, Criminal Justice TD/SMI Instructor Training Course, Re-Certification for RADAR Instructors, Re-Certification Training for TD/SMI Instructors, and Driver Training Modules.

Accomplishments, tasks, and responsibilities:
- Develop, evaluate, coordinate, and deliver training programs to law enforcement officers throughout SC seeking certification to instruct in driver training programs conducted within the state.
- Prepare program materials and translate enforcement issues into cohesive programs which are understood, accepted, and utilized by the law enforcement community.
- Provide guidance to develop, promote, and market program concepts and materials for use by law enforcement leaders, national associations, and state and local governments.
- Gather the results of program findings and evaluations and incorporate these findings into materials which can be used in functional areas of police traffic services.
- As School Director for the South Carolina Justice Academy's Specialized Driver Instructor Training Course, have trained more than 350 officers currently certified as Specialized Driver Instructors.
- Have developed and implemented a revised driver training curriculum for the Basic Law Enforcement Training Program which increased the training of basic recruits from 16 hours to 44 hours while also mandating training in emergency response and pursuit driving.
- Am School Director for the Academy's RADAR and Time-Distance Instructor Training Courses, and am responsible for development, revision, coordination, and delivery of training for law enforcement officers seeking certification to instruct in RADAR and Time-Distance Operator Training courses in the state (have personally trained all of the approximately 150 current instructors).

INSTRUCTOR/COORDINATOR. South Carolina Department of Justice, South Carolina Justice Academy, Columbia, SC (1985-90). Was responsible for coordination and instruction of training programs to law enforcement officers throughout South Carolina.

TROOPER. South Carolina Department of Crime Control and Public Safety, Division of State Highway Patrol, Columbia, SC (1978-85). Excelled in varied assignments:
- Patrolled state highways within assigned area to monitor traffic, to arrest or warn persons guilty of violating motor vehicle law, criminal law, or safe driving practices; provided road information and assistance to drivers.
- Instructed newly employed cadets in accordance with training schedules and orders; oriented cadets in fundamentals of physical fitness, discipline, pride, and loyalty to patrol; trained cadets in close-order drills and in care and use of equipment and uniforms; instructed cadets in physical training and provided guidance in areas of dietary needs and weight training; secondary instructor in areas of defensive tactics, accident investigations, firearms, riot control, and vehicle operations; made daily inspections of cadets' personal appearance and living quarters.

EDUCATION B.A. degree, **cum laude**, in Justice and Public Policy, South Carolina State College, Maryville, SC, 1995. **A.A.S.** degree in Criminal Justice, Nash Technical College, Nash, SC, 1984.

Date

Exact Name of Person
Exact Title
Exact Name of Company
Address
City, State, Zip

INTELLIGENCE &   Dear Exact Name of Person (or Dear Sir or Madam if answering a blind ad):
DATA MANAGER

With the enclosed resume, I am expressing my interest in exploring employment opportunities with your organization.

As you will see from my resume, I established a track record of accomplishments along with a reputation as one who achieves results while advancing to the rank of Lieutenant Colonel in the U.S. Army. Throughout my career, both as a military officer and earlier as a teacher, I have always been recognized for my outstanding communication skills. With an energetic and outgoing personality, I offer a persuasive leadership style and exceptional effectiveness as a public speaker.

Selected for highly visible roles predominately in the international intelligence community, I have built organizations from scratch, and I have brought about improvements in team spirit, productivity, and work quality in every position I have held. With a reputation as an excellent manager of resources, I have frequently been called upon to take on the management of programs which were understaffed and improperly resourced.

Selected for advanced executive training, my educational background includes a bachelor's degree in French, a graduate-level program for management professional, and several technical courses for intelligence operations managers. Known for unquestioned personal integrity and high standards, I was entrusted with a Top Secret security clearance. In addition to numerous prestigious medals and honors from the military, I have been recognized with inclusion in "The World Who's Who of Women" and "2,000 Notable American Women."

I have earned respect for my sound judgment, ability to gain cooperation and motivate others to give their best efforts, and talent for motivating personnel to excel. If you can use a mature, articulate, persuasive, and intelligent professional, I hope you will contact me soon to suggest a time we might meet to discuss how I could contribute to your organization. I can provide excellent professional and personal references at the appropriate time. Thank you for your time and consideration.

Sincerely,

Anne J. Darwin

ANNE J. DARWIN

1110½ Hay Street, Fayetteville, NC 28305   •   preppub@aol.com   •   (910) 483-6611

OBJECTIVE

To offer a background of results achieved in the process of building a reputation as an exceptionally articulate, persuasive speaker and writer who excels at motivating others and maximizing resources while gaining respect in a career as a respected military officer.

EDUCATION & TRAINING

Received a B.A. in French, Washington State University, Seattle, WA..

Excelled in numerous courses and schools for military executives including a graduate-level management program and technical courses in intelligence/data management.

Completed extensive training in counterterrorism and surveillance sponsored by the U.S. Army and the Department of Defense; the locations and dates of such training are classified information.

HONORS

Listed in the 12th edition (1996-97) of "The World Who's Who of Women" and in the sixth edition (1997) of "2,000 Notable American Women," received numerous prestigious military medals and honors in recognition of my professionalism and accomplishments.

LANGUAGES

Speak, read, and write French; can speak Turkish, Korean, and Spanish and have used these languages in business.

CLEARANCE

Hold one of the nation's highest security clearances: Top Secret with SBI/SCI.

EXPERIENCE

Advanced to the rank of Lieutenant Colonel in the U.S. Army where I was widely recognized for my public relations, communications, and planning skills:

CHIEF, ANTITERRORISM OPERATIONS AND INTELLIGENCE. Washington, DC (2000-present). Evaluated as a brilliant performer and superb communicator, served as principal advisor on technical issues relating to personnel protection and antiterrorism issues; was the Army liaison with agencies such as the FBI, CIA, and State Department.

- Met challenges head on and was credited with always getting the job done in a difficult, ever-changing, and fast-moving environment.
- Brought about steady improvements and accomplishments which included development of a tracking system for getting information to personnel in high-threat areas.
- Brought about steady improvements and accomplishments which included development of a tracking system for getting information to personnel in high-threat areas.
- Advised key government officials, including the President and his Cabinet officials, in the aftermath of the September 11th tragedy. Am involved daily in briefing members of Congress as well as VIPs from other countries on antiterrorism.

INTELLIGENCE OPERATIONS CHIEF. Locations in the Middle East (1990-1999). Was praised for my emphasis on quality of life and personnel issues in a unique organization which provided intelligence analysis support for the largest NATO joint intelligence center.

- Managed an independent 24-hour center; oversaw administrative and personnel, budget, ADP, logistics, security, and training resources; formulated policy and procedures.
- Was commended for my managerial expertise in an organization with an extremely fluid and heavy operations tempo throughout Europe, the Middle East, and Africa.

Highlights of other military experience: Excelled as Company Commander three times.

PERSONAL

Outstanding personal and professional references upon request.

Date

Exact Name of Person
Exact Title
Exact Name of Company
Address
City, State, Zip

INTELLIGENCE OPERATOR

Dear Exact Name of Person (or Dear Sir or Madam if answering a blind ad):

With the enclosed resume, I would like to make you aware of my interest in exploring employment opportunities with your organization and introduce you to my background related to intelligence. I hold a Top Secret security clearance with an SSBI. I offer a proven ability to apply knowledge of national-level operational intelligence production, policies, and programs that support the Unified Commands and their components, and I am experienced in crisis management and skilled in accomplishing liaison throughout the DoD/Intelligence Community.

After graduating from the U.S. Air Force Academy in 1991, I commanded a 250-person tri-service signal intelligence collection and processing unit at the world's largest Air Intelligence Agency/Joint Cryptologic Operations Center. After excelling in that job, I was promoted to Chief, Satellite and Printer Systems Management. In that role, I ensured the efficient tasking of 1,200 people while managing multimillion-dollar radioprinter, voice, and satellite communications resources.

I was handpicked for subsequent positions with the National Security Agency (NSA) as Chief, Air Force Liaison Office, and as Field Operations Officer. With NSA, I led 45 highly skilled engineers in Signal Intelligence (SIGINT) support to Special Operations Forces and covert intelligence teams. I served as the NSA's senior representative to the Joint Special Operations Command (JSOC), AF Special Operations Command, US Navy SEALS, and US Army Special Operations. I gained considerable crisis management experience during Operation Deliberate Force in Bosnia, and a NATO commander commended my leadership ability during high-visibility missions.

Most recently I have worked with the Special Operations Command at Ft. Campbell, KY, and as the group's Senior Combat Intelligence Officer, I managed nine officers and NCOs while conducting compartmented combat missions tasked by the NCA. I was commended as "an incisive, imaginative leader and visionary" and praised for forging effective partnerships with Joint Task Force (JTF) staff and NSA specialists.

While serving my country I received numerous medals and honors in recognition of exemplary performance. I can provide outstanding references at the appropriate time. I would appreciate your contacting me if you feel my expertise and knowledge related to the intelligence community would be of value to you.

Yours sincerely,

Suzie G. Strike

SUZIE G. STRIKE

1110½ Hay Street, Fayetteville, NC 28305 • preppub@aol.com • (910) 483-6611

OBJECTIVE

To benefit an organization that can use an accomplished young professional who has excelled as a military officer while gaining expertise related to intelligence, skills in managing multiple analysts, as well as experience in briefing and working with intelligence professionals and customers worldwide.

CLEARANCE

Top Secret with SSBI

**EDUCATION
& TRAINING**

Completing **M.A., Human Resources Management,** Webster University.
Earned **B.S., Humanities,** United States Air Force Academy, 1991.
Advanced Survival Training (SV-91), (JPRA), June 1999
Advanced Cryptologic Course (CY-500), Feb 1998
Sensitive Operations Training Course (SS-209), March 1998
Squadron Officer School (Resident Course), June 1997
Signals Intelligence Officer Course, July 1992

EXPERIENCE

COMMANDER OF INTELLIGENCE OPERATIONS. Special Operations Command, Ft. Campbell, KY (2000-present). As the group's Senior Combat Intelligence Officer, managed nine officers and NCOs while conducting compartmented combat missions specifically tasked by the National Command Authority (NCA). Tailored intelligence products for five diverse flying units and a Special Operations battlestaff charged with low-vis infil/exfil of special teams in denied areas.
*   On a formal evaluation, was described as *"an incisive, imaginative leader and visionary"* and praised for *"forging partnerships with Joint Task Forces (JTF) staff and National Security Agency (NSA) specialists."*
*   Was praised in writing as *"the most polished briefer among 10 handpicked officers with the ability to masterfully focus on the most complex issues."*
*   Evaluated newest technologies for intelligence distribution, and generated improvements to specialized resistance training for combat aircrews and forward mission liaisons. Formulated synergistic intelligence/force protection policies in support of U.S. policies.
*   Was strongly encouraged to remain in the Air Force and recommended for promotion as the USAF's rep in the White House Situation Room; however, I decided to resign my commission and seek employment in the civilian intelligence community.

FIELD OPERATIONS OFFICER & CHIEF, SPECIAL OPERATIONS BASE. National Security Agency (NSA), Fort George G. Meade, MD (1998-99). Led 45 highly skilled and tactically trained engineers in Signal Intelligence (SIGINT) support to Special Operations Forces and covert intelligence teams; served as the NSA's senior representative to the Joint Special Operations Command (JSOC), A.F. Special Operations Command, U.S. Navy SEALS, and U.S. Army Special Operations.

CHIEF, SATELLITE AND PRINTER SYSTEMS MANAGEMENT & SECTION COMMANDER. U.S.A.F., Japan (1992-97). Excelled as Section Commander (1992-94) of a 250-person tri-service signal intelligence collection and processing unit at the world's largest Air Intelligence Agency/Joint Cryptologic Operations Center, and was promoted to Chief, Satellite and Printer Systems Management (1994-95). As Chief, managed enciphered radioprinter, voice, and satellite communications resources, and ensured efficient tasking of 1,200 people.

PERSONAL

Highly motivated individual. Outstanding references. Outstanding communicator.

CAREER CHANGE

Date

Exact Name of Person
Exact Title
Exact Name of Company
Address
City, State, Zip

INTELLIGENCE OPERATIVE

Dear Exact Name of Person (or Dear Sir or Madam if answering a blind ad):

With the enclosed resume, I would like to make you aware of my experience, skills, and knowledge as well as of my strong interest in contributing to the effectiveness of law enforcement activities through my hard work and dedication. I am interested in exploring employment opportunities with your agency as an Intelligence Operative.

As you will see from my enclosed resume, I am pursuing an A.S. degree in Law Enforcement and have completed the San Antonio College Police Academy program from which I received a certificate in Law Enforcement. Other training has led to placement on the National Register of Emergency Medical Technicians as an EMT-Basic. Qualified as an Expert Marksman with the M-16 rifle, I received extensive military training in subject matter ranging from leadership and training management techniques, to defensive driving and threat recognition, to rifle and bayonet fighting, to combat lifesaving.

While serving in the U.S. Army, I was awarded U.S. Army Commendation and Achievement Medals in recognition of my accomplishments as a supervisor, instructor, and maintenance mechanic. In each case I was evaluated for "exceptionally meritorious service" and described as a dedicated professional who was willing to accept responsibility and meet challenges head on.

If you can use a mature professional with experience, education, and training related to security and law enforcement operations, I hope you will contact me to suggest a time when we might talk about your needs. I can provide outstanding references at the appropriate time.

Sincerely,

Thomas C. Gartner

Alternate last paragraph:
If you can use a mature professional with experience, education, and training related to security and law enforcement operations, I hope you will welcome my call soon to discuss how I could contribute to your organization. I can provide outstanding references at the appropriate time.

THOMAS C. GARTNER

1110½ Hay Street, Fayetteville, NC 28305   •   preppub@aol.com   •   (910) 483-6611

OBJECTIVE

To offer a strong interest in law enforcement to an organization that can use a hardworking and dedicated young professional with a background in providing security for personnel and material assets as well as a reputation for dealing with pressure and deadlines.

EDUCATION & TRAINING

Am pursuing an A.S. in Criminal Justice; have completed the San Antonio College Police Academy and received a certificate in Law Enforcement, San Antonio College, TX, 2002. Completed military training programs emphasizing hazardous material handling, risk management, combat lifesaving, and power generation equipment repair as well as courses in such areas as:

signal communications	marksmanship	training management
NBC operations	defense and first aid	rifle and bayonet fighting
defensive driving	threat recognition	land navigation
individual combat techniques	maintenance procedures	

SPECIAL SKILLS & KNOWLEDGE

Am on the **National Register of Emergency Medical Technicians** as an EMT-Basic.
Weapons: am qualified as an Expert Marksman with the M-16 and M-4.
Physical conditioning and training: consistently score above 290 on a 300-point test and have been recognized for scoring a perfect 300.

EXPERIENCE

Received several medals for my professionalism and accomplishments while serving in the U.S. Army:
TEAM LEADER. Ft. Sam Houston, TX (2002-present). Refined supervisory and training skills as the leader of two subordinate personnel while maintaining and controlling $125,000 worth of sensitive equipment used in support of Special Operations teams worldwide.

INTELLIGENCE TEAM LEADER. Korea (1998-01). Displayed the ability to build cooperation and accomplish results as supervisor of four subordinate personnel while also working closely with Korean national personnel.
- Achieved a 95% equipment readiness rate while involved in supporting the gathering and deciphering of intelligence used for decision making at higher operational levels.

TECHNICAL INSTRUCTOR and **SECTION SUPERVISOR.** Ft. Sam Houston, TX (1994-98). Oversaw the day-to-day operation of a power generation section which provided support for training activities at the U.S. Medical Center and School.
- Applied technical expertise related to the operation of power generation equipment as an instructor for a program which trained an average of 55,000 students annually.
- Was awarded a U.S. Army Commendation Medal for "exceptionally meritorious service" and "technical knowledge and expertise."
- Provided leadership for a $40,000 motor pool self-help renovation project.

ASSISTANT SECTION SUPERVISOR. Germany (1992-94). Assisted in the day-to-day running of a power generation equipment repair section for an ammunition depot.
- Planned and scheduled maintenance and repair activities so that adequate personnel and equipment were always available.
- Received a U.S. Army Achievement Medal which cited "willingness to assume responsibilities and accept challenging missions" and for my impact on unit success.

PERSONAL

Have basic working knowledge of German. Am a mentally and physically tough professional.

Date

Exact Name of Person
Exact Title
Exact Name of Company
Address
City, State, Zip

**INTELLIGENCE
OPERATIONS MANAGER**

Dear Exact Name of Person (or Dear Sir or Madam if answering a blind ad):

With the enclosed resume, I would like to express my interest in exploring employment opportunities with your organization.

I offer a versatile management background and a history of advancement based on expertise in analyzing situations, developing innovative solutions, and building diverse groups of people into exceptional teams. Highly respected as a U.S. Air Force officer, currently holding the rank of Captain, I am recognized as one of the Department of Defense's highest rated performers. Although I have been strongly encouraged to remain in military service and assured of continued rapid promotion, I have made the decision to seek opportunities in the civilian community.

In every job I have held throughout my military career, I have been recognized as a key figure in developing methods for improving productivity, customer satisfaction, and employee performance. In my current job I have applied my special abilities to identify and solve problems which have resulted in new standards and procedures. I was singled out from among 15 talented military executives as "Outstanding Officer of the Year" for 2002 based on my personal initiative and reputation as a team player.

In earlier jobs as an intelligence manager, I was handpicked for high-visibility roles requiring expertise related to planning and managing international projects, developing improvements to databases, and testing/fielding technologically advanced equipment. In one job as a Detachment Commander in charge of 13 people, I led my team in conducting special counter-narcotics projects in numerous countries throughout Central and South America. I am an effective public speaker known for research, analytical, and communication skills which were described in a formal evaluation as "impeccable."

Respected for sound judgment, I am known for my ability to deal effectively with people. If you can use a versatile and mature management professional, I hope you will contact me to suggest a time we might meet to discuss how I could contribute to your organization. I can provide excellent professional and personal references. Thank you in advance for your time.

Sincerely,

Abraham Ingracias

ABRAHAM INGRACIAS

1110½ Hay Street, Fayetteville, NC 28305   •   preppub@aol.com   •   (910) 483-6611

OBJECTIVE   To contribute through a versatile background of accomplishments and reputation as an assertive, articulate, and highly intelligent professional who has excelled as a military officer known for the ability to improvise, overcome challenges, and solve problems.

EDUCATION   B.A., Political Science, University of Mississippi, Oxford, MS, 1992.
· Received a full four-year scholarship and graduated with honors with a 3.64 GPA.
· Completed a year of Electrical Engineering studies with a 4.0 GPA before changing majors.

LANGUAGE   Extensively schooled in Spanish; could quickly become conversational again.

TRAINING &   Completed extensive U.S. Air Force technical and management training with an emphasis
CERTIFICATIONS on intelligence operations management. FAA licensed single-engine land private pilot, PADI licensed advanced open-water SCUBA diver, certified personal trainer and strength coach, and rated at the genius aptitude level by MENSA and the Department of Defense (DOD).

CLEARANCE   Hold a **Top Secret/SCI** security clearance with SSBI and Special Access Program.

EXPERIENCE   Have advanced to the rank of Captain in the U.S. Air Force ahead of my peers while earning official ratings placing me in "the top three percent" of Air Force officers:
MANAGER FOR INTELLIGENCE OPERATIONS. Classified locations worldwide (2000-present). Praised for my vision and described as possessing "impeccable" skills in motivating and leading employees to exceptional levels of performance, developed and conducted worldwide operations.
  • Recognized by numerous **"Officer of the Quarter"** honors, was selected **"Outstanding Officer of the Year 2002"** from among 15 top-notch managers based on my personal initiative and for being a team player.
  • Cited for strong research and presentation skills, analyzed threats to personnel and **developed procedures which reduced risk 30%** during seven overseas missions requested by the Secretary of Defense and National Security Command.

MANAGER, DATA COLLECTION AND ANALYSIS DEPARTMENT. Ft. Dix, OK (1994-00). Directed ten collection managers in planning, coordinating and executing counternarcotics and other national security missions throughout Central and South America and the Caribbean.
  • Served as the **operations personnel liaison throughout the world** to ensure the timely collection of information and its dissemination to appropriate users.

TECHNICAL   Operate and troubleshoot systems and equipment to include T-43 Navigation Radar, GPS,
EXPERTISE   SABER, and SILO; navigate by sextant at 600+ knots, compass and chart; software programs for air, land, and sea; operate a variety of secure phones and cryptographic equipment. Operate over 20 leading-edge military and government computer systems.
Certified instructor in counterterrorism, surveillance, reconnaissance, and all phases of security support. Am certified to provide remote emergency medical care.
Experienced in creating multimedia presentations using National Imagery, signals intelligence (SIGINT), and human intelligence (HUMINT) products.

PERSONAL   Earned recognition which has included two prestigious Joint Service Achievement Medals and numerous Letters of Commendation. Achieved the honor of Eagle Scout.

Date

Exact Name of Person
Exact Title
Exact Name of Company
Address
City, State, Zip

Dear Exact Name of Person (or Dear Sir or Madam if answering a blind ad):

With the enclosed resume, I would like to make you aware of my interest in exploring employment opportunities with your organization and introduce you to my background related to your business.

Technical communications knowledge: As you will see from my resume, I offer extensive technical expertise related to radio and satellite communications, and I have applied my knowledge worldwide in countries throughout Central America and South America. In my most recent position, I served as Communications Chief of a high-tech communications center as I managed the installation, operation, and maintenance of radio and data communications equipment, photographic, and video services. In numerous overseas Special Forces projects, I have planned and implemented communications training for individuals from other countries. As a Communications Manager for the U.S. Army Special Forces, I traveled throughout South America and Central America to manage training activities, counter-narcotic projects, and other operations. Proficient in Spanish, I communicated in Spanish as I trained officers and instructors from Chile, Bolivia, Colombia, and other countries.

Strong investigative and problem-solving skills: The recipient of more than 20 medals, honors, and other awards for exceptional work, I have been commended for "strong initiative" and described as "a manager of dynamic character with unlimited capacity." In every position I held in the military, I applied my strong investigative and problem-solving abilities. From my resume you will also see that I possess considerable knowledge and skills related to law enforcement. I hold a B.S. degree in Criminal Justice and have completed extensive law enforcement and Special Forces training which also refined my investigative and problem-solving skills.

If you can use an individual known for unquestioned loyalty and dedication, I hope you will contact me to suggest a time when we could meet in person to discuss your needs. Thank you.

Yours sincerely,

Chuck P. Vinston

CHUCK P. VINSTON

1110½ Hay Street, Fayetteville, NC 28305   •   preppub@aol.com   •   (910) 483-6611

OBJECTIVE   To benefit an organization that can use an experienced professional with strong problem-solving and management skills acquired through distinguished service as a military professional.

EDUCATION   **College: Bachelor of Science (B.S.) degree, Criminal Justice,** Winston State University (a campus of the University of Tennessee), 1999.
- Excelled academically with a 3.4 GPA.

Law enforcement: Received a Law Enforcement Certificate, NC Department of Justice, after 604 hours of Basic Law Enforcement Training at Fayetteville Technical Community College.
- Am a sworn police officer.

Language training: Completed five-month language courses in both **Portuguese** and **Spanish.**

Management and leadership training: Graduate of numerous leadership development and technical training courses related to quality control and safety management, human resources and training management, and other areas.

Completed **Special Forces' 8-month Qualification Course** designed to refine management skills and leadership ability. Graduated from the four-month **Special Forces Operations and Intelligence Course** designed to strengthen analytical and problem-solving skills.

EXPERIENCE   **COMMUNICATIONS CHIEF.** U.S. Army Special Forces, Ft. Campbell, KY (2000-present). Supervised 60 people while managing operations of a high-tech communications center; managed the installation, operation, and maintenance of radio and data communications equipment, photographic, and video services.
- Controlled $10 million in vehicles, generators, and equipment.
- Was evaluated in writing as "a manager of dynamic character with unlimited capacity."
- Planned and implemented communications training for six overseas Special Forces projects.

COMMUNICATIONS MANAGER. U.S. Army, Ft. Sill, OK (1995-99). Received several prestigious medals, letters of appreciation, and certificates of achievement while traveling extensively throughout South America and Central America to manage training activities, counter-narcotic projects, and other operations.
- Instructed 22 officers from Colombia on counter-narcotics matters.
- Supervised 14 instructors from Chile during the training of 535 South American soldiers.
- On a special project in Bolivia, trained Bolivian counter-narcotics police on advanced communications techniques and law enforcement skills.
- In Ecuador, spoke Spanish while training Ecuadoran Special Forces organizations.
- Maintained long distance communications, both voice and CW, via HF, VHF, and UHF.
- Conducted numerous sensitive counter-drug operations worldwide.

SQUAD LEADER. U.S. Army, Korea (1991-94). Motivated, trained, and supervised 10 people in an armor organization; trained personnel in aircraft, armor identification, and communication procedures.

PERSONNEL RECRUITER. U.S. Army, Newburgh, New York (1988-91). Received a prestigious Commendation Medal, Certificate of Achievement, and the Gold Army Recruiter's Badge for excelling in attracting qualified men and women for military careers. Exceeded sales goals by 300%.

PERSONAL   Excellent references. Held Secret security clearance. Computer skills include Word and Excel.

Date

Exact Name of Person
Title or Position
Name of Company
Address (no., street)
Address (city, state, zip)

**INVESTIGATOR &
CHILDREN'S ADVOCATE**

Dear Exact Name of Person (or Dear Sir or Madam if answering a blind ad):

I would appreciate an opportunity to talk with you soon about how I could contribute to your organization through my enthusiastic, energetic, and friendly personality.

As you will see from my resume I am a mature professional who offers a proven ability to work with people of all ages and walks of life. My versatile background has included working with legal and social services personnel in a child advocacy program, factory workers and supervisors in a manufacturing environment, medical personnel and patients in a hospital setting, and adolescents in counseling.

I have a reputation as an enthusiastic and friendly person who excels in putting others at ease and developing rapport. I have experience in working under pressure and in handling emergencies and critical situations in my current job as a Juvenile Corrections Officer and as an Investigator and Children's Advocate in the Guardian Ad Litem program. My year-and-a-half of study in the social sciences (criminal justice) also contributed to my understanding of people.

I enjoy traveling and feel that I offer the right combination of maturity, personality, and enthusiasm that your organization would want in its personnel.

I hope you will welcome my call soon to arrange a brief meeting at your convenience to discuss your current and future needs and how I might serve them. Thank you in advance for your time.

Sincerely yours,

Ida V. Pepperoni

Alternate last paragraph:
I hope you will call or write soon to suggest a time convenient for us to meet and discuss your current and future needs and how I might serve them. Thank you in advance for your time.

IDA V. PEPPERONI

1110½ Hay Street, Fayetteville, NC 28305 • preppub@aol.com • (910) 483-6611

OBJECTIVE

To apply my outstanding communication skills and ability to meet people and quickly develop rapport with them to an organization that can use an enthusiastic, friendly, and energetic professional.

EXPERIENCE

JUVENILE CORRECTIONS OFFICER. Dade County, Miami, FL (2000-present). Counsel children/adolescents from nine to 16 who are either delinquents or severely undisciplined and placed in the county's juvenile detention center.
- Acquired a great deal of experience in dealing with all types of people from the children and their parents, to professionals including social workers, detectives, and counselors.

INVESTIGATOR AND CHILDREN'S ADVOCATE. Guardian Ad Litem, Miami, FL (1997-00). Officially commended for my "initiative" and "great commitment," handled a variety of activities related to protecting and helping children who had been abused, neglected, or were alcohol or drug dependent.
- Interviewed interested parties to gather information and investigate reported situations to determine actions to be taken.
- Used the results of my investigations while appearing in court to make recommendations on what actions would best protect and help the child.
- Gained experience in dealing with people from all walks of life and of all ages including professionals from the legal, medical, social work, and law enforcement fields.
- Discovered the personal satisfaction of seeing children and adolescents receive guidance.
- Was cited for my "high energy level" and "willingness to learn."

ASSISTANT PRODUCTION SUPERVISOR. Sportswear, Inc., Miami, FL (1990-96). Advanced to a supervisory role based on my performance, flexibility, and dedication working at this major manufacturer of sportswear.
- Displayed flexibility and a willingness to learn and try new things in jobs including making dyes used in machine fabric cutting.
- Was recognized as a dedicated hard worker who could work well with others and contribute to a pleasant and productive work atmosphere.

Highlights of other experience:
- Became skilled in handling multiple responsibilities including packing completed products, working on an assembly line, and using a die-cutting machine to prepare doll house parts at the manufacturer of Little Golden Books and other leisure activities.
- Was known for my ability to build rapport with patients and their families in a hospital pediatrics ward assisting in discharge/admittance procedures as well as by helping the nursing staff and delivering mail and flowers.

EDUCATION

Have completed approximately one-and-one-half years of a two-year course in **Criminal Justice**, Westin Technical Community College, Westin, TN.

TRAINING

Attended numerous seminars and training courses in subjects including:

crisis intervention in dealing with teenagers	first aid
procedures for dealing with youth services	substance abuse awareness
community awareness of occult practices	reality therapy

PERSONAL

Offer well-developed motivational and counseling skills. Excellent references on request.

Date

Exact Name of Person
Exact Title
Exact Name of Company
Address
City, State, Zip

JUVENILE CORRECTIONS OFFICER

Dear Exact Name of Person (or Dear Sir or Madam if answering a blind ad):

With the enclosed resume, I would like to make you aware of my background as a motivated and highly experienced human services professional with a strong background in juvenile corrections and the counseling of at-risk juveniles and their families.

In my most recent job, I have proven my dedication and ability, performing a dual role as Juvenile Corrections Officer and Case Manager. I have consistently excelled in these positions, supervising as many as 70 juvenile offenders while reviewing the cases of 6-8 clients to determine possible eligibility for reduction in sentencing or other rewards for good behavior. In previous positions as a Resource Teacher, Rehabilitation Technician, and volunteer for the Guardian ad Litem program, I have shown my commitment to protecting and promoting the best interests of at-risk juveniles and insuring that they are provided with the counseling and services they need.

As you will see, I hold an Associate of Applied Science degree in Human Services which I have supplemented with additional training courses. I believe that my strong combination of education and experience will be a great asset to any organization. Although I am highly regarded by my present employer and can provide excellent references at the appropriate time, I feel that my skills and talents would be better utilized in a direct service, family support environment.

If you could use a highly motivated, experienced human services professional with exceptional organizational and problem-solving skills and a background in providing support and services to at-risk juveniles, then I hope you will contact me soon to discuss your needs, and how I might serve them. I can assure you in advance that I have an excellent reputation within the community, and would quickly become a valuable addition to your organization.

Sincerely,

Adam Smith

ADAM SMITH

1110½ Hay Street, Fayetteville, NC 28305   •   preppub@aol.com   •   (910) 483-6611

OBJECTIVE   To benefit an organization that can use a highly motivated, experienced human services professional with exceptional organizational and problem-solving skills and a strong background in the counseling of at-risk juveniles and their families.

EDUCATION   Associate of Applied Sciences in Human Services, Redding Community College, Redding, SD (1997).
Atlantic Behavioral Health Services Training course, Redding Mental Health Center, Seven Lakes, SD (2001).
Effective Teaching Training course, Pinehurst Community College, Pinehurst, SD (2001).
Certified Nursing Assistant program, Pinehurst Community College, Pinehurst, SD (1988).

EXPERIENCE   **JUVENILE CORRECTIONS OFFICER/CASE MANAGER.** South Dakota Department of Corrections, Morrison Youth Institution, Hoffman, SD (2002-present). At Morrison, currently perform two jobs with one salary, serving on the case management team in addition to my regular duties as a Juvenile Corrections Officer.
* Supervise as many as 70 juvenile offenders in addition to handling a caseload of six to eight clients whose cases have come up for review by the team.
* As a member of the Case Management Team, perform client assessments and make recommendations for changes in custody status.
* Counsel juvenile offenders and act as liaison between families and clients.
* Transport inmates to and from the facility in approved departmental vehicles.
* Give supervisory direction to juvenile offenders, and ensure compliance with local, state, and federal guidelines and policies.
* Perform computer data entry of client information and specifics of case files.

RESOURCE TEACHER. Redding County Board of Education, Redding, SD (2001-02). Excelled in this position while working full-time and accepting increasing responsibilities at Morrison; was responsible for 17 students who were classified as "slow learners".
* Gathered materials to supplement regular classroom assignments and ensured that students stayed on-task with regular class work.
* Created and implemented lesson plans to maximize the interest and participation of the class and stimulate intellectual and emotional growth of each student.
* Divided the class into groups of 5-6 students each in order to better provide for the special needs of each student; developed different educational plans for each sub-group.

REHABILITATION TECHNICIAN. R.H.A. Services, Inc., Maxton, SD (1998-1901). Educated and assisted mentally handicapped adults in a group home setting, helping them to recognize and achieve their potential and work towards living more independently.
* Observed and assessed the mental and emotional state of clients to ensure the health and well-being of those in my care.
* Implemented individual plans of care and documented client's progress accordingly.

VOLUNTEER, GUARDIAN AD LITEM PROGRAM. 20th Judicial District, Richmond County Court House, Maxton, SD (1995-1997). Protected and promoted the best interests of at-risk juveniles entering the court system due to allegations of abuse or neglect.
* Represented the juvenile in court and conducted follow-up investigations to determine the facts, assess the needs of the juvenile, and locate resources within the community.

PERSONAL   Outstanding personal and professional references are available upon request.

JUVENILE COUNSELOR   Dear Sir or Madam:

Can you use a poised communicator and effective problem solver with proven skills in the area of counseling?

As you will see by my enclosed resume, I offer extensive counseling experience through a combination of training, volunteer work, and positions in intake counseling, dispute resolution, and as a Social Worker with the Newport County Department of Social Services.

In addition, you would find me to be a friendly professional with solid decision making skills and the ability to be firm and remain fair and unbiased. I relate very well to people of all backgrounds. I would like to contribute my dedication and strong work ethic to become a valuable and productive member of your team.

I hope you will contact me soon to suggest a time convenient for us to meet and discuss your current and future needs and how I might serve them. Thank you in advance for your time.

Sincerely,

Randy Castillo

RANDY CASTILLO

1110½ Hay Street, Fayetteville, NC 28305 • preppub@aol.com • (910) 483-6611

OBJECTIVE

To benefit an organization needing a versatile young professional with "top-notch" abilities in communication, leadership, and problem solving.

EDUCATION

Bachelor of Science in **Criminal Justice** with a concentration in **Social Work**, Newport State University, Newport, RI, 1996; selected to **Who's Who Among College Students**.
- Completed internship with the Newport County Adult Probation Division.
- Wrote an abstract paper presented at the National Criminal Justice Conference.

EXPERIENCE

HUMAN RESOURCES PLACEMENT SPECIALIST and **SOCIAL WORKER.** Newport County Department of Social Services, Newport, RI (2001-present). Provide placement counseling and assistance to a heavy caseload of client families under the Work First program (TNF, FS, MIC).

CASE WORKER I. Nashua County Department of Social Services, Nashua, RI (1998-2001). Interviewed clients to determine if they were eligible for food stamps and processed cases in a timely manner; suggested alternate programs they might be eligible for.
- Received Computer-Based Training (CBT) in Aid for Families with Dependent Children (AFDC) and Adult Medicaid — extensive classroom training in adult Medicaid.
- Served as Chairman of I MAAC, an in-house group of caseworkers selected by our peers to represent all caseworkers concerning training and testing needs.

DISPUTE RESOLUTION MEDIATOR. Newport County, Newport, RI (1995-97). Licensed by the State of Rhode Island to mediate the resolution of conflicts in court-referred cases involving juveniles and adults.

JUVENILE INTAKE COUNSELOR. Victim/Offender Reconciliation Program, Newport County, RI (1993-95). Use problem-solving techniques to help juvenile offenders and their victims understand the causes and effects of crime while providing counseling and mediation.

JUVENILE COUNSELOR. Newport Juvenile Detention Center, Newport, RI (1991-93). Maintained security and safety for 20-30 young men and women between 8-17.
- Conducted group and one-on-one counseling sessions at any given time; counseled the families along with their child at the request of the family.
- Disciplined those children who disobeyed the rules of the center and made firm, but fair, decisions on whether to counsel them or remove them from the group.

PURCHASING CLERK. Newport Medical Center, Newport, RI (1990-91). Handled the purchasing, shipping, and receiving of hospital supplies at a major medical center, which involved interpreting inventory data to make appropriate ordering decisions.
- Worked closely with administrators and medical personnel to coordinate the proper distribution of supplies; processed hospital mail.

Highlights of other experience: Served as the **VICE PRESIDENT** of Armchair Quarterbacks United Against (A.Q.U.A.), one of Newport's newest non-profit organizations designed to enable contributors to actually participate in the giving process (1999-2000); excelled at public relations while recruiting and supervising volunteers.

PERSONAL

Relate well to people of all backgrounds. Excellent problem-solving and organizational skills.

Date

Exact Name of Person
Exact Title
Exact Name of Company
Address
City, State, Zip

**JUVENILE
PROBATION OFFICER**

Dear Exact Name of Person (or Dear Sir or Madam if answering a blind ad):

With the enclosed resume, I would like to make you aware of my education and extensive experience related to social work and human services. I offer a reputation as a compassionate, dedicated, and enthusiastic professional with a proven willingness to go the extra mile to help my clients.

Most recently I have served as a Juvenile Probation Officer for Dale County Youth Services in New York. In that position, I managed a caseload of over 100 active probationary juveniles, counseling them and their families and acting as liaison between my clients and local law enforcement, school systems, and other supporting agencies. I reported directly to the Chief Probation Officer, and I was being groomed to take over that position when my father passed away and I decided to return home to Arkansas to be with my mother.

With a Master's degree in Counseling and Psychology and a Bachelor of Science in Social Work, I have a solid educational background in addition to my years of experience. In previous positions, I have utilized my proven ability to coordinate services between agencies as well as my strong skills in youth counseling, patient evaluation and assessment, and substance abuse counseling. Though my main experience has been in providing crisis intervention, rehabilitation, and guidance to at-risk youth, I feel that my exceptional counseling skills and highly developed organizational, supervisory, and communication skills would be a strong asset in any counseling environment.

If your organization can use the skills of a highly experienced, motivated counselor or program director, I look forward to hearing from you to arrange a convenient time when we could meet to discuss your present and future needs and how I might serve them.

Sincerely,

Ebony Haigler

EBONY HAIGLER

1110½ Hay Street, Fayetteville, NC 28305   •   preppub@aol.com   •   (910) 483-6611

OBJECTIVE

To offer my reputation as a compassionate, dedicated, and enthusiastic professional to an organization that can use my education and experience related to social work and human services along with my willingness to go the extra mile for my clients.

EDUCATION

Master's Degree in Counseling and Psychology, Troy State University, Gotham, NY, 1996. Bachelor of Science in Social Work, Troy State University, Gotham, NY, 1991.

EXPERIENCE

JUVENILE PROBATION OFFICER. Dale County Youth Services, Ozark, NY (2000-present). As the frontline officer for more than 100 active probationary juveniles and their families, was involved in a wide range of human resources management activities in addition to providing crisis counseling; on any given day, provided leadership and problem-solving related to multiple crises arising in clients' family/home environment, school situation, and community activities.

- Acted as liaison between local law enforcement, school systems, the judicial system, and other agencies charged with the care and supervision of these juvenile offenders.
- Prepared and maintained accurate paperwork for court procedures, state commitments, and case maintenance.
- Counseled clients and their families to assist them in dealing with problems arising within the family/home environment, school, and community.
- Dealt with day-to-day issues and crises confronting clients while providing oversight for the home, school, and community activities of more than 100 juveniles aged eight to 18.
- Scheduled and conducted probationary supervision meetings with clients and families.

YOUTH SERVICES SPECIALIST. Southeast Alabama Youth Services, Gotham, NY (1996-2000). Performed individual, group, and family counseling for clients in this regional office.

- Coordinated with directors of other agencies and assisted clients in obtaining referrals.
- Prepared and maintained complete and accurate records on all clients.
- Provided support counseling to local group homes as well as the diversion center.
- Ensured compliance with all local, state, and federal guidelines and maintained the confidentiality of all materials.

ADDICTIONS COUNSELOR I. Chemical Addictions Recovery Effort, Inc., Panama City, FL (1992-1995). Counseled and offered rehabilitative guidance to adolescents with identified chemical dependency problems.

- Performed preliminary intake and evaluation of assigned clients, and developed psychosocial assessments to determine a proper course of counseling and treatment.
- Acted as liaison between local agencies and youths in my care to assure that each client was provided with comprehensive, high-quality services.
- Participated in an addiction team formulated to educate and assist at-risk children in the local school system with drug and alcohol-related issues.

OUTPATIENT COUNSELOR. Northwest Florida Drug Council, Inc., Panama City, FL (1991). Provided outpatient treatment and counseling.

- Assessed each assigned referral client to determine services needed.
- Provided individual, group, and family counseling and worked with clients to establish treatment plans.
- Coordinated with other counselors for quality assurance, and reviewed all case closures.

PERSONAL

Excellent personal and professional references are available upon request.

Exact Name of Person
Title or Position
Name of Company
Address (no., street)
Address (city, state, zip)

LAW ENFORCEMENT SPECIALIST

Dear Exact Name of Person (or Dear Sir or Madam if answering a blind ad):

I would appreciate an opportunity to talk with you soon about how I could contribute to your organization through my eight years of experience in the law enforcement field where I have become known as an exceptional performer who offers outstanding interpersonal, investigative, and leadership skills.

You will see by my resume that most of my time in law enforcement has been spent in personal protection and VIP protection. Throughout my career I have been cited for my coolness under pressure and ability to think on my feet while responding to volatile or emergency situations. I have experience in handling actions ranging from providing first aid and comfort to injured people, to controlling crowds during public activities or disturbances, to investigating accidents and incidents. I have provided physical security for multimillion-dollar aircraft and facilities as well as for personnel.

I feel that I offer valuable experience, skills, and knowledge that will allow me to move into positions where persistence, tact, and dedication are necessary. My good judgment and common sense approach have enabled me to be effective in responding to potentially serious events by taking control and keeping them from escalating.

I hope you will welcome my call soon to arrange a brief meeting at your convenience to discuss your current and future needs and how I might serve them. Thank you in advance for your time.

Sincerely yours,

Dennis W. Oliver

Alternate last paragraph:
I hope you will call or write me soon to suggest a time convenient for us to meet and discuss your current and future needs and how I might serve them. Thank you in advance for your time.

DENNIS W. OLIVER

1110½ Hay Street, Fayetteville, NC 28305   •   preppub@aol.com   •   (910) 483-6611

OBJECTIVE   To contribute my knowledge and experience in law enforcement to an organization that can use a mature young professional who offers outstanding communication skills and a reputation for attention to detail.

TRAINING   Excelled in 400 hours of specialized law enforcement/leadership training:
&   Police procedures and weapons use — the Montana Security Police Academy
EDUCATION   Resource protection and facilities defense techniques
                         Radar use and traffic management
                         Leadership, counseling, and communications
                  Am studying **Criminal Justice**, the University of Montana campus at Flowers, MT.

CLEARANCE   **Top Secret** with Special Background Investigation (SBI).

EXPERIENCE   **LAW ENFORCEMENT OFFICER.** City of Flowers, MT (2001-present). Have earned a reputation as a highly proficient and knowledgeable security specialist while handling multiple responsibilities as a Desk Sergeant, Patrolman, Armorer, and Administrative Specialist:
                  Desk Sergeant: monitor a communications network which consists of a base station, backup network, crime-stop line, and direct commercial lines; dispatch personnel to investigate reports of incidents; prepare reports for higher headquarter; receive reports and ensure proper handling; advise authorities of changes in security conditions; regulate entry into secure areas using an interior intrusion detection system.
                  Patrolman: enforce law and order; maintain a high profile to discourage pilferage of money and property; investigate minor incidents & crimes; receive admissions/statements from witnesses; prepare written reports; make physical checks of facilities to protect aircraft and equipment.
                  Armorer: conduct inventories, account for, and issue weapons, equipment, and ammunition worth approximately $75,000.
                  Administrative Specialist: prepare performance reports and decorations and proofread to guarantee they are error free.
                  • Earned recognition for my ability to react quickly in crisis situations and under pressure in responding to alarm activations, aircraft emergencies, and traffic accidents.

                  HONOR GUARD. State of Montana, Missoula, MT (1995-01). Was handpicked as a member of the U.S. Air Force Honor Guard, a unique ceremonial high-visibility unit which supported nationwide recruiting and public relations activities.
                  • Performed in numerous official ceremonies for the President of the United States and foreign heads of state.
                  • Singled out for a special assignment, was one of 12 people selected from a field of 150 to handle special security arrangements for the Secretary of Defense and his Deputy Secretary.
                  • Received the prestigious honor of participating in the escort unit for President Bush during the inauguration ceremonies.
                  • Documented travel costs and prepared travel plans while staying within a $200,000 annual budget.
                  • Evaluated and counseled two people; prepared annual performance reports.
                  • Earned commendation and achievement medals for "meritorious service."

COMPUTERS   Offer experience in using the SPAS (Security Police Automated System) for documentation.

PERSONAL   Was certified by the U.S. Customs Service as a Customs Official, 1999.

Date

Exact Name of Person
Title or Position
Name of Company
Address (number and street)
Address (city, state, and ZIP)

**LAW ENFORCEMENT
SUPERVISOR**

Dear Exact Name of Person (or Dear Sir or Madam if answering a blind ad):

I would appreciate an opportunity to talk with you soon about how I could contribute to your organization through my extensive experience in law enforcement and security where I have built a reputation as an exceptional performer.

As you will see from my enclosed resume, I have served with distinction in positions requiring the ability to react quickly to emergency and danger, make sound decisions on the spot, and take charge so that the proper procedures are followed.

Presently a Law Enforcement Supervisor, I oversee responses to traffic accidents, limited criminal investigations, crime prevention, resource protection, and military customs. I was entrusted with a Top Secret security clearance and completed a B.A. in Criminal Justice and Social Science in 1992. I am especially proud of the fact that I will have earned this degree while working in demanding full-time jobs in a career field where frequent special projects and overseas assignments come with the job.

I hope you will welcome my call soon to arrange a brief meeting at your convenience to discuss your current and future needs and how I might serve them. Thank you in advance for your time.

Sincerely yours,

Derek M. Asparagus

Alternate last paragraph:
I hope you will call or write me soon to suggest a time convenient for us to meet and discuss your current and future needs and how I might serve them. Thank you in advance for your time.

DEREK M. ASPARAGUS

1110½ Hay Street, Fayetteville, NC 28305 • preppub@aol.com • (910) 483-6611

OBJECTIVE   To offer a reputation as an assertive professional with a talent for making sound decisions, maximizing resources, and applying tact and diplomacy under difficult conditions to an organization that can benefit from my background in law enforcement, security, and management.

EDUCATION   **B.A., Criminal Justice and Social Science,** University of Colorado, 1992.
&   Completed extensive training emphasizing law enforcement and security skills including
TRAINING   supervision, management, and leadership.

SKILLS   Hold a **Top Secret** security clearance.
Offer extensive experience in liaising with representative of international civilian and military law enforcement agencies including British, Italian, and Saudi Arabian.
Possess specialized experience in VIP and asset protection, surveillance, investigations, customs, and in the supervision of law enforcement and security operations.

EXPERIENCE   **LAW ENFORCEMENT SUPERVISOR.** City of Los Angeles, CA (2000-present). Direct and supervise law enforcement personnel during investigations of traffic accidents as well as handling limited criminal investigations, overseeing traffic control, crime prevention, resource protection, customs, and the operational use of working dogs.
- Establish duty schedules and rosters, review and approve reports, and directly supervise training and standardized evaluations given after training completion.
- Managed a special project related to Cuban refugees; supervised 80 security police personnel controlling five separate migrant populations with a total of 6,000 people; in four weeks transformed a shell camp into a community with a supply issue area, a school with more than 100 students, three churches, and a recreation area.
- Established new reporting and recordkeeping procedures which resulted in improved response and tracking of incident reports as well as entry control procedures so that sensitive resources were more effectively secured and protected in a temporary assignment at a classified location in the desert.
- Led hostage rescue teams on multiple occasions.

SUPERVISORY PATROLMAN. Malibu, CA (1992-00). Began as a Patrolman and was promoted rapidly; provided physical security for a highly sensitive controlled area as well as conducting investigations of traffic accidents, minor incidents, and complaints; submitted the appropriate incident reports; escorted visitors and operated the special section which destroyed classified waste.
- Revamped the on-the-job training program which resulted in ensuring the quality of place services while also reducing the volume of security violations.
- As a Senior Patrolman/member of the Emergency Services Team (SWAT), was involved in incidents including an off-base sniper and hostage situation where two police officers were killed, and I led a reconnaissance team and worked with a local task force investigating beach break-ins and drug offenses.

Highlights of earlier experience: Was described as a professional with a natural talent for making sound decisions while gaining experience in security and law enforcement.

PERSONAL   Am a thoroughly trained and experienced law enforcement and security professional who enjoys volunteering my time in community, sports activities, and travel.

Exact Name of Person
Title or Position
Name of Company
Address (number and street)
Address (city, state, and ZIP)

LOSS PREVENTION DETECTIVE

Dear Exact Name of Person (or Dear Sir or Madam if answering a blind ad):

I would appreciate an opportunity to talk with you soon about how I could contribute to your organization through my extensive experience in loss prevention.

As you will see from my enclosed resume, I am current working as a Loss Prevention Detective with TJ Maxx, and I have established procedures which increased apprehension of shoplifters 50%. While providing security for store premises, I have demonstrated my ability to maintain composure during tense situations. I have trained store employees in numerous procedures which reduced theft and pilferage.

Although I am held in high regard by my current employer, I am selectively exploring opportunities with other quality retailers. I hope you will welcome my call soon to arrange a brief meeting at your convenience to discuss your current and future needs and how I might serve them. Thank you in advance for your time.

Sincerely yours,

Lance T. Spears

Alternate last paragraph:
I hope you will call or write me soon to suggest a time convenient for us to meet and discuss your current and future needs and how I might serve them. Thank you in advance for your time.

LANCE T. SPEARS

1110½ Hay Street, Fayetteville, NC 28305   •   preppub@aol.com   •   (910) 483-6611

OBJECTIVE

To offer my education in finance and analytical, sales, and communication skills to an organization that can benefit from my strong interest in financial planning and banking as well as from my personal reputation for integrity, high moral standards, and a strong work ethic.

EDUCATION

Pursuing a bachelor's degree in Finance, The University of North Carolina at Wilmington (UNCW); degree expected spring 2003.
- Placed on the university's Dean's List in recognition of my academic accomplishments.
- Received an "A" on an intensive class project: performed a company analysis on Harley-Davidson including keeping records, analyzing price and volume data as well as technical data, gathering and analyzing information about the industry, and making determinations on the economic outlook for the company and industry as a whole.
- Completed specialized course work such as Finance 330 (principles of finance, stock valuation, options, etc.) and Finance 331 (real estate investing).

EXPERIENCE

Learned to manage time wisely while maintaining at least a 3.0 GPA thus far in my college career and excelling in demanding part-time jobs including this track record of accomplishments with TJMaxx, Wilmington, NC:

LOSS PREVENTION DETECTIVE. (2000-present). In only 18 months with the company, progressed to the highest level available to a part-time employee based on my maturity, willingness to take on hard work, and communication skills.
- Increased apprehensions of shoplifters 50%, thereby greatly reducing losses from theft.
- Displayed the ability to remain calm and in control and act as an arbitrator under intense conditions.
- Provided security for the store premises, researched discrepancies in cash accounts, and generated surveillance programs.
- Gained a thorough understanding of the importance of confidentiality while guarding privileged information.

FRONT-LINE SUPERVISOR. (1995-00). Supervised approximately 50 employees in order to ensure that customers received the highest quality of service and satisfaction.
- Opened cash drawers and initiated changeovers while register contents were transferred as well as changing large denominations of bills for smaller ones as needed.
- Approved refunds, lay-a-ways, and purchases by associates.
- Conducted new employee orientation which included such areas as cash handling procedures, customer service techniques, and company policy.
- Was honored as "Associate of the Quarter" by management and other associates.

CASH OFFICE ASSOCIATE. (1992-95). Was given the opportunity to apply my knowledge gained in college in a real-life situation while handling day-to-day retail store office activities including:

Inputting financial data into computers	Creating and filing financial reports
Auditing and making daily cash deposits	Balancing registers with cash in vault
Auditing cash variances of sales associates	Preparing reports for the home office
Determining and reporting weekly after-tax cash sales totals	

- Learned the value of accuracy and attention to detail.

TRAINING

Completed several seminars and training programs including loss prevention training (detecting losses, detaining suspects, and making reports).

Date

Exact Name of Person
Title or Position
Name of Company
Address (number and street)
Address (city, state, and ZIP)

NATIONAL GUARDSMAN

Dear Exact Name of Person (or Dear Sir or Madam if answering a blind ad):

With the enclosed resume, I would like to make you aware of my interest in exploring employment opportunities with your organization and acquaint you with my background.

Currently as a National Guardsman, I am involved in Language School and am studying the Thai language. I have recently been promoted to Staff Sergeant. It is my desire to obtain full-time employment in the civilian sector, and I would remain with the National Guard part-time.

You will notice from my resume that I previously served my country in the U.S. Army, and I served with distinction as a Guard and Infantry Team member. During my military service, I was a member of a peacekeeping mission in the Sinai.

I can provide outstanding references at the appropriate time, and I hope you will welcome my call soon to arrange a brief meeting at your convenience to discuss your current and future needs and how I might serve them. Thank you in advance for your time.

Sincerely yours,

Vince Jamison

VINCE JAMISON

1110½ Hay Street, Fayetteville, NC 28305 • preppub@aol.com • (910) 483-6611

OBJECTIVE   I want to contribute to an organization that can use a versatile young professional who offers strong management and communication skills along with law enforcement knowledge, radio and satellite communications skills, as well as personnel training and supervision.

EDUCATION   **Bachelor of Arts in Criminal Justice,** California State University, San Bernardino, CA, 1996.
Associate of Arts, San Bernardino Valley College, San Bernardino, CA, 1994.
Management and technical training: Completed numerous technical and management courses.
Graduated from San Gorgonio High School, San Bernardino, CA, 1987.

SPECIAL SKILLS **Firearms:** Extensive familiarity with firearms.
Clearance: Hold a Secret security clearance.
Computers: Proficient with Microsoft Word and have used other programs.

EXPERIENCE   **NATIONAL GUARDSMAN.** Fort Lewis, WA (2002-present). Have completed extensive training sponsored by the U.S. Army and National Guard.
- Currently am involved in language school, and am studying the Thai language.
- Have decided to seek civilian employment and remain in the National Guard part-time.
- Recently promoted to the rank of Staff Sergeant (E-6) in the National Guard.

NIGHT COUNSELOR. Olive Crest, Redlands, CA (2001-02). For a facility with six boys aged 14-18, was the night counselor and the adult supervisor in charge.
- Maintained records; oversaw morning meals; administered medications and paperwork.

TEAM LEADER. U.S. Army, Schofield Barracks, HI (1997-01). Entered the Army as an E-4 after earning my college degree, and became a team leader in charge of three people. Continuously involved in the training and mentoring of junior soldiers.
- Was responsible for maintaining equipment in addition to training and leading team members.
- Was promoted to E-5 and received an Honorable discharge; then entered the National Guard, and worked as a Night Counselor in the job described above while waiting for an assignment.
- Received excellent ratings on performance evaluations and was strongly encouraged to remain in the Army and assured of continued rapid advancement.
- Gained valuable skills related to law enforcement as well as management.

ASSISTANT SUPERVISOR. St. Katherine's Boys Home, Corona, CA (1996-97). Conducted group and individual counseling sessions and other activities for delinquent and troubled youth. Managed three counselors who interacted with the 16 boys on my unit.
- Refined my skills in coaching youth, and helped many develop a better attitude.

GUARD and INFANTRY TEAM MEMBER. U.S. Army, Ft. Campbell, KY, and Germany. (1993-96). Joined the Army and served as a Guard protecting access to classified materials while in Germany; while stationed at Ft. Campbell, served as a team member and was involved in a six-month assignment with a multinational peacekeeping force in the Sinai.

PERSONAL   Earned five medals for exceptional performance as well as other military awards.

**OPERATIONS &
INTELLIGENCE MANAGER**

Dear Sir or Madam:

I would appreciate an opportunity to talk with you soon about how I could contribute to your organization through the managerial and supervisory skills I have developed while serving in the Central Intelligence Agency.

Through my experience in numerous international assignments, I have become highly proficient with intelligence gathering and physical security procedures, including with numerous software applications. In my present job as an Operations and Intelligence Manager, I have been selected to fill several critical roles in a 455-person organization during the past four years.

In addition to my accomplishments and numerous medals and citations for professionalism and superior performance, I am pursuing a college degree. In spite of the demands of relocating and travel, I am only a few hours short of a bachelor's degree in Psychology from Georgetown University. You will see that I have also studied criminal justice.

My CIA has provided me opportunities to receive extensive training and experience in law enforcement, and it is now my desire to offer my considerable experience and knowledge to a local police force.

I hope you will call or write me soon to suggest a time convenient for us to meet and discuss your current and future needs and how I might serve them. Thank you in advance for your time.

Sincerely,

Leroy B. Peacemaker

LEROY B. PEACEMAKER

1110½ Hay Street, Fayetteville, NC 28305　　•　　preppub@aol.com　　•　　(910) 483-6611

OBJECTIVE　　To contribute to an organization through my supervisory and operations management abilities as well as through my knowledge and experience related to security and law enforcement gained while serving my country in the U.S. Army.

EDUCATION　　Completed 64 credit hours in a Bachelor of Arts degree program with a major in Psychology, Georgetown University, Washington, DC.
- Specialized course work included critical thinking, psychological tests and measures, research methods, and experimental psychology.
- Earlier courses transferred from other schools and completed while serving in demanding jobs requiring frequent relocation and travel included:

Crime and delinquency	Juvenile procedures
Human resource management	Stress management
Criminal justice seminar on narcotics	Police community relations
Criminal justice seminar on street survival	Microcomputer operations

Earned an Associate in General Studies degree from Central Texas College, 1988.

EXPERIENCE　　*Gained a strong, well-rounded background in supervision, management, operations, and security while advancing with the Central Intelligence Agency, worldwide locations:*

OPERATIONS AND INTELLIGENCE MANAGER. Washington, DC (2002-present). Earned a reputation as a versatile self-starter with excellent organizational and leadership skills and was selected to hold critical and highly visible roles worldwide.
- Fill several positions such as directing information gathering and analysis efforts, controlling classified records and physical security activities, and supervising 50 people.
- Received an Achievement Medal for "superb performance" which allowed the organization to receive a "no deficiencies noted" rating in a demanding inspection of physical security procedures and practices.
- Planned a detailed physical security program which was accepted and implemented.
- On a daily basis, utilize a variety of software applications used to gather intelligence.
- Contributed to flood relief activities in Ohio as a member of a special task force.

WEAPONS OPERATIONS SUPERVISOR. Classified locations worldwide (1995-02). Received a Service Medal for my accomplishments while ensuring quality training and performance of weapons systems operations and maintenance crews.
- Cited for sound judgment, initiative, and devotion to providing enthusiastic and professional leadership, produced thoroughly trained and competent employees.

WEAPONS SECTION SUPERVISOR. Germany (1990-94). Was awarded an achievement medal for my contributions and professionalism while supervising a team of skilled weapons operations and maintenance specialists and providing an example for them in all aspects of unit operations.
- Provided the leadership which allowed my department to earn recognition as technically competent and capable field artillery systems specialists.

TRAINING　　Completed extensive training programs in areas including instructors' training, substance abuse awareness, technical writing, leadership development, maintenance management, security operations management, and airborne operations.

PERSONAL　　Known for my personal integrity, moral courage, and character, was entrusted with a Top Secret security clearance following a special Background Investigation.

Exact Name of Person
Exact Title
Exact Name of Company
Address
City, State, Zip

OPERATIONS MANAGER

Dear Exact Name of Person (or Dear Sir or Madam if answering a blind ad):

With the enclosed resume, I would like to make you aware of my interest in exploring employment opportunities with your organization.

As you will see from my resume, I offer extensive security and law enforcement knowledge based on my experience as a part of elite Rangers and Special Forces organizations. Entrusted with an ENTNAC security clearance, I have undergone extensive background investigations. I am skilled in utilizing numerous types of weapons and weapons systems, and I completed Spanish language training at the John F. Kennedy Special Warfare Center and School.

In my most recent position at the nation's largest military base, I worked as an Operations Manager coordinating resources needed for live-fire activities conducted all over the east coast. In my previous assignment in Hawaii, I was promoted to increasing supervisory levels until I was placed in charge of 22 people and a fleet of vehicles. I led employees in numerous training activities in rugged field environments, and I shared the extensive training I had gained through the Special Forces and Rangers. You will see from my resume that I graduated from the Special Forces Assessment and Qualification Course as well as Ranger School, the military's 72-day school designed to test the physical and mental limits of the Army's best soldiers. I am in excellent physical condition, and in my spare time I enjoy running marathons.

Although I was strongly encouraged to remain in military service and assured of continued advancement in rank, I decided to leave the military and enter the civilian work force. I am certain that I could become a valuable member of an organization that can use a dedicated professional with expert security skills and knowledge.

I am single, and I could relocate worldwide and travel as your needs require. If you can make use of my versatile background, I hope you will contact me to suggest a time when we could meet in person to discuss your needs. I can provide excellent personal and professional references. Thank you.

Yours sincerely,

Alphonse Miragaldo

ALPHONSE MIRAGALDO

1110½ Hay Street, Fayetteville, NC 28305 • preppub@aol.com • (910) 483-6611

OBJECTIVE   I want to contribute to an organization that can use an accomplished professional who offers a versatile background which includes management experience as well as security and law enforcement skills.

CLEARANCE   Received **ENTNAC** security clearance; have undergone extensive background investigations.

LANGUAGE   Graduate, Spanish language training, John F. Kennedy Special Warfare Center and School, 2000.

EDUCATION   *College:* Completed approximately two years of college courses, Memphis State University and University of Tennessee.
Security and law enforcement training: Completed extensive security training including:

Ranger School
Special Forces Pre-SCUBA training   Air Assault Course
Pre-Combat Diver Qualification Course   Special Forces Engineer Course
Munitions Equipment Maintenance Course   Advanced Mountaineering Course
Jumpmaster Course   Airborne Course
Advanced Infantry Training   Fire Direction Center Operation
Advanced Land Navigation Course   Infantry Training
Special Forces Assessment and Qualification Course

Management training: Completed the Army's Noncommissioned Officer Course and the Primary Development Course for mid-level managers.
Driver's Training: Gained professional driving certifications; licensed to drive cargo trucks, armored tow carriers, and tractor trailers; trained in hazardous materials handling and transportation.

WEAPONS EXPERTISE   Skilled in utilizing and maintaining weapons including the .50 cal M2 machine gun, M249 machine gun, the M16A1/M16A2 rifle, M136 grenade launcher, and all types of pistols.

EXPERIENCE   **OPERATIONS MANAGER.** U.S. Army, Ft. Gordon, GA (2002-present). At the nation's largest U.S. military base, was specially selected for this position which involved coordinating the land resources and equipment needed for live-firing exercises conducted as training.
- Controlled an inventory of hazardous materials including ammunition and weapons.
- Provided flawless support for training activities in Georgia, Virginia, and North Carolina.

GENERAL MANAGER. U.S. Army, Schofield Barracks, HI (2001-2002). Was promoted from Team Leader in charge of 4 people, to Squad Leader in charge of eight employees, to Platoon Leader responsible for supervising 22 people in an organization with 22 vehicles.
- Continuously trained personnel in military/security skills as well as technical job skills.

Other U.S. Army experience:
SPECIAL FORCES ENGINEER SERGEANT. Ft. Gordon, GA (1999-00). Was a member of an African-oriented organization; maintained demolitions and construction equipment.
RANGER SQUAD LEADER. Ft. Lewis, WA (1996-99). Trained and managed a nine-person Airborne Ranger Squad which had to remain ready to relocate worldwide in 18 hours.
RIFLE TEAM LEADER. Ft. Lewis, WA (1995-96). Trained/managed a four-person rifle team in three separate organizations.

PERSONAL   Single and willing to relocate worldwide. In my spare time, enjoy hunting, reading history.

Date

Exact Name of Person
Exact Title
Exact Name of Company
Address
City, State, Zip

PARALEGAL ASSISTANT   Dear Exact Name of Person (or Dear Sir or Madam if answering a blind ad):

With the enclosed resume, I would like to make you aware of my background as an educated young professional with exceptional communication and organizational skills who offers a track record of success in paralegal, community probation, and juvenile counseling environments.

In my current job as a Paralegal Assistant, I read and analyze blotter reports to prepare fact sheets for new cases. While serving in this position, I simultaneously work as a Community Probation Officer, providing administrative support, including composing and typing correspondence sent to the client to inform them of the action being brought against them and the date and time of their community appointment. In addition, I prepare files on new clients and close out files on those who had completed their sentences and were scheduled to be released.

In a prior position, I served as a Juvenile Counselor for the Juvenile Detention Center, providing counseling services and in-processing for new female residents being admitted to the Center. I instructed new residents in the rules of the center, informed them of what would be expected of them, and conducted individual and group counseling sessions.

As you will see, I have completed a Bachelor of Science degree in Criminal Justice, graduating **magna cum laude.** I was awarded an Honor Scholarship for academic excellence in Criminal Justice and was named to the National Dean's List for two consecutive years. I feel that my strong combination of educational excellence and practical work experience would make me a valuable addition to your organization.

If you can use an enthusiastic, hard-working professional whose skills related to human services, social work, and counseling have been tested in challenging environments worldwide, I look forward to hearing from you soon. I assure you in advance that I have an excellent reputation, and would quickly become an asset to your organization.

Sincerely,

Rolanda Perkins

ROLANDA PERKINS

1110½ Hay Street, Fayetteville, NC 28305 • preppub@aol.com • (910) 483-6611

OBJECTIVE

To benefit an organization that can use an educated young professional with exceptional communication and organizational skills who offers a track record of excellence in paralegal, community probation, juvenile counseling, and library environments.

EDUCATION

Earned a **Bachelor of Science** degree in **Criminal Justice**, Macon State University, Macon, GA, 1995. Course work included a class on diversity in the workplace.
- Graduated **magna cum laude**, maintaining a cumulative GPA of 3.5.
- Awarded an Honor Scholarship in Criminal Justice for academic excellence.
- Named to the National Dean's List for two consecutive years.
- Nominated for the National Collegiate Minority Leadership Award.
- Nominated for the Honor Society.

EXPERIENCE

PARALEGAL ASSISTANT. Office of the Attorney General, Criminal Law Division, Richmond, VA (2001-present). Performed paralegal duties and provided clerical, administrative and general office support to this busy government agency.
- Read and analyzed information contained in blotter reports in order to prepare fact sheets for new cases.
- Gained the confidence of judges and other legal personnel while learning the inner workings of the court system.

COMMUNITY PROBATION OFFICER. Richmond, VA (2001-present). While simultaneously serving in the above position, I provided administrative support to the probation office, gaining valuable experience related to the types and length of punishment imposed for certain offenses.
- Composed and typed correspondence sent to the client to inform them of their community appointment as well as the action being brought against them.
- Prepared files on new clients in addition to closing out files on clients who were being released from their sentences.

JUVENILE COUNSELOR. Juvenile Detention Center, Richmond, VA (1998-01). Contributed to the operation of the detention center through my excellent communication and organizational skills, providing counseling services and in-processing to new residents; notified parents that their child was being held at the center.
- Conducted individual and group counseling for up to nine female students.
- Performed in-processing of new female residents, instructing them of the rules of the center and what would be expected of them; performed complete body searches.

LIBRARY TECHNICIAN. Library of Congress, Washington, DC (1995-98). Provided customer service, clerical, and administrative support while assisting patrons and performing general upkeep, shelving, bookkeeping, and documentation for this busy branch library.
- Supervised seasonal employees, training them in library procedures, including proper shelving using the Dewey Decimal system and in-processing of new materials.
- Assisted library patrons in locating information using sources such as the card catalog, Books in Print, and other reference materials.
- Instructed library patrons in the use of computers and the operation of computer-based library resources and databases, such as Sirs and Newsbank.

PERSONAL

Excellent personal and professional references are available upon request.

PATROL SERGEANT   Dear Mr. Smith:

With the enclosed resume, I would like to make you aware of my background as an educated young law enforcement professional with strong communication and motivational skills who offers a background in supervision and training of new recruits as well as experience in all aspects of police work.

In my present position as a Patrol Sergeant and Field Training Officer, I supervise, schedule, and assign the work of the uniformed officers in my section, as well as overseeing the training and job performance of these personnel. I was promoted to this position after serving as a Field Training Officer and as a Narcotics Agent, where I performed liaison with the County Sheriff's Department and Bureau of Narcotics as well as with numerous federal, state, and local agencies. While investigating drug activity in multiple jurisdictions, I participated in covert operations which often involved large cash purchases of controlled substances. I was named Police Officer of the Year in recognition of my outstanding performance in this position.

You will see that I graduated from the Basic Law Enforcement Training (BLET) program at Youngstown Technical Community College, and have supplemented that education with numerous advanced law enforcement training courses and certifications. I am currently completing the Management Development Course for law enforcement professionals, an extensive ten-month program which encompasses all aspects of departmental management.

Although I am highly regarded by my present employer and can provide excellent references at the appropriate time, I am interested in pursuing other opportunities where I can make use of my leadership ability and strong supervisory and training skills. I trust that you will hold my inquiry in the strictest confidence until after we have had a chance to meet.

If you can use an accomplished law enforcement professional who offers outstanding staff development and training skills, then I look forward to hearing from you soon. I assure you in advance that I have an outstanding reputation and would quickly become an asset to your organization.

Sincerely,

Ricky Gonzalez

RICKY GONZALEZ

1110½ Hay Street, Fayetteville, NC 28305   •   preppub@aol.com   •   (910) 483-6611

OBJECTIVE

To benefit an organization that can use a motivated young law enforcement professional with strong communication and motivational skills as well as extensive education and experience in supervision and training of new recruits, narcotics operations, and investigation.

EDUCATION

Completing the **Management Development Course** for law enforcement professionals, a ten-month advanced training program with segments covering gathering and analyzing information, employment law, communication skills, media relations, leadership, motivation and achievement, performance management, project management, budget management, and policy development.

Graduated from the **Basic Law Enforcement Training (BLET) program**, Youngstown Technical Community College, Youngstown, MA, 1998.
Completed a number of advanced law enforcement training courses, including:
   First Line Supervision course, 80 hours, MA Justice Academy, 2001.
   Field Training Officer Program, 40 hours, Mass Community College, 2000.
   D.C.I. Certification course, 40 hours, County Sheriff's Department, 1999.

EXPERIENCE

With the Boston Police Department, have advanced in the following "track record" of increasing responsibility:
2001-present: **PATROL SERGEANT** and **FIELD TRAINING OFFICER.** Promoted from Patrol/Field Training Officer to this position, where I command, direct, and supervise a uniform patrol section as well as performing the regular duties of a police officer.
- Supervise, schedule, and assign the work of up to 15 uniformed officers.
- Gained hands-on experience as a Narcotics Agent; played a key role in seizing millions of dollars in illegal substances.
- Develop and implement performance standards for employees in my section; provide employee counseling to ensure that job performance meets or exceeds expectations.
- Monitor section personnel in their interactions with the public and assist or instruct them when necessary.
- Oversee maintenance of equipment and inspect all personnel under my supervision to ensure they present a professional image.
- Ensure that all personnel comply with departmental policies and procedures; investigate certain types of complaints against officers in my section.

1998-01: **PATROL OFFICER** and **FIELD TRAINING OFFICER.** Performed patrol, traffic enforcement, investigative, and training duties while serving as a "role model" for new recruits.
- Provided training for new recruits in all aspects of police work, including but not limited to effecting arrest, policies and procedures, officer safety, and completion of paperwork.

1992-98: **POLICE OFFICER.** Received training and hands-on experience in a variety of police activities including the K-9 patrol.
- Was selected to travel to various high schools and middle schools to promote the DARE Program, designed to educate youth about the dangers of drug use and the potential of drug addiction.

PERSONAL

Excellent personal and professional references on request.

Date

Exact Name of Person
Title or Position
Name of Company
Address (no., street)
Address (city, state, zip)

PATROLMAN   Dear Exact Name of Person (or Dear Sir or Madam if answering a blind ad):

I would appreciate an opportunity to talk with you soon about how I could contribute to your operations in the law enforcement field through my experience and training as a police officer.

You will see by my resume that I offer experience in teaching police procedures and primary marksmanship and that I am qualified as an **Expert** with numerous weapons. I have a record of rapid promotion and outstanding performance in providing physical security, deterring crime through high-visibility patrolling, investigating accidents and incidents, preparing clear and concise reports, and handling switchboards and dispatching. I have provide protection for facilities ranging from nuclear power plants to coal mines, and I am skilled at all aspects of personal protection,

In my present job, I have been in charge of training and supervising employees during shifts which can range from eight to 24 hours. I am widely recognized as a professional who has the ability to remain calm and in control under pressure while communicating and working well with others.

I am very proud of the fact that I am a third-generation police officer and that I am achieving my long-held personal dream of success in the field of law enforcement.

I hope you will welcome my call soon to arrange a brief meeting at your convenience to discuss your current and future needs and how I might serve them. Thank you in advance for your time.

Sincerely yours,

Steven E. Bouillibaise

Alternate last paragraph:
I hope you will call or write soon to suggest a time convenient for us to meet and discuss your current and future needs and how I might serve them. Thank you in advance for your time.

STEVEN E. BOUILLIBAISE

1110½ Hay Street, Fayetteville, NC 28305   •   preppub@aol.com   •   (910) 483-6611

OBJECTIVE   To contribute my law enforcement skills to an organization that can use a calm, level-headed young professional who can handle pressure and who offers problem-solving and decision-making abilities refined through experience.

TRAINING   Excelled in intensive training including the following:
The three-month Kentucky Police School
40-hour courses in site security, physical security, intrusion detection systems, and custodial agent procedures
Eight credit hour courses in prisoner corrections and physical security —
The Kentucky Institute for Professional Development

CERTIFICATIONS   Completed five credit hour course in **Emergency Medical Services** which included CPR, techniques for moving people with spinal injuries, and many other aspects of "first-response" medical care.
- Am licensed by the U.S. Government to drive hazardous cargo.

SPECIAL SKILLS & KNOWLEDGE   Am qualified as an **Expert** with the 9 mm pistol, .45 caliber pistol, M-16 rifle, M-70 machine gun, and 12-gauge shotgun.
Through experience and training, perform minor maintenance on and use intrusion detection systems.
Have been trained in **counterterrorism** and personnel/material security.
Was entrusted with a **Secret** security clearance.

EXPERIENCE   **PHYSICAL SECURITY SPECIALIST** and **PATROLMAN**. National Security Operators, Bowling Green, KY (2002-present). Under a contract with a private security firm, am providing security for coal mining assets as well as company VIPs.
- Monitored security cameras and checked for clearance to provide access to secure documents, assets, and locations.
- Refined my proficiency in conducting searches and making arrests.
- Investigated and prepared reports on accidents as well as fight, assaults, robberies, and other incidents.
- Trained and supervised team members in surveillance and counterterrorism.

SENIOR SECURITY TEAM LEADER. Security Forces International, Plymouth, West Virginia (1998-01). For a private security services firm, supervised a team of eight personnel required to work in pairs to guarantee "error-free" security for a nuclear power plant by escorting personnel and confirming clearances.
- Responded to alarms and arrested or detained intruders.
- Became skilled in performing minor maintenance on security alarms.

MILITARY POLICEMAN. Wesley Grove, TN (1995-97). Earned rapid promotion and recognition for my skills in security and law enforcement while monitoring alarms, handling a switchboard, and dispatching 11 police units responding to an average of 25 emergency calls a night.
- Taught classes on subjects including weapons and search and arrest.
- Was a contributing member of a police section named "the best for the quarter."

PERSONAL   In excellent physical condition, have often worked long hours such as 24- and 12-hour shifts. Am the son and grandson of police officers.

Date

Exact Name of Person
Exact Title
Exact Name of Company
Address
City, State, Zip

PERSONAL BODYGUARD

Dear Exact Name of Person (or Dear Sir or Madam if answering a blind ad):

With the enclosed resume, I would like to make you aware of my interest in exploring employment opportunities within your organization in some capacity in which you could utilize my skills related to security and personal protection.

In my most recent position, I worked seven days a week at the Georgia Pacific Corporation in Seattle, Washington, where hundreds of workers were out on strike. As a Shift Supervisor for Security Operations, I played a key role in managing a security force which grew to 100 people at its height. I had broad responsibility for supervising plant personnel and equipment during the labor dispute, and I acted as a liaison with union members.

During that time, I undertook a special assignment as a Security Consultant for Exxon Corporation of America. While providing executive protection for senior executives, I developed a new cost-effective alternative for maintaining the in-house guard force, and I assisted in producing a proposal for a new video surveillance system. I briefed corporate decision makers on the system's features and benefits.

A Certified Personal Protection Specialist, I have provided personal protection services for numerous VIPs who retained my services in a highly confidential manner.

Single and available for worldwide relocation and frequent travel as your needs require, I can provide outstanding personal and professional references. I would appreciate an opportunity to meet with you personally to discuss your needs.

Sincerely,

Hayden E. Orenson

HAYDEN E. ORENSON

1110½ Hay Street, Fayetteville, NC 28305   •   preppub@aol.com   •   (910) 483-6611

OBJECTIVE   I want to contribute to an organization that can use a Personal Protection Specialist who offers experience in performing surveillance and reconnaissance, developing and implementing site security, managing security professionals, and safeguarding executives.

TRAINING   Completed the **Executive Protection Institute's Personal Protection Course,** 2000. Attended Nine Lives Association (NLA) Conference, San Antonio, TX, 2000.
Completed extensive training sponsored by the U.S. Army including Airborne School, the Primary Leadership Development Course, and technical training related to the gunner field.

CERTIFICATIONS Certified Personal Protection Specialist; CPR/AED Certified (current).

WEAPONS   Expert marksman; skilled in using semi-automatic and automatic weapons.
Hold a Washington state concealed firearms permit.

EXPERIENCE   **SHIFT SUPERVISOR, SECURITY OPERATIONS.** Alternative Management Corporation, Seattle, WA (2000-present). For two years, worked seven days a week at Georgia Pacific as part of the company's security force when hundreds of workers went on strike.
- Played a key role in managing a security force of up to 100 people.
- Provided oversight for the safety of plant personnel and equipment during a labor dispute.
- Conducted and delegated vehicular patrol of facility and outlying satellites.
- Implemented policy for off-road equipment operation.
- Coordinated with facility security in operation of $200,000 video surveillance system.
- Supervised the distribution of more than $3,500 weekly for personnel.
- Performed site assessment for manpower allocation; instructed and evaluated personnel.
- Acted as liaison with union members, employees, and security force.
- Coordinated with city and county law enforcement during volatile and hostile situations.

Special Project: SECURITY CONSULTANT, EXECUTIVE PROTECTION. Exxon Corporation of America, Grand Rapids, MI (1999). Was selected for a special assignment providing executive protection services for corporate executives.
- Conducted security assessment for client and facility; developed standard operating procedures for static and roving patrol of in-house security force; performed security reconnaissance.
- Utilized video/camera equipment to document security weakness and equipment inventory.
- On my own initiative, developed a new cost-effective alternative for maintaining in-house guard force.
- Assisted in producing a proposal for a new video surveillance system and briefed corporate decision makers on the features and benefits of the system.

TEAM LEADER. City of Merced, CA (1996-98). Trained, managed, and evaluated seven individuals while assuming responsibility for ½ million dollars in weapons systems, communication systems, vehicles, and other equipment.
- Interacted with VIPs during special events.

DRIVER. Various VIPs whose names I cannot reveal, various locations (1991-95).

LANGUAGES   Speak some Arabic; completed 2 years of Spanish; understand Italian.

PERSONAL   Received numerous letters recognizing my professionalism. Excellent references.

POLICE CAPTAIN   Dear Sir or Madam:

With the enclosed resume, I would like to formally initiate the process of becoming considered for the job of Chief of Police for your city.

As you will see from my resume, I am currently serving the Howard Police Department as a Police Captain in charge of one of the city's three Patrol Divisions. As one of the department's six Captains, I have transformed the city's newest Patrol Division into a highly respected and productive operating unit known for the high morale and productivity of its 62 personnel.

In previous jobs with the City of Howard, I performed with distinction as Lieutenant in charge of both the Major Crimes Investigative Division and Emergency Operations. I began working for the City of Howard as a Patrol Officer in 1982 after serving my country briefly in the U.S. Army as a Military Policeman. I have enjoyed a track record of promotion because of my hard work and common sense, my outstanding police work in all functional areas, as well as my excellent administrative skills and ability to deal articulately and tactfully with everyone, from employees to citizens' groups.

I can provide outstanding references at the appropriate time, and I can assure you that you would find me to be an individual who is known as a gifted strategic thinker, powerful motivator, and fair supervisor.

Please contact me if you would like me to make myself available for a personal interview at your convenience. Although I am held in high regard within the Howard Police Department, I have a strong interest in exploring ways in which my leadership ability and extensive experience in all aspects of police work could be put to use for your city as its Chief of Police.

Sincerely,

James Babylon

JAMES BABYLON

1110½ Hay Street, Fayetteville, NC 28305　　•　　preppub@aol.com　　•　　(910) 483-6611

OBJECTIVE

I want to contribute to your city as its Chief of Police through my experience in all aspects of police operations as well as through my outstanding community relations skills, administrative abilities, and highly respected personal and professional style.

EXPERIENCE

Have excelled in this track record of promotion to increasing responsibilities within the Howard Police Department, Howard, WY:

POLICE CAPTAIN, PATROL SUPPORT DIVISION. (2001-present). In July 2001, was assigned to command the Patrol Support Division.

- In addition to motivating, supervising and evaluating a 55-man division comprised of Lieutenants, Sergeants, and Officers, skillfully handle a wide range of administrative responsibilities ranging from strategic planning to statistical analysis.
- Develop the overall budget for the Division and Sub-Station.
- Am responsible for the Traffic Section, Neighborhood Improvement Team, Housing Officers (Safe Streets Program), School Resource Officers, Mounted Police Unit, and Park Unit. Am working on strategic initiatives to improve public safety.

POLICE CAPTAIN, PATROL. (2000-2001). In 2000, was promoted to the rank of Captain and became one of the six Captains in this 320-person police department; was placed in charge of the newly formed 3rd Patrol Division and transformed the division's 62 employees into a highly respected and productive operating unit.

- Motivated, supervised, and evaluated a 62-person division comprised of Lieutenants, Sergeants, and Officers, skillfully handled a wide range of administrative responsibilities ranging from strategic planning to statistical analysis.

LIEUTENANT, MAJOR CRIMES INVESTIGATIVE DIVISION. (1998-00). While still serving in 1998 as Lieutenant in charge of Emergency Operations, was specially selected to take over as Lieutenant of the Major Crimes Investigative Division comprised of nine Officers and one Sergeant. Provided strong leadership to a division which had a 100% clearance rate in homicides and an 84% clearance rate in robbery cases.

LIEUTENANT, EMERGENCY OPERATIONS. (1990-98). Commanded operations of the department's S.W.A.T. Team and Narcotic Vice Task Force; earned widespread respect for my work in revitalizing this area of police operations.

- Took over a team which had made 200 felony arrests in the first eight months of 1997; led the team to make 365 felony arrests in only four months.

Highlights of other experience within the Howard Police Department:
Unit Supervisor, Major Crimes Investigative Division. As Sergeant of Police, supervised nine Investigators assigned to Crimes Against Persons and Property and was credited with producing an unusually high arrest rate.
Sergeant of Police, Street Crimes Unit. Planned and coordinated unit operations while supervising five Officers; also worked on active investigations.
Investigator, Street Crimes Unit. Handled a wide range of duties as an Investigator related to vice, narcotics, drug operations, and intelligence gathering.

EDUCATION

B.S. degree in Political Science, Howard State University, Howard, WY, 1989.
A.S. degree in Criminal Justice, Rockland Community College, Suffern, NY.
Hold Advanced, Intermediate, and Basic Law Enforcement Certificates.

CAREER CHANGE

Date

Exact Name of Person
Title or Position
Name of Company
Address (no., street)
Address (city, state, zip)

POLICE OFFICER INTERN

Dear Exact Name of Person (or Dear Sir or Madam if answering a blind ad):

With the enclosed resume, I am formally expressing my desire to work in your organization, and I can assure you that I offer a solid commitment to the law enforcement and criminal justice field.

You will see from my resume that I excelled as a Chemical Specialist while working in the Department of Defense. While acquiring expertise in the handling, storage, and disposal of toxic and hazardous substances, I was promoted ahead of my peers and selected to train other young people. It was during my employment with the Department of Defense that I decided to earn my degree in criminal justice and dedicate myself to a career in law enforcement. I believe my self control and calm temperament are well suited to police work.

Subsequently I completed my B.S. degree in Criminal Justice in only three years instead of the usual four years. I give much credit for my academic success to my disciplined work habits.

Most recently I have excelled as a Police Officer Intern with the Watkins Police Department, and during that internship I became skilled in resolving domestic/personal disputes, conducting surveillance, handling auto accidents, retrieving stolen goods, writing up police documentation, and detecting illegal activities related to drugs, shoplifting, and other areas. Obviously this brief experience in law enforcement does not make me an "expert" in any area, but I hope you will conclude from my military and academic track record that I am committed to becoming an outstanding law enforcement professional.

Please be assured that I can provide outstanding personal and professional references. I can also assure you that you would find me in person to be an enthusiastic and dedicated young person who prides myself on being the best and doing the best at all times.

I hope you will welcome my call soon to arrange a brief meeting at your convenience to discuss your current and future needs and how I might serve them. Thank you in advance for your time.

Sincerely yours,

Richard E. Beanstalk

RICHARD EDWARD BEANSTALK

1110½ Hay Street, Fayetteville, NC 28305 • preppub@aol.com • (910) 483-6611

OBJECTIVE

To benefit an organization that can use a disciplined, hard-working, and resourceful young professional who offers skills related to law enforcement and the criminal justice field along with planning, management, and communication abilities transferrable to any field.

EDUCATION

Earned my **Bachelor of Science (B.S.) degree in Criminal Justice,** Martin Luther King State University, Watkins, OH, 2000.
- Completed this rigorous degree program in only three years by applying my hard-working nature as well as disciplined habits.
- In the computer lab, gained familiarity with Excel, Word, and Java.

Excelled in the Department of Defense Chemical School studying chemical warfare and decontamination; also completed training as a Drug and Alcohol Abuse Counselor.

EXPERIENCE

POLICE OFFICER INTERN. Watkins Police Department, Watkins, OH (2001-present). Gained experience in many aspects of police work in this internship completed after receiving my B.S. degree; was commended for demonstrating excellent judgement and exhibiting a patient approach to public relations and problem solving while working in hostile and often dangerous situations.
- *Police documentation:* Wrote citations while handling the normal duties of a police officer; learned to complete police reports and other documentation.
- *Personnel protection/transport:* Transported mental patients to and from hospitals.
- *Domestic disputes:* Refined my skills in handling domestic/family problems.
- *Stolen goods:* Retrieved stolen vehicles and coordinated their disposition.
- *Auto accidents:* Learned how to handle all aspects of auto accidents from arranging for medical help to writing up all the documentation required at accident scenes.
- *Illegal drugs:* Became knowledgeable of procedures used to detect the sale and use of illegal drugs and to apprehend suspects.
- *Property protection:* Became skilled in dealing with shoplifters and trespassers.
- *Surveillance:* Learned techniques of police surveillance and attended Community Watch meetings.

ADMINISTRATIVE ASSISTANT. V.A. Hospital, Watkins, OH (July 2000-August 2000). While excelling in this work-study job to finance my college degree, became skilled in completing medical forms and paperwork particular to the medical field.
- Scheduled students for work study interviews and other administrative duties.
- Answered telephones in a personnel placement operation.

ALCOHOL/DRUG ABUSE COUNSELOR. V.A. Hospital, Watkins, OH (1995-1998). Was cited for my compassionate personality and kind nature while dealing with people experiencing multiple personal problems; screened and counseled veterans abusing alcohol and drugs and determined appropriate treatment remedies.

CHEMICAL SPECIALIST. Department of Defense, Washington, DC (1990-94). Gained expertise in the handling and disposal of toxic and hazardous substances while participating in numerous field exercises and projects in the chemical field.
- Became certified as a **Chemical Operations Specialist.**

PERSONAL

Am an energetic individual who has a positive and optimistic outlook. Pride myself on my self control and ability to remain calm in stressful situations.

CAREER CHANGE

Date

Exact Name of Person
Title or Position
Name of Company
Address (no., street)
Address (city, state, zip)

POLICE OFFICER

Dear Exact Name of Person (or Dear Sir or Madam if answering a blind ad):

With the enclosed resume, I wish to make you aware of my interest in exploring employment opportunities with your security firm.

You will see from my resume that I am currently working as a Police Officer for the Topeka Police Department. In a prior position, I worked for a private contractor and I excelled in assignments worldwide. During that time, I supervised people involved in assuring security at a U.S. embassy in the Middle East, and I supervised an eight-person team in Egypt controlling access to a construction site.

I also worked previously for the Topeka Police Department in the early 1990s, and during that time I gained specialized experience as a Burglary Investigator.

Although I am held in high regard by the police department where I am currently employed, I have decided that I wish to offer my considerable skills to a private contracting firm. I am single and available for worldwide relocation and extended travel as your needs require.

I hope you will welcome my call soon to arrange a brief meeting at your convenience to discuss your current and future needs and how I might serve them. Thank you in advance for your time.

Sincerely yours,

Jason Hunter

JASON HUNTER

1110½ Hay Street, Fayetteville, NC 28305   •   preppub@aol.com   •   (910) 483-6611

OBJECTIVE

I want to contribute to an organization that can use a **Police Monitor** and experienced law enforcement and police professional who offers a background which includes Special Forces training and experience, extensive international participation in special projects, and a wealth of training related to antiterrorism, search and seizure, crime scene and investigations.

EDUCATION

Graduate of the KS Justice Academy's courses and training in these and other areas:

Arrest, Search Warrants, Search & Seizure   **Crime Scene Searches**
Basic Juvenile Officer Training   Advanced School Resource Officer
Graduate of the State Bureau of Investigation (SBI), Division of Criminal Information DCI Statewide Mobile Certification Class; am an **authorized DCI Terminal Operator.**
• Also completed the SBI's training leading to **Specialized Certification.**
Completed **Operator Certification** training by the KS Department of Justice.
Completed training related to **Street Gangs**, Syracuse Police Department.
At Miami Technical Community College, completed instruction related to:

Time Distance Operator   **EMS First Responder Recertification**
Certification Training for Radar Operators Firearms Recertification
Response to High Risk Situations   Cardiopulmonary Resuscitation
Law Enforcement Pursuit Driving   Crime Scene Searches
HAZMAT for Law Enforcement Officers   CPR - Heartsaver
Report Writing for Law Enforcement Officers
Radar Operators Training Update   Standardized Field Sobriety Testing
Was trained by the Miami Police Department in **Special Weapons and Tactics (S.W.A.T.)**

CLEARANCE

Top Secret security clearance

EXPERIENCE

POLICE OFFICER. Topeka Police Department, Topeka, KS (2000-present). Served as a Police Officer enforcing city, state, and federal laws while also safeguarding life and property;
• For two of these years, performed as a School Resource Officer for Massey Hill Alternative School, a school for at-risk children in grades 7-12.

SUPERVISOR. DVD, Inc., Falls Church, VA (1997-2000). Was involved in three separate assignments:
1999: Supervised an 8-man team in the East African country of Djbuti.
1998: Supervised two people in charge of security at the U.S. Embassy in the Middle East.
1997: Was Supervisor of an 8-man team in Egypt, on access to construction site for a new embassy; ensured area was not compromised and that electronic and other threats were rebuffed.

POLICE OFFICER. Topeka Police Department, Topeka, KS (1990-96). After receiving an honorable discharge from a military career in which I received numerous awards recognizing my accomplishments, became a valued member of the Topeka police force.
• Was loaned to the Department of Alcohol, Firearms, and Tobacco (ATF) for one year, and performed as an undercover investigator in the breakup of the White Patriot Party; the group's leaders received prison sentences.
• Worked for two years as a burglary investigator.

PERSONAL

Member of Masons; Police Association of KS; Special Forces Association.

Date

Exact Name of Person
Exact Title
Exact Name of Company
Address
City, State, Zip

POLICE OFFICER   Dear Exact Name of Person (or Dear Sir or Madam if answering a blind ad):

With the enclosed resume, I would like to make you aware of my experience as a law enforcement professional with excellent investigative, communication, and supervisory skills and a strong background in the training of personnel. I am particularly interested in the job as Airport Security Chief which you recently advertised in the Albany Gazette.

As you will see, I have extensive law enforcement experience in a number of diverse metropolitan areas. While with the Albany police department, I have served as a uniformed Police Officer and Police Sergeant. I have also served as a Major Crimes Investigator. I have been "loaned" by the Albany Police Department to an international police task force and to Dulles Airport, where I served as Deputy Chief of Airport Security.

With a Bachelor of Science in Criminal Justice from Albany College, I have a strong educational background to support my years of practical experience. I have also been awarded an Advanced Law Enforcement Certification from the New York Criminal Justice Training and Standards Commission. I feel that this combination of experience, education, and the proven ability to train and supervise personnel will be a great asset to any organization.

If you would benefit from the services of a highly experienced and motivated law enforcement professional with a strong background in supervision, training, and investigation, then please contact me to arrange a time when we might meet to discuss your needs. I thank you in advance for your time and consideration.

Sincerely,

Candice Royal

CANDICE ROYAL

1110½ Hay Street, Fayetteville, NC 28305   •   preppub@aol.com   •   (910) 483-6611

OBJECTIVE   Seeking a career-enhancing opportunity in Law Enforcement or a related field.

QUALIFICATIONS
- Over fifteen years experience as a law enforcement officer with supervisory, investigative, and instructor experience.
- Awarded the Advanced Law Enforcement Certification by the New York Criminal Justice Training and Standards Commission.
- Over eleven years of active duty military service.
- Possess extensive background in police procedure; investigative technique; and the supervising, training, and mentoring of personnel.

EDUCATION   Bachelor of Science degree in Criminal Justice, Albany College, Albany, NY.
CIVILIAN POLICE EDUCATION: New York Justice Academy, Salemburg, NY.
> First-Line Supervision
> Interaction Management
> Basic Criminal Investigations
> Police Law Institute

EXPERIENCE   **POLICE OFFICER.** Albany Police Department, Albany, NY (2000-present). Provide full-service policing in diverse metropolitan environments while serving as a uniformed Patrol Officer, Supervisor, and Major Crimes Investigator.

DEPUTY CHIEF OF AIRPORT SECURITY. Albany County Sheriff's Department, Albany County, NY (1998-00). Worked on special assignment as Chief of Airport Security at Dulles Airport.

POLICE MONITOR & INSTRUCTOR. Grumman Aerospace Technology, Ft. Worth, TX (1990-97). Served on special assignment with the International Police Task Force as a Police Monitor, Patrol Team Leader, Advisor, and trainer of local police.
- Also served as a local police instructor at the Syracuse Regional Local Police Training and Development Unit.
- Developed and implemented a master program of instruction which served as the blueprint for a 40-hour Program of Instruction in Traffic Enforcement.

POLICE OFFICE & POLICE SERGEANT. Albany City Police Department, Albany, NY (1987-90). Also served as a local police instructor at the Syracuse Regional Local Police Training and Development Unit.
- Developed and implemented a master program of instruction which served as the blueprint for a 40-hour Program of Instruction in Traffic Enforcement.

MILITARY EXPERIENCE. locations worldwide. Served in the U.S. Army as a Heavy Anti-Armor Infantryman, with a secondary occupational specialty as a Military Police Supervisor.
- Trained, supervised, and guided the professional development of subordinate soldiers.
- Maintained the operational readiness of complex anti-armor missile systems.
- Developed and expanded my personal expertise through service in various assignments with both rapidly deployable and forward-based combat divisions.

PERSONAL   Excellent personal and professional references are available upon request.

CAREER CHANGE

Date

POLICE SPECIALIST

This individual hopes to
become a Special Agent
with the FBI.

Dear Ms. Smith:

With the enclosed resume, I would like to initiate the process of being considered for an appointment as a Special Agent with the FBI.

As you will see from my resume, I offer approximately nine years of experience with the Rochester Police Department in Rochester, NY, a city which is rated as the fourth largest metropolitan area in the state. After excelling in earlier jobs requiring strong investigation, communication, and training skills I was selected to receive additional training and certified as a K-9 handler. Recently I have been filling dual roles as a K-9 Officer and Police Specialist. Presently leading the department in the number of criminal apprehensions by K-9 teams for the year to date, I am also considered highly effective in training and supervising new officers in areas which include police safety, criminal enforcement, traffic enforcement, public safety, crime prevention, investigation techniques, and report writing.

Since joining this police force in 1995, I have met the challenges of working with the public and my fellow officers while earning a reputation as an articulate, self-motivated professional with exceptional communication and organizational skills. I am known as a patient and persistent investigator who will follow all leads and pursue a case to its conclusion. A persuasive speaker, I have been effective in giving testimony when my cases come to trial.

I am confident that the qualities that have made me effective as a representative of this city's law enforcement community would easily translate to success with the Federal Bureau of Investigation. I appreciate the opportunity to meet and discuss the Bureau's requirements, needs, and goals and how my background might serve them. I can provide outstanding references at the appropriate time.

Sincerely,

Alexis Sanders

ALEXIS SANDERS

1110½ Hay Street, Fayetteville, NC 28305   •   preppub@aol.com   •   (910) 483-6611

OBJECTIVE   To obtain a position as a Special Agent with the FBI.

EDUCATION   Bachelor of Arts in Visual Arts Management, Simmons College, Rochester, NY, 1991. Graduated with a 3.2 GPA.

EXPERIENCE   *Am earning a reputation as a quick learner and skilled trainer who relates well to others and offers a strong ability to work with the public as a member of the Rochester Police Department, Rochester, NY:*

K-9 OFFICER and **POLICE SPECIALIST.** (2001-present). Have quickly become recognized as a highly effective dog handler and am leading the department in the number of criminal apprehensions for the year to date while also contributing through my knowledge and experience in the capacity of training specialist.
- Completed training which allows me to work as a team with my dog in areas including narcotics searches of vehicles, buildings, and interdiction.
- Have learned that well-trained K-9 officers are useful in calming scared children.
- Work with my dog during tracking and trailing lost children or law violators, land and water cadaver recovery, and for handler protection such as during building searches.
- As a Police Specialist, train new officers who are recognized for their efficiency in accident investigations and report writing.
- Provide training in officer safety, criminal enforcement, traffic enforcement, public safety, crime prevention, investigative techniques, and report writing.

POLICE INVESTIGATOR. (1998-2001). Was offered an opportunity to become a homicide investigator on the basis of my skills displayed while investigating serious criminal acts.
- Oversaw cases from conducting the investigation, through charging the criminal, to presenting evidence in the case before a court of law.
- Led the department with most arrests resulting in closed cases over eight months.

POLICE SPECIALIST. (1995-97). Recognized for my outstanding ability to communicate both verbally and in writing as well as for my skill as a trainer .
- Produced effective officers while involved in internal training in areas which included officer safety, criminal investigation, crime prevention, criminal enforcement, traffic enforcement, public safety, and report writing.
- Created a new city citation book for the City of Rochester.

CERTIFICATIONS
- **New York Basic Law Enforcement Training:** Traffic & Criminal Enforcement, Criminal Apprehension, Weapons: .357 Caliber Handgun, 12-Gauge Shotgun.
- **New York Advanced Law Enforcement Training:** 500 hours of in-service training and six years of patrol experience, culminating in a four-year college degree.
- **Police Law Institute:** course of study included units on search & seizure, search warrants, and surveillance.
- **K-9 Certifications:** North American Police Work Dog Association, and Certificate of Training, Police K-9 Patrol.
- **Radar Certifications:** Radar Operator Certification Training, 1997; Operator Certification for Radar, 1999; re-certification.
- **Intoxilyzer Certification:** (40 hours), re-certification, Intoxilyzer Recertification
- **Search and Seizure Certification:** (80 hours); re-certification, sponsored by the Police Law Institute (8 hours).

Date

Exact Name of Person
Title or Position
Name of Company
Address (no., street)
Address (city, state, zip)

**POLICE
TRAINING OFFICER**

Dear Exact Name of Person (or Dear Sir or Madam if answering a blind ad):

I would appreciate an opportunity to talk with you soon about how I could contribute to your organization by offering the experience I have gained as a U.S. Army Special Forces officer planning and conducting international operations with an emphasis on Central and South America. I am responding to your recent advertisement for a Police Training Officer.

As you will see from my enclosed resume, the bulk of my experience has been in Central America including Mexico where I have been effective in taking concepts and turning them into realities. I am fluent in Castilian and Latin American Spanish and this asset has enabled me to represent the U.S. military during sensitive projects including training foreign security forces in antinarcotics actions as well as metropolitan police force operations. I have frequently briefed top-level military and civilian leaders, U.S. and foreign, on programs I have planned and managed. I have extensive experience in multi-agency coordination, including dealing with high-ranking personnel in the DEA, Department of Defense, and State Department, as well as host nation officials.

I have been selected by the Department of the Army for an advanced civil degree (master's degree) program and as a Foreign Area Officer with a Latin American orientation. I hold a Top Secret security clearance with Special Background Investigation. In addition to my bachelor's degree in Criminal Justice, I excelled in the military's graduate-level executive training program, the Combined Arms Staff Services School.

I feel that my practical experiences in living and working in international settings have allowed me to become an area specialist. I am especially proud of the fact that wherever I have worked, I have been able to instill my own belief in hard work and striving to do one's personal best in people I have trained and instructed. I am the proud recipient of three Meritorious Service Medals and four Commendation Medals — all of which were awarded for extraordinary accomplishments and superior performance.

I hope you will welcome my call soon to arrange a brief meeting at your convenience to discuss your current and future needs and how I might serve them. Thank you in advance for your time.

Sincerely yours,

Eldon L. Souffle

ELDON L. SOUFFLE

1110½ Hay Street, Fayetteville, NC 28305   •   preppub@aol.com   •   (910) 483-6611

OBJECTIVE

To offer my expertise in turning concepts and plans into realities through my outstanding analytical, research, and managerial abilities honed as a military officer experienced in dealing with security, internal defense, and law enforcement activities on international levels.

EXPERIENCE

Advanced to the rank of Major in the U.S. Army while excelling in training program development and operational advisory assistance; have extensive overseas experience working with foreign nationals in their native language:

PLANS AND OPERATIONS OFFICER. The Pentagon, Washington, DC (2001-present). As the principal advisor to a three-star general, am the resident expert on Special Forces operations and missions in Central and South America; act as liaison between the Department of the Army (DA), commands in the region, and individual units.
- Am program manager for overseas training and the Counterdrug Program.

TRAINING ADVISOR and **OPERATIONS MANAGER.** Central America (1998-01). As the chief of a team of training specialists headquartered in the American Embassy, assisted the Mexican National Police Antinarcotics Division in reorganizing and improving every facet of their operations.
- Trained and advised more than 200 antinarcotics police personnel in operations planning, intelligence, and light infantry skills.
- Excelled in reaching all objectives in a region which was politically very turbulent and extremely dangerous.
- Cited as an example of integrity and professionalism, performed aggressively in a multi-agency environment while working closely with personnel from the DEA (Drug Enforcement Administration), Department of Defense (DOD), State Department, and Mexican National Police.
- Translated my experiences, which included frequent exposure to the front lines of the drug war, into assistance for updating policies of U.S. counterdrug agencies.

TRAINING CHIEF. The Pentagon, Washington, DC (1995-97). Continued to use my fluency in Spanish and operations expertise while coordinating, planning, evaluating, and making improvements to internal training activities in a 1500-member Special Forces Group conducting low-intensity conflicts throughout Central and South America.
- In charge from concept development through implementation, carried out a successful "war" exercise which included personnel from El Salvador, Venezuela, and Ecuador.
- Worked closely with officers from other participating countries and prepared them to integrate smoothly into the multi-national staff by developing solid rapport with them.
- Used my diplomatic and language skills to effectively translate for foreign VIP visits.

SENIOR ADVISOR. The Middle East (1990-94). Handpicked for this sensitive assignment, actively developed lines of communication between U.S. and Middle East officials.

EDUCATION & TRAINING

Bachelor's degree in Criminal Justice, Loyola University, New Orleans, LA.
- Placed on the Dean's List for my academic accomplishments.

Completed extensive training programs including the graduate-level Combined Arms Staff Services School and additional courses such as:

Airborne, Special Forces Military Freefall, and Jumpmaster Schools

Special Forces Qualification Course

SERE — Survival, Evasion, Resistance, and Escape

Infantry Officer Basic and Advanced Courses

Date

Exact Name of Person
Title or Position
Name of Company
Address (number and street)
Address (city, state, and zip)

POLICEMAN   Dear Exact Name of Person (or Sir or Madam if answering a blind ad):

With the enclosed resume, I would like to make you aware of my background and experience related to law enforcement, and I would also like to express my strong desire to put my skills to use for the benefit of the Denver Police Department.

As you will see from my resume, after graduating from high school I served my country with distinction and was promoted ahead of my peers to E-4. I was aggressively recruited to remain in military service and assured of continued rapid advancement ahead of my peers, but I decided to leave military service after three years of excellent performance and embark on a career in law enforcement.

In my most recent position I was handpicked for a job as Unit Armorer, to take charge of a disorganized section which had failed to pass inspection in several key areas. I transformed the section into a model of efficiency and received a "Coin" in recognition of my achievements after a major inspection which gave the inspection outstanding ratings. I received six Achievement Medals, a Certificate of Achievement, and five "Coins" for exceptional contributions and accomplishments.

Highly proficient in operating, maintaining, and repairing weapons including pistols, rifles, machine guns, and grenade launchers, I was the Distinguished Graduate from Armor School after graduating as Distinguished Graduate from Advanced Individualized Training, where I learned to disassemble and reassemble weapons and identify deficiencies.

Single and able to relocate worldwide, I have specially selected the Denver Police Department as the place I would most like to work because of your reputation for excellence. I can provide excellent references at the appropriate time, and I hope you will contact me to suggest a time when we might meet in person. I feel confident that I could make valuable contributions to the Denver Police Department.

Yours sincerely,

Chris Burgos

CHRIS BURGOS

1110½ Hay Street, Fayetteville, NC 28305   •   preppub@aol.com   •   (910) 483-6611

OBJECTIVE
I want to contribute to the Denver Police Department through my strong desire to become a vital part of a top-notch law enforcement organization that can use a hard-working young professional with excellent firearms knowledge and experience as a military professional.

EDUCATION & TRAINING
Excelled in military training and completed school including the following:
- Armor School, **Distinguished Graduate**: Training in small arms and artillery repair.
- Advanced Individualized Training, **Distinguished Graduate,** 2000: Completed training related to disassembling and reassembling weapons; learned to identify deficiencies.
- Driver's Training, 2001: Learned professional driving skills and techniques.
- Airborne School, 2001: Became airborne qualified; subsequently performed 27 jumps.
- Basic Training, 2000; Learned valuable military skills.

Completed college-level course work in Psychology and English.
Graduated from East Juniata High School, Cocolamus, PA, 2000.

MEDALS & HONORS
Received six Army Achievement Medals, a Certificate of Achievement, and five Coins for distinguished performance.
Received Master Driver's Badge for driving thousands of accident-free miles.
Won the brigade Driving Competition in an annual skills competition.
Received Venezuelan Foreign Wings.

WEAPONS
Am highly proficient in operating, maintaining, and repairing weapons including these:

.9mm Beretta	M119 howitzer	M4 carbine
M16 rifle	M198 howitzer	M203 grenade launcher
M60 machine gun	M240B machine gun	M249 squad automatic
M2 .50 cal		Mark MK19 grenade launcher

EXPERIENCE
UNIT ARMORER. U.S. Army, Ft. Benning, GA (2000-present). Was handpicked for this position because of my reputation as an outstanding young leader with excellent organizational skills; took charge of a disorganized and inefficient section and transformed it into a model of efficiency, improving inspection scores in several key areas.
- Train and supervise one individual.
- Underwent a rigorous quarterly inspection and received a "Coin" award signifying my outstanding technical knowledge and management skills.
- Am accountable for thousands of dollars in equipment; assure perfect accountability while managing the issuing and distribution of weapons and Night Vision Devices to an 80-person company.
- Although aggressively recruited by re-enlistment personnel and assured of continued rapid advancement if I remained in military service, I decided to seek civilian employment.

SMALL ARMS & ARTILLERY REPAIR SPECIALIST. U.S. Army, Ft. Benning, GA (1998-00). Prior to graduating from Armor School, worked as a repair specialist as a member of a 9-person Small Arms and Artillery Repair Section supporting the needs of a 1,500-organization at the nation's largest military base.
- Due to my exceptional leadership ability, was entrusted with a leadership role normally held by an individual of higher rank; while still an E-2, was placed in charge of a squad of four people during the unscheduled absence of the E-6 supervisor.

PERSONAL
Hold a Secret security clearance. Enjoy hunting, fishing, skiing, watching NASCAR races.

Date

Career Trainee Division
P.O. Box 12002
Arlington, VA 22209-8727

Dear Sir or Madam:

I would appreciate an opportunity to talk with you soon about how I could contribute to your organization through my managerial talents and my specialized experience in special operations along with my expertise as an instructor.

As you will see from my resume, I have a strong background in these areas through my years of service as a Special Forces officer in the U.S. Army. I completed more than two years of specialized training which has led to qualification as an instructor and specialist in technical aspects of Army Special Operations including close quarter combat and counterterrorism.

I am especially effective in training, both on the individual level and for groups. I am highly skilled in turning personnel into cohesive teams known for their high level of readiness and professionalism.

Known as a dependable leader and manager, I also offer a reputation for being able to handle challenges and pressure through my decision-making skills and sound judgment.

I hope you will call or write me soon to suggest a time convenient for us to meet and discuss your current and future needs and how I might serve them. Thank you in advance for your time.

Sincerely yours,

Rockford N. Isley

ROCKFORD N. ISLEY

1110½ Hay Street, Fayetteville, NC 28305   •   preppub@aol.com   •   (910) 483-6611

OBJECTIVE

To offer my experience in security and personal protection to an organization that can benefit from my technical skills and my ability to manage both human and fiscal resources.

EXPERIENCE

POLICE OFFICER. City of Delta, VA (2000-present). Provide law enforcement and police services for this city with a population of over 100,000 and am entrusted by supervisors to work independently; organize and implement officer-initiated law enforcement and problem solving.
* Was one of eleven specially selected to attend the Delta Police Department Academy; scored in the top 10% on the VA Law Enforcement Certification Exam.

As a military officer in the U.S Army Special Forces, advanced to increasing responsibilities:
COUNTERTERRORISM PROJECT DIRECTOR. Okinawa (1995-00). Reporting directly to top-level military and civilian officials, planned and conducted special operations, foreign internal defense, and counterterrorism missions throughout Southeast Asia.
* Managed the training and performance of a combat-ready detachment which was responsible for classified and highly sensitive missions vital to international security.
* Was cited for my knowledge and organizational skills after creating and conducting a no-notice mission which was officially described as "splendidly planned and executed."
* Ensured constant preparedness of 33 personnel and $175,000 worth of equipment.

OPERATIONS MANAGER. Okinawa (1991-94). Promoted ahead of my peers to take over a totally disorganized and ineffective company, developed it into one recognized as the most highly organized and respected in the parent organization; led my team in planning, coordinating, and managing all activities related to the development of up-to-1500-person, indigenous, para-military organizations trained to preserve U.S. security interests.
* Was handpicked to assemble and lead a 15-person team which traveled to Bangladesh to train their military's high-ranking officers in disaster relief operations.

GENERAL MANAGER. Ft. Lewis, WA (1990-91). Directed a staff which provided administrative, logistical, training, and personnel support for personnel from a headquarters facility with 13 separate staff sections, consisting of 90 personnel.

TRAINING AND SUPPORT SERVICES MANAGER. Ft. Lewis, WA (1987-89). As second-in-command, oversaw personnel in a range of occupational specialities including aviation, logistics, maintenance, medical, and administrative fields.
* Received an achievement medal for my leadership while organizing and leading a pistol team which placed first in competition among all companies throughout Ft. Lewis.

EDUCATION & TRAINING

B.A., History, University of Washington, Seattle, WA, 1986.
Completed more than two years of intense training including the following:
    Infantry Officer Basic and Advanced courses
    Combined Arms and Services Staff School
    Special Forces Qualification Course/Special Operations Language Course (Thai)
    Ranger School, the military's "stress test" of mental and physical limits
    Survival, Evasion, Resistance, and Escape (SERE) Course/SERE instructor qualified
    Airborne and Jumpmaster courses
    Winter Operations Instructor Course and Jungle Warfare Course
    Advanced Reconnaissance, Target Analysis, and Exploitation Techniques Course
    Basic Law Enforcement Training

Exact Name of Person
Exact Title
Exact Name of Company
Address
City, State, Zip

**POLICE
SUPERVISOR-TRAINER**

Dear Exact Name of Person (or Dear Sir or Madam if answering a blind ad):

With the enclosed resume, I would like to make you aware of my skills and abilities in law enforcement and security with an emphasis on operations management and personnel supervision.

Handpicked for my present assignment as a Police School Instructor for the Justice Academy in the state of Connecticut, I am producing well-trained and knowledgeable law enforcement professionals. Earlier assignments as a Patrol Supervisor and Desk Sergeant allowed me opportunities to serve the community through my skills and abilities in law enforcement and security operations. I also briefly served the Hartford community as its Airport Security Supervisor.

In earlier experience as a U.S. Army professional, I gained a reputation as a skilled problem solver with a rare talent for motivating and guiding others to achieve success and consistently exceed the established standards. Because of my positive approach and willingness to give my time to counsel and lead others, I was frequently sought out by my superiors and peers for advice and to share my knowledge. I earned numerous honors as a top performer and as the best in my field and have earned five prestigious U.S. Army Commendation Medals and two Achievement Medals for my professionalism and accomplishments.

If you can use an experienced and mature leader who has long been recognized as a reliable and honest individual with uncompromising personal standards, I hope you will contact me soon to suggest a time when we might meet to discuss your needs. I can assure you in advance that I can provide outstanding references and could quickly become an asset to your organization.

Sincerely,

Allan Thomas

ALLAN THOMAS

1110½ Hay Street, Fayetteville, NC 28305　　•　　preppub@aol.com　　•　　(910) 483-6611

OBJECTIVE

To offer experience and knowledge in law enforcement and security operations to an organization that can benefit from my managerial and supervisory abilities as well as from my reputation as an honest, reliable, and enthusiastic professional.

EDUCATION & TRAINING

Received extensive military training which included a Law Enforcement Command Certification Course, Police Basic Course, and the Police Sergeant School as well as other programs for HIV/AIDS awareness instructors, rifle marksmanship, radio operations, and German and Italian language courses. Am certified breathalyzer operator.
Completed approximately 60 credit hours of general studies at the college level.

EXPERIENCE

POLICE SCHOOL INSTRUCTOR. State of Connecticut Justice Academy, Hartford, CT (2000-present). Consistently develop student groups recognized as "the best" while providing individual and group training and supervision for up to 80 students in nine-week class cycles.

AIRPORT SECURITY SUPERVISOR. Hartford Regional Airport, Hartford, CT (1999). Cited for setting new standards through direct involvement and motivational skills, supervised and trained 30 people who provided airport security services.
- Oversaw the maintenance and utilization of more than $2.3 million worth of equipment.
- Was officially described as possessing "an unusually high level of technical expertise in law enforcement duties" and as a calm and patient leader.

DESK SERGEANT. Hartford, CT (1996-98). Recognized for my "uncompromising integrity" and for an energetic and positive attitude that others wished to follow, received and handled complaints and requests for assistance from more than 10,000 military personnel and their family members.
- Maintained liaison with the community and personnel from the FBI and CIA.

Highlights of military experience, U.S. Army:
TRAINING PROGRAM MANAGER. Ft. Bragg, NC (1992-95). Handpicked ahead of my peers based on my reputation as "a consummate trainer," am known for my ability to produce well-qualified Military Police professionals by supervising, monitoring, and instructing 55 new personnel during 17-week training cycles.

RADIO TRANSMISSION OPERATOR. Ft. Stewart, GA (1990-92). Monitored 15 MP patrols by way of their radio transmissions while also retrieving calls and taking action as operator of the 911 emergency systems at a major military installation.
- Entered and retrieved information from the National Crime Information Center System and was credited with training personnel who earned certification in system operations.

SUPERVISORY MP. Ft. Stewart, GA (1989). Performed law enforcement duties; supervised a three-person team; controlled maintenance and use of $50,000 in equipment.
- Chosen from a pool of more than 40 qualified individuals as the representative at the 51st annual "MP Noncommissioned Officer of Excellence" competition, was cited as a key factor in the unit's recognition as the best MP company in the region.

PERSONAL

Received five respected U.S. Army Commendation Medals and two Achievement Medals in recognition of my accomplishments and "exceptional meritorious service."

Date

Exact Name of Person
Exact Title
Exact Name of Company
Address
City, State, Zip

PRISON GUARD   Dear Exact Name of Person (or Dear Sir or Madam if answering a blind ad):

With the enclosed resume, I would like to make you aware of my background as an experienced U.S. Marine Corps Security Guard who offers a reputation for being able to quickly adapt to any circumstances and meet challenges head on with professionalism and control. I am particularly interested in applying for the Prison Guard position which you recently advertised.

I entered the Marine Corps with a personal goal of becoming a team leader and achieving the rank of sergeant in four years and am extremely proud of the fact that I was promoted ahead of my peers and reached these goals in only three years. My current assignment at the American Embassy in Mexico ends soon, and although I am highly regarded and proud of being a Marine, I am ready to make a career change into the civilian work force.

With a Top Secret security clearance with SCI Access, my accomplishments as a Marine, and my international experience, I feel that I have a great deal to offer to the security or law enforcement communities. I have been involved in providing security for the President of the United States on two occasions and earned praise for my professionalism, knowledge, and leadership skills displayed in these critical assignments.

If you can use a talented and intelligent young professional who enjoys meeting challenges head on, I hope you will contact me to suggest a time when we might meet to discuss your needs. I can provide outstanding personal and professional references at the appropriate time and can assure you in advance that I could rapidly become an asset to your organization.

Sincerely,

Paul Johnson

PAUL JOHNSON

1110½ Hay Street, Fayetteville, NC 28305 • preppub@aol.com • (910) 483-6611

OBJECTIVE

To apply my knowledge and experience in the field of physical security and law enforcement to an organization that can benefit from my reputation as a skilled professional who can be counted on to remain in control and take charge while excelling under pressure.

EDUCATION & TRAINING

Have completed one year of college course work in pursuit of a bachelor's degree.
Excelled in extensive training which included the Marine Corps Security Guard School emphasizing the protection and storage of classified materials, a course in military operations in urban terrain, Combat Lifesaving, and professional leadership development.

SPECIAL SKILLS

Security clearance: Top Secret with SCI Access
Weapons: qualified and familiar with numerous weapons systems
Other: counterterrorism, physical security, and law enforcement in international settings

EXPERIENCE

Achieved leadership roles ahead of my peers in the U.S. Marine Corps:
ASSISTANT COMMANDER, MARINE SECURITY GUARD. **American Embassy, Mexico City, Mexico** (2001-present). Have received a meritorious promotion and numerous letters of commendation in recognition of my leadership and team-building abilities in this sensitive environment where my diplomacy and strong motivational skills are valued.

- Received the prestigious Meritorious Mast for my professionalism as a Security Guard during an official visit by President Bush; was cited for my enthusiasm and positive attitude during a period of frequent change and stress.
- Commanded a security detachment during a presidential visit to Armagh, Northern Ireland, and earned respect for my ability to mold six people from different units around the world into a cohesive and effective team.
- Received a letter of commendation from the Special Agent in Charge of the Presidential Protective Division for my team's actions in securing a hotel wing and keeping track of more than 800 security badges during the presidential visit.

ASSISTANT COMMANDER, MARINE SECURITY GUARD. **American Embassy, Kuwait** (2000-01). Became known as a young professional who quickly adapted and made contributions to the success of embassy security support; assisted in preparing work schedules, managing a residence facility, ensuring the protection of classified materials and personnel, providing entry and exit control, and preparing budgets.

- Implemented a system of keeping important information concerning exterior defense positions in one accessible binder which included photographs and descriptions of likely approaches and danger areas.
- Played a leadership role which allowed the embassy (rated the least desirable assignment among 122 embassies) to become **"Detachment of the Year" for Kuwait** despite the hardships of no potable water, poor sanitary conditions, limited communications, a high AIDS infection rate, and internal strife.
- Received a Letter of Appreciation from the Regional Security Officer noting that my arrival was during a period of civil war when the embassy compound was full of refugees and in turmoil; was described as being the first to volunteer for any assignment and cited for my initiative in always finding a way to get things done.

RIFLEMAN and **TEAM LEADER**. Fort Sill, OK (1996-00). Gained a strong base of exposure to working with people from diverse backgrounds and experience levels while sharpening my leadership skills as a supervisor of infantry personnel.

Date

Exact Name of Person
Exact Title
Exact Name of Company
Address
City, State, Zip

PROBATION & PAROLE
OFFICER

Dear Exact Name of Person (or Dear Sir or Madam if answering a blind ad):

With the enclosed resume, I wish to make you aware of my interest in seeking employment with your organization. I am interested in applying for the position of Corrections Officer which you recently advertised.

In my current position as a Probation and Parole Officer, I supervise a caseload of probationers and parolees who are not eligible for regular probation and parole but who are in their unique situation because of prison overcrowding. In a prior position I taught a course in Probation and Parole at Savannah Community College. I have also served as a Sheriff's Deputy in Savannah County, where I worked in the detention facility supervising inmates. I have earned a B.S. in Criminal Justice.

I offer an intense dedication to my field, and I am confident that I could excel as a Corrections Officer in the federal system. I would appreciate your advising me about the next step I should take in pursing my goal of becoming a federal Corrections Officer.

Sincerely,

Dwight Barry Corning

DWIGHT BARRY CORNING

1110½ Hay Street, Fayetteville, NC 28305   •   preppub@aol.com   •   (910) 483-6611

OBJECTIVE

To contribute to an organization that can use an exceptional administrator and program manager who offers proven decision-making and problem-solving skills along with a reputation as a resourceful, well-organized professional with excellent communication skills.

EDUCATION

Bachelor of Science degree in Criminal Justice, Shippensburg University, Shippensburg, PA, 1992.

EXPERIENCE

PROBATION AND PAROLE OFFICER. Savannah Department of Corrections, Division of Adult Probation and Parole, Savannah, GA (2000-present). Carry a badge and weapon as a Surveillance Officer supervising up to 25 probationers and parolees who are not eligible for regular probation and parole, but who are under intense supervision because of prison overcrowding.
- See each probationer or parolee at least three times a week.
- Make nightly curfew checks.
- Investigate any suspicious activity involving a probationer or parolee.
- Monitor their employment, supervise weekly drug testing, and make criminal record checks.
- Write regular reports and make arrests as needed.

INSTRUCTOR. Savannah Community College, Savannah, GA (1998-00). Taught a course in probation and parole during the winter quarter.

SHERIFF'S DEPUTY. Savannah County, Savannah, GA (1992-98). Worked in the detention facility supervising inmates incarcerated there as well as transporting inmates, writing reports, and performing all other required duties.

FULL-TIME COLLEGE STUDENT. Shippensburg University, Shippensburg, PA (1988-92).

CORRECTIONAL OFFICER. Missouri Department of Corrections (summers 1988 and 1989).
Central Missouri Correctional Center, Jefferson City, MO, June-August 1988
St. Mary's Honor Center, St. Louis, MO, June-August 1989
- Was a full-time uniformed Correctional Officer supervising inmates, writing reports, transporting inmates, and conducting all other required duties; was qualified to carry a weapon.

VOLUNTEER CORRECTIONS OFFICER. Missouri Eastern Correctional Center, Pacific, MO (1986-87). Completed a two-week course at the institution and performed duties as a Correctional Officer in a pilot volunteer program.

PERSONAL

Have consistently been known as a "hands-on" professional who could be counted on to efficiently handle any situation or task. Handle pressure extremely well. Have a keen eye for detail and the ability to "read" people.

CAREER CHANGE

Date

Mr. Rick Smith
Camp Director
Eckerd Youth Alternatives, Inc.
Camp Miracles Happen

**PROBATION OFFICER
WHO HAS
TRANSITIONED TO
FAMILY WORKER**

Dear Rick:

With the enclosed resume, I would like to formally make you aware of my interest in the position as Social Services Coordinator with Eckerd Youth Alternatives, Inc., at Camp Miracles Happen.

As you already know, I have proudly played a key role in the successful establishment and implementation of the facility as a Family Worker. While providing a positive role model to the youth we serve, I have always gone out of my way to encourage and assist my peers, and I have consistently and cheerfully shouldered the heaviest and most complex case load. When I joined the Eckerd organization in 2002, I excelled in handling extensive public relations responsibilities, and my efforts played a key role in generating the referrals we needed in order to make the program a success.

It is now my desire to serve the Eckerd program as Social Services Coordinator, and I offer strong communication, mediation, consensus-building, and problem-solving skills which would be useful in such a supervisory role. I am respected by my peers for my ability to develop innovative and effective treatment plans, and other Family Workers routinely seek my guidance in a variety of areas. Because of my previous 10 years as an Adult Probation Officer, I am very knowledgeable of the resources available within the law enforcement and social services community, and I have established an extensive network of contacts within the public and private sector.

I am well known for my desire to take initiative and provide leadership when new concepts and new programs need a disciplined and resourceful professional. For example, when I was an Adult Probation Officer, I was honored by being selected as one of the state's first three House Arrest Officers, and I played a key role in pioneering the house arrest concept in Wyoming which was subsequently adopted statewide. Similarly as a Family Worker, I used my initiative to start up a parents' group, and I now teach a monthly class attended by 12 or more parents. My public speaking and communication skills have been refined through my teaching responsibilities as well as through my involvement in graduation and other activities.

My commitment to the Eckerd program is proven, and I am confident I could further enhance the program in Elizabethtown by assuming a supervisory role. I am confident that my strong skills in mediation, arbitration, consensus-building, and problem solving would be valuable assets in such a supervisory capacity.

Sincerely,

Robert Raynor

ROBERT RAYNOR

1110½ Hay Street, Fayetteville, NC 28305 • preppub@aol.com • (910) 483-6611

OBJECTIVE
I want to contribute to an organization that can use an experienced problem solver and decision maker who offers strong communication and organizational skills along with a proven ability to motivate, persuade, and inspire others.

EDUCATION
Bachelor of Arts (B.A.) degree in Human Services, Elon College, Burlington, WY, 1990.
• Extensive coursework in Business Administration, Accounting, Economics, and Psychology. Extensive professional training related to arbitration, mediation, and problem solving; also completed extensive training in first aid and emergency procedures.

EXPERIENCE
FAMILY WORKER. Eckerd Youth Alternatives, Inc., Elizabethtown, WY (2002-present). Played a key role in the start-up of a new facility which provides a wilderness therapeutic environment with fully accredited school services for 60 youth aged 10-16 in grades 5-12; the Eckerd retail drug family started this organization over 30 years ago, and now the organization provides services in five states, mostly through state contracts.
• Performed extensive public relations in an effort to help establish this new facility; my activities helped to generate needed referrals as I "sold" the facility and the concept of the program to principals, guidance counselors, the social services community, and others.
• Served on the budget committee and assisted in fundraising efforts.
• Have been a member of school accrediting committees and quality assurance committees; have conducted inspections of other camp operations.
• Work as part of a professional team comprised of three Family Workers and a supervisor; consistently manage the largest and most difficult caseload.
• Perform extensive interviewing and assessment while interviewing families and youth for potential placement in this out-of-home environment for youth at risk.
• Provide a positive role model for youth while also teaching a group class for parents attended by 12 people monthly; lead discussions on topics designed to facilitate good decision making and refine parents' ability to communicate with their children.
• Assist youth in learning coping skills and techniques related to anger management.
• Handle a case load of 20 youth, and prepare extensive written reports and correspondence.
• Have become known as an effective public speaker while participating in activities including graduations and teaching activities.
• Have established a track record as an effective mediator through my ability to resourcefully build consensus and mediate/arbitrate controversial situations.

ADULT PROBATION OFFICER. N.C. Department of Corrections, Cheyenne, WY (1990-02). Supervised a caseload of 147 probationers with 75% of them being felons.
• Communicated extensively with hundreds of social services agencies and law enforcement professionals in the course of doing my job.
• As an entry-level Probation Officer, handled a heavy volume of collections as I handled collection of restitution and court costs.
• In 1994, was honored by being selected as one the state's first three House Arrest Officers; pioneered the concept of house arrest and played a key role in the successful implementation of this new program. The program was subsequently adopted for use statewide and all probation officers simultaneously became House Arrest Officers.
• Learned how to interact effectively with judges, attorneys, and other agencies and professionally carried out the duties of an officer of the court.

PERSONAL
Motivated individual with outstanding skills in influencing and motivating others.

Date

Exact Name of Person
Exact Title
Exact Name of Company
Address
City, State, Zip

PROPERTY CRIMES DETECTIVE

Dear Exact Name of Person (or Dear Sir or Madam if answering a blind ad):

With the enclosed resume, I would like to express my interest in exploring employment opportunities with your organization.

As you will see from my resume, I offer strong analytical, investigative, and problem-solving skills which have been refined in a distinguished track of performance with the Richmond County Sheriff's Department. In my current position as a Detective in the Property Crimes Division, I investigate a wide range of crimes on residential and commercial property. I have become respected for my common sense as well as my highly effective style of interviewing suspects, victims, and witnesses.

In a previous assignment with the Sheriff's Department as a School Resource Officer in Richmond County, I had an opportunity to work with youth in the #1 county in the state for juvenile crime. The two years I spent working in the school system helped me acquire great insight into the juvenile population and into human behavior in general as I performed simultaneously as a law enforcement officer, counselor, and educator. While working with the schools, I gained extensive public speaking experience, and I am comfortable working with people one-on-one or in groups of all sizes.

You will see from my resume that I hold a Bachelor of Science as well as an A.A.S. in Criminal Justice, and I also hold numerous law enforcement certificates.

Although I am held in high regard within the Sheriff's Department and can provide outstanding references at the appropriate time, I have decided to make a career change into the private sector. I am confident that my strong investigative background would be a valuable asset to a company such as yours.

If you can use an experienced investigator and problem solver known for unquestioned integrity and a disciplined work ethic, I hope you will contact me to suggest a time when we might meet to discuss your needs and how I might serve them. Thank you in advance for your time.

Sincerely,

Evan W. Andrews

EVAN W. ANDREWS

1110½ Hay Street, Fayetteville, NC 28305 • preppub@aol.com • (910) 483-6611

OBJECTIVE   To contribute to an organization that can use a highly trained investigative professional who offers experience as a detective along with strong analytical and problem-solving skills.

EDUCATION   **Bachelor of Science degree in Criminal Justice,** Richmond College, Richmond, VA, 2000.
Associate of Applied Science degree in Criminal Justice, Richmond Technical Community College, Richmond, VA, 1995.
Complete extensive training sponsored by the Virginia Justice Academy, the Richmond County Sheriff's Office, and federal law enforcement agencies related to these and many other areas:

Firearms/Weapons	OSHA Training	Missing and Abducted Children
Tactical Restraints	K-9 Defense	Search Warrants
Youth Protection	Community Policing	Street Gangs
Infectious Control	Drug Investigations	Case Management
Interviewing Skills	Search and Seizure	Case Law
False Documents	Death Investigations	Crime Scene Preservation

Advanced Interviewing and Interrogation Techniques

CERTIFICATIONS   Advanced Law Enforcement Certificate in progress; Intermediate Law Enforcement Certificate; Basic Law Enforcement Certificate; Law Enforcement Certificate. Certified as a Star Instructor. Enrolled in the Criminal Investigator's Certificate Program.

EXPERIENCE   **Have advanced in the following track record of promotion with the Richmond County Sheriff's Department, Richmond, VA (1991-present):**
1998-present: PROPERTY CRIMES DETECTIVE. Investigate property crimes to residential and commercial property in Cumberland County; make arrests as appropriate and prepare felony files on the crimes. Turn cases over to the District Attorney for prosecution.
- Played a role in implementing the Juvenile Protective Ordinance in the #1 county in the state for juvenile crime. Trained as a member of the Hostage Negotiation Team.
- Work in close cooperation with 10 other detectives as well as with outside agencies including the FBI, DEA, AFT, and state regulatory officials.

1995-98: JUVENILE DETECTIVE & DEPUTY SHERIFF. Entered the Detective Division as a Juvenile Detective for the first three years, and came into contact with many of the students I knew as a School Resource Officer; investigated many "crimes of impulse" such as shoplifting and fighting. Worked with the Gang Unit in preventing gang activities.

1993-95: SCHOOL RESOURCE OFFICER. Was promoted to work with middle schools and was a resource to schools; helped implement the Students Against Violence Everywhere (S.A.V.E.) Program.
- Performed this job according to training I had received in the Triad Concept, which balances the roles of law enforcement officer, educator, and counselor.
- Performed extensive public speaking, and developed all aspects of formal presentations; met with community watch groups and other citizen organizations.

1991-93: ROAD PATROL OFFICER.

PERSONAL   Member of VA Juvenile Officers Association and National School Resource Officers Association. Have never had a reprimand or disciplinary action. Excellent references.

Date

Exact Name of Person
Exact Title
Exact Name of Company
Address
City, State, Zip

SECURITY ADMINISTRATOR & DIRECTOR OF COUNTERTERRORISM OPERATIONS

Dear Exact Name of Person (or Dear Sir or Madam if answering a blind ad):

With the enclosed resume, I would like to express my interest in exploring employment opportunities with your organization.

As you will see from my resume, I offer a distinguished record of accomplishments built while managing physical, information and industrial security operations. While advancing ahead of my peers in the Department of Defense, I have consistently earned recognition as a subject matter expert who can be counted on to achieve excellent results while exceeding expected standards. Presently completing an assignment as the Director of Personnel Security Support Operations for three organizations in Kuwait, I was described as "the only candidate" for this newly created position to act as the senior advisor and consultant on antiterrorism and force protection issues. In this capacity, I manage a $2.9 million annual operating budget while developing programs which reduce vulnerability to terrorist attacks on the 1,500-person task force. Based on my reputation, I was requested by name as an advisor to the Kuwaiti Ministry of Defense to carry out vulnerability assessments of their protection measures for Top Secret information.

Prior to my selection for this high-visibility job, I held several positions at The Pentagon where I developed security programs, oversaw security support operations, and inspected internal security programs in order to advise and guide efforts to correct deficiencies. I have been singled out for recognition with the prestigious Meritorious Service Medal, six Commendation Medals, and one Achievement Medal for accomplishments which included ensuring the security of human, material, and fiscal assets in international settings.

If you can use an articulate and forceful manager who excels in developing innovative solutions while responding decisively in environments where there is no "margin for error," I hope you will contact me soon to suggest a time we might meet to discuss how I could contribute to your organization. I can provide excellent professional and personal references at the appropriate time. Thank you for your time and consideration.

Sincerely,

Ronald T. Pound

RONALD T. POUND

1110½ Hay Street, Fayetteville, NC 28305 • preppub@aol.com • (910) 483-6611

OBJECTIVE
To offer a distinguished background in the management of physical, information, and industrial security to an organization that can use a seasoned security administration professional with a reputation for innovatively achieving results and exceeding standards.

EDUCATION & TRAINING
Associate degree, **Security Administration,** The Community College of the Army. Completed numerous advanced leadership and technical programs including Hostage/Crisis Negotiations and Dynamics of International Terrorism as well as programs emphasizing records management, instructional systems, and interpretation of training codes.

CLEARANCE
Hold a **Top Secret** security clearance.

EXPERIENCE
Have received numerous awards and honors while advancing in the Department of Defense:
DIRECTOR OF PERSONNEL SECURITY & COUNTERTERRORISM OPERATIONS. Kuwait (2000-present). Handpicked and described as "the only candidate" for this newly created job, served as the senior advisor and consultant on antiterrorism force protection issues in support of 1,500 personnel in three organizations; managed a $2.9 million budget.
- Developed and monitored all aspects of physical and operational security in order to deter terrorist and criminal acts against aircraft, weapons systems, and personnel.
- Cited as a "technical genius," developed innovative measures and equipment which reduced man-hours and saved hundreds of thousands of dollars to include researching, securing funding, procuring, and installing a $150,000 thermal imaging system.
- Developed guidelines for toxic waste handling and water/food poisoning detection; solved a case involving possible terrorist poisoning of a water supply.
- Detected six attempts by Third World nationals to gather intelligence for hostile forces and then developed the briefings for presentation to the highest government levels.
- Requested by name by the Kuwaiti Ministry of Defense to carry out vulnerability assessments of their National Security Agency, achieved results which increased their protection measures for Top Secret information.
- Reduced security vulnerability 73% in under seven months for the best record in the Army. Was awarded the prestigious Meritorious Service Medal for accomplishments which included developing a Security Escort Program accepted as the model in Asia.

MANAGER OF FORCE PROTECTION OPERATIONS. The Pentagon, Washington, DC (1997-99). Officially described as a "phenomenal" senior manager and expert in personnel security issues, directed operations in a 24-hour computer and intrusion detection center providing security for more than 6,300 people and vital assets/equipment.
- Implemented new standard operating procedures for the control center which reduced delays 100% and ensured immediate notification of 500 crisis response team members.
- Developed and managed a project to provide protection for 17,000 people, 380 aircraft, and 23,474 pounds of vehicles, mail, and supplies during a major operation in Kuwait.

Highlights of other experience: Directed utilization of the Starwatch Intrusion Detection Alarm System used to protect highly classified defense information and personnel in 65 Secure Compartmented facilities. As a Sensors System Supervisor, developed guidance and provided advice on sensor alarm operations while ensuring security for restricted areas and COMSEC (communications security) coded materials.

PERSONAL
Have been honored with six Commendation Medals, one Achievement Medal, and the Meritorious Service Medal. Can provide outstanding references on request.

SECURITY OFFICER   Dear Sir or Madam:

With the enclosed resume, I would like to make you aware of my background as a skilled professional with experience in various high-security environments, and of the excellent supervisory, planning, and organizational skills which I could put to work for your company.

As you will see from my resume, I have excelled in various positions as a Security Officer, controlling access to high-security compounds through such means as checking photo security badges and access logs, as well as providing visual surveillance to personnel and vehicles entering these facilities. I have been entrusted with additional responsibilities as Assistant Shift Leader on weekends, and I have built a reputation as a reliable and conscientious security professional whose integrity is beyond reproach.

Throughout my successful career in the U.S. Army, I excelled in numerous supervisory roles, advising and assisting higher-ranking personnel from Platoon Leaders and Company Commanders to the Deputy Post Commander of a military installation. While supervising as many as 20 personnel in various demanding environments, I honed the discipline and leadership skills that have led to my success in the security field.

I am highly regarded by my employer, and I can provide excellent personal and professional references at the appropriate time.

Sincerely,

Linda Howell

LINDA HOWELL

1110½ Hay Street, Fayetteville, NC 28305 • preppub@aol.com • (910) 483-6611

OBJECTIVE	To benefit an organization that can use an experienced security professional with strong supervisory, planning, and organizational skills who offers a background of excellence in security operations.
EDUCATION	Completed nearly two years of college studying Business Administration, Wurton Technical Community College, Wurton, OK. Completed extensive military training in both technical skills and leadership development, to include courses in staff development and training, small unit leadership, and management.
CLEARANCE	Hold a Top Secret security clearance.
SKILLS	Qualified as an expert in a wide range of firearms, including handguns, shotguns, semi-automatic and automatic rifles, and others.
EXPERIENCE	**SECURITY OFFICER.** Triple P. Services, Inc., Mount Olive, OK (2000-present). Control the front gate of a high-security compound, checking photo security badges and access logs to ensure that only authorized personnel are allowed to enter. • Assume additional responsibility as Assistant Shift Leader on Saturday and Sunday. • Maintain the guard report for the shift, noting any incidents; brief the shift leader coming on duty prior to leaving the premises at shift change. • Inspect the guard vehicle and equipment to ensure that they are in proper condition. **SECURITY OFFICER.** United International Investigative Services, Anaheim, CA (1993-1999). Ensured that front gate access to a high-security compound was restricted to authorized personnel only; checked photo security badges and access logs as well as providing visual surveillance of vehicles and personnel entering the facility. **SECURITY OFFICER.** Crawford Technical Services, Inc., Austin, TX (1990-1992). Provided front gate security and surveillance, controlling access to a high-security compound; checked photo security badges and the access log to ensure that no unauthorized personnel were granted access to the premises. **FULL-TIME COLLEGE STUDENT.** Wurton Technical Community College, Wurton, OK (1986-90). After leaving military service, enrolled full-time in college and studied Business Administration. *Highlights of earlier military experience, U.S. Army:* **SUPERVISOR** and **ADVISOR.** Served as the principal advisor to the Deputy Post Commander with regards to matters concerning enlisted personnel and their families; also assisted the Provost Marshal on matters related to enlisted personnel living in government housing, and worked with the Director of Engineering and Housing and all Command Sergeants Major to ensure maintenance of the post according to all regulations. **PERSONNEL ADMINISTRATIVE SUPERVISOR.** Assisted the Company Commander in planning the training of all units, to include authoring the training schedule and coordinating the use of firing ranges and other training areas throughout the installation.
PERSONAL	Excellent personal and professional references on request.

Exact Name of Person
Title or Position
Name of Company
Address (no., street)
Address (city, state, zip)

SECURITY OPERATIONS SUPERVISOR

Dear Exact Name of Person (or Dear Sir or Madam if answering a blind ad.)

I would appreciate an opportunity to talk with you soon about how I could contribute to your organization through the managerial and supervisory skills I refined while excelling in positions usually held by more experienced professionals.

While serving my country with the Department of Defense, I earned numerous medals for my dedication, supervisory abilities, and high performance standards. I have a proven ability to train and motivate others through my "leadership by example."

In one earlier job I was in charge of security patrols at the United States Military Academy at West Point, NY, where I regularly trained and supervised nine specialists. During special events and ceremonies I oversaw as many as 20 personnel providing traffic control.

I feel certain that you would find me to be an articulate and dedicated individual who can adapt to pressure and rapidly changing circumstances with maturity and professionalism.

I hope you will welcome my call soon to arrange a brief meeting at your convenience to discuss your current and future needs and how I might serve them. Thank you in advance for your time.

Sincerely yours,

Cherry T. Pigh

Alternate last paragraph:
I hope you will call or write soon to suggest a time convenient for us to meet and discuss your current and future needs and how I might serve them. Thank you in advance for your time.

CHERRY T. PIGH

1110½ Hay Street, Fayetteville, NC 28305 • preppub@aol.com • (910) 483-6611

OBJECTIVE

To contribute through my supervisory and managerial abilities to an organization that can use an aggressive and hard-working young professional with specialized expertise in law enforcement operations ranging from administration, to training, to industrial security.

EXPERIENCE

DEPUTY SHERIFF. Pisgah County, Pisgah, CA (2001-present). Perform routine patrol duties including serving civil process, enforcing motor vehicle laws, responding to all calls from the county dispatcher, completing field notes and arrest forms, as well as processing/arresting offenders.
- Investigate misdemeanor crimes and testify in court.

SUPERVISORY LAW ENFORCEMENT SPECIALIST. Department of Defense, Turkey (1998-2000). As a police supervisor and desk sergeant, trained and oversaw the activities of five employees involved in controlling access to operational headquarters facilities in an area vital to national security.
- Applied my technical knowledge to develop, implement, and train personnel in new emergency response procedures to be used in the event of terrorist intrusion.

SECURITY OPERATIONS SUPERVISOR. U.S. Army, The United States Military Academy, West Point, NY (1992-97). Supervised nine employees on four teams which ensured security and safety of personnel and facilities throughout the academy complex.
- Was in charge of as many as 20 employees providing traffic control during special events and ceremonies.
- Excelled in producing well-trained and qualified specialists.
- Earned a Meritorious Service Medal for my performance as a supervisor and leader.

SENIOR TEAM LEADER. Department of Defense, Dallas, TX (1989-91). Polished my motivational abilities and became the leader of a covert three-person team of law enforcement personnel.
- Gained experience in administrative functions as a desk sergeant.
- Selected for special training in nuclear/biological/chemical (NBC) defense, was the honor graduate for the course.

POLICE OFFICER. Department of Defense, Dallas International Airport, Dallas, TX (1985-89). Earned a reputation as a highly knowledgeable and well-trained professional and was given responsibilities usually reserved for more experienced and higher-ranking personnel.
- Became skilled in a variety of related work areas including investigating traffic accidents, handling administrative paperwork and details, patrolling, acting as desk sergeant.

EDUCATION & HONORS

Basic Law Enforcement Training Academy, GPA: 4.0.
Associate Degree in General Education, Dallas Community College, Dallas, TX, 1989.
- Graduated with "Highest Honors" GPA: 4.0

CLEARANCE & WEAPONS

Hold a **Top Secret** security clearance, effective until May 1997.
Offer weapons expertise including qualifying with the M-16 rifle, .38 cal. revolver and .45 cal. pistol, .357 cal. pistol, 9mm, and the 12-gauge shotgun.

PERSONAL

Offer the ability to interact with others and pass my enthusiasm and dedication to them. Am an aggressive and dedicated professional with well-developed managerial abilities.

Date

SECURITY POLICEMAN   Dear Mr. Smith:

With the enclosed resume, I would like to make you aware of my interest in exploring employment opportunities in the security field.

As you will see from my resume, I have served my country with distinction in the U.S. Air Force. With a Top Secret security clearance, I have been selected for special assignments in direct support of the President of the United States. In my previous position at Andrews Air Force Base, I performed top-notch protective security for the President, Vice President, and other diplomatic and distinguished visitors.

On numerous occasions, I have been commended for my resourcefulness, initiative, and technical expertise. Formal performance evaluations have praised my "tireless dedication and attention to detail." In one incident, I was cited for utilizing a by-the-book approach that prevented a border violation. In another situation, I was commended for quickly coordinating medical, fire, and police units to the scene of an accident. An Air Force Audit Agency and AMC Staff Assistance Team praised my attention to detail when they found zero discrepancies during an audit of thousands of badges in a restricted area.

In my job as a Security Policeman at Andrews Air Force Base, I have provided security services for three Air Force wings, the Air National Guard Headquarters, a Naval Air Facility, and 250,000 customers annually. I have operated databases of personnel who approve entry onto military bases, supervised vehicle registration, provided surveillance of alarmed facilities, conducted anti-hijack inspections, and worked as an Installation Entry Controller. On my own initiative, I once created a new, comprehensive tracking program for weapons and illegal, confiscated property. I also developed a new, detailed quick reference book for the Customs Element which enabled the section to reduce the time to research key information.

If my background and skills interest you, I hope you will contact me to suggest a time when we could meet in person to discuss your needs. I can provide excellent references. Thank you in advance for your time.

Yours sincerely,

Shelly Raines

SHELLY RAINES

1110½ Hay Street, Fayetteville, NC 28305   •   preppub@aol.com   •   (910) 483-6611

OBJECTIVE

To benefit an organization that can use an accomplished security and law enforcement professional who offers strong investigative, problem-solving, and customer skills.

CLEARANCE

Top Secret security clearance

EDUCATION

College: Completed 1½ years (43 credits) of college coursework toward Associate's degree, University of Maryland.

Security and Military Training: Extensive Air Force training included:

Airman Leadership School   Ground Combat Skills Course
Criminal Justice Information System   National Crime Center Course
Hazardous Materials Training Course.   Radar Certification Course

EXPERIENCE

SECURITY POLICEMAN. U.S. Air Force, Andrews AFB, MD (2002-present). Was selected for special assignment in direct support of the President of the United States; handled the responsibility for issuance and control of various identification media required for installation entry and circulation control.

- Provided security services supporting three Air Force wings, the Air National Guard Headquarters, a Naval Air Facility, and 250,000 customers annually.
- Operated a database of more than 7,300 personnel who approved the entry of more than 125,000 visitors onto the installation annually.
- Supervised registration and distribution of decals for 9,000 vehicles annually and supported 23 separate agencies; provided oversight for the issuance and control of more than 3,400 installation restricted area badges.
- Issued identification media for mobility personnel; was responsible for securing more than $1 billion in Presidential and Special Air Mission aircraft including Air Force One.

Accomplishments:

- On a formal performance evaluation, was commended as an "excellent worker" and praised for providing "100% customer satisfaction; flawlessly processed over 250,000 customers onto Andrews."
- Was praised by the Air Force Audit Agency and AMC Staff Assistance Team for "zero discrepancies during audit of restricted area badges program—accounted for 3,400 badges."

SECURITY POLICEMAN & INSTALLATION ENTRY CONTROLLER. U.S.A.F., Andrews AFB, MD (1998-02). Was specially selected for this position supporting the President, Vice President, and various foreign and domestic distinguished visitors; provided law enforcement response and security for more than 26,000 military and civilian personnel who reside and are employed on the installation.

- Provided surveillance of 65 alarmed facilities, including 19 major weapons and vaults.
- Apprehended violators of military, local, state, and federal laws.
- Performed top-notch protective security for the President, Vice President, and other diplomatic and distinguished visitors who transit Andrews AFB.

Accomplishments:

- On a formal evaluation, was recognized for outstanding initiative and problem-solving skills; was commended for quickly coordinating medical, fire, and police units during an accident, for taking actions which confiscated over 30 expired ID cards, and for confiscating ammunition found in a vehicle trying to gain access to a Base Entry Point Check.
- Earned written praise for "articulate communication and writing skills."

Date

Exact Name of Person
Title or Position
Name of Company
Address (number and street)
Address (city, state, and ZIP)

SECURITY SPECIALIST

Dear Exact Name of Person (or Dear Sir or Madam if answering a blind ad):

I would appreciate an opportunity to talk with you soon about how I could contribute to your organization through my experience in law enforcement and security gained while serving my country in the U.S. Marine Corps.

As you will see from my resume, I am a Team Leader in a Fleet Antiterrorist Security Team company based in Norfolk, VA. After being selected early in my career for leadership roles, I first led a four-person team and then was selected to manage a team of 15 specialists within a 50-person organization.

Through training and experience, I have become skilled in weapons use and qualified as an urban scout sniper and primary marksmanship instructor. Having been entrusted with a Secret security clearance, I am skilled in high-risk personal protection, counterterrorism, surveillance, reconnaissance, and basic security guard activities.

During a five-month period providing perimeter and mobile security for the U.S. Liaison Office in Mogadishu, Somalia, I earned several medals for my accomplishments. I am certain that I possess the knowledge of and experience in security and law enforcement activities to allow me to make a difference through my exceptional training and motivational skills.

I hope you will welcome my call soon to arrange a brief meeting at your convenience to discuss your current and future needs and how I might serve them. Thank you in advance for your time.

Sincerely yours,

Glen R. Oliver

Alternate last paragraph:
I hope you will call or write me soon to suggest a time convenient for us to meet and discuss your current and future needs and how I might serve them. Thank you in advance for your time.

GLEN R. OLIVER

1110½ Hay Street, Fayetteville, NC 28305   •   preppub@aol.com   •   (910) 483-6611

OBJECTIVE   To offer my experience in providing security for human and material resources to an organization that can use a highly disciplined and motivated leader who offers excellent weapons skills along with knowledge of law enforcement and industrial security.

EXPERTISE
- Through training and experience, have become skilled in high-risk personal protection, counterterrorism, surveillance, reconnaissance, and basic security guard activities.
- Offer expertise related to weapons use including special qualifications as an urban scout sniper (designated marksman), primary marksmanship instructor, and 0311-rifleman along with being qualified to use the PR-24 police baton.
- Am licensed by the military as a driver of 1 1/4-ton trucks, 36-passenger buses, 1-ton trucks, and explosive ordnance trucks.

CLEARANCE   Have been entrusted with a Secret security clearance.

EXPERIENCE   *Became known as a skilled team leader, instructor, and weapons specialist while earning promotion as a member of a "Fleet Antiterrorist Security Team (FAST)" company with the U.S. Marine Corps, Norfolk, VA:*
TEAM LEADER. (2002-present). Was promoted ahead of my peers to lead a 15-person team of specialists who were one element of a 50-person organization.
- Learned how to lead and motivate others to achieve team goals and accomplish difficult assignments.
- Excelled in passing on my knowledge to others and in providing guidance which guaranteed that the job was always done — and done right.

SECURITY SPECIALIST. (1995-01). Singled out as leader of a 5-person team, was selected to receive advanced training while refining my practical skills in worldwide assignments as part of a 50-person organization.
- Earned several medals and ribbons in recognition of my professionalism while serving in Bosnia.
- Earned the Combat Action Ribbon, Armed Forces Expeditionary Medal, and Sea Service Medal for my accomplishments.
- Provided perimeter and mobile security for the U.S. Liaison Office which included two ambassadors and several senators among other VIPs.
- Was singled out to receive a Letter of Commendation while providing security for special weapons at the Naval Weapons Station in Yorktown, VA, and was also selected to provide security for a special weapons movement at the Naval Shipyards.

TRAINING   Completed extensive advanced Marine Corps training including:
security force battalion rifle and pistol team — eight weeks — 2000
designated marksman skills — four weeks — 1999
marksmanship instructor training — eight weeks — 1998
basic security guard school — four weeks — 1998
the USMC infantry school with an emphasis on weapons training — eight weeks— 1997
basic infantry skills — four weeks — 1996
Marine Corps "boot camp" basic training — 13 weeks — 1995

PERSONAL   Enjoy challenge and can handle the pressures of emergency situations and high-stress environments. Enjoy taking a job through to completion and seeing the results of what I have done.

CAREER CHANGE

Date

Wanda Smith
Human Resource Department
BB & T Bank
P.O. 1847
Wilson, NC 27893

SECURITY SUPERVISOR

This individual hopes to return to a career in banking after working in the security field for a while.

Dear Mrs. Smith:

I would appreciate an opportunity to talk with you soon about my strong interest in becoming a Branch Manager at BB & T Bank. I feel strongly that I could contribute to your organization through my education, computer knowledge, and background of success in roles requiring outstanding verbal and interpersonal communication skills as well as my experience working for First Citizens Bank & Trust Co., where I became knowledgeable of systems used in the banking industry, namely the Integrated Deposit and Customer Information Systems.

As you will see from my resume, I attend North Carolina State University, Raleigh, NC, and will receive a B.S. degree in Business Administration (with a concentration in Management) in December. I have also studied Accounting and Computer Information Systems and have been active in campus organizations for those areas of interest.

I offer a reputation as a very hard worker who can handle the challenge of managing my time effectively while simultaneously attending college, working, and involving myself in community activities. I am very proficient with computers and have some programming experience.

I hope you will welcome my call soon to arrange a brief meeting at your convenience to discuss your current and future needs and how I might serve them. Thank you in advance for your time.

Sincerely yours,

Edward R. Mince

EDWARD R. MINCE

1110½ Hay Street, Fayetteville, NC 28305 • preppub@aol.com • (910) 483-6611

OBJECTIVE

To apply my business administration and accounting education as well as my in-depth computer knowledge to an organization in need of a mature young professional with excellent communication skills in addition to a background of community involvement.

EDUCATION

Am pursuing a B.S. in Business Administration with a concentration in Management, North Carolina State University, Raleigh, NC; degree expected in December 2004.
- Hold membership in the Accounting Society Today Club which involved participating in projects with local business and accounting firms.

Studied Accounting with a minor in Computer Information Systems, North Carolina Central University, Raleigh, NC.
- Was elected co-chairman of the Computer Information Systems Club executive board; arranged for area business people to speak and attended regular board meetings.
- Refined listening and communicating skills in a work-study program at the University's Learning Resources Center: answered phones and set up video equipment.

EXPERIENCE

While attending college full time, gained experience in jobs including the following:
SECURITY SUPERVISOR. Guardian Security International, Raleigh, NC (2002-present). Work as an armed security guard in order to insure safety for clients and employees by preventing thefts, damage, and vandalism on the customer's property.
- Maintain accurate, up-to-date, and complete records of activities on my shift.
- Polished my ability to communicate effectively and concisely under extreme conditions.
- Am often called on to act as the site supervisor for three employees.

AIRPORT SECURITY OPERATIONS SUPERVISOR. Ogden Allied Contract Co., Raleigh/ Durham International Airport, NC (2001-02). Supervised from eight to 12 employees while screening passenger luggage using state-of-the-art X-ray equipment and working closely with law enforcement and customs authorities to guarantee security throughout the terminal.
- Was known for my ability to remain calm and controlled in pressure situations.
- Calmed airline passengers delayed by increased security precautions due to the war in Afghanistan.

BANK TELLER. First Citizens Bank & Trust Co., Raleigh, NC (1992-01). Served an average of 150 customers a day at the main branch — the busiest on the military post — while managing customer transactions inside the facility as well as at the drive-in windows.
- Handled at least $500,000 daily in funds which were distributed to other branches.
- Acted as a courier delivering important documents between several branches, thereby saving the bank the cost of hiring another employee to handle courier responsibilities.
- Gained "real-world" knowledge of banking system laws, rules, and procedures by participating in and observing various tests and examinations.
- Became familiar with computer systems unique to the banking industry including the Integrated Deposit System and Customer Information System.

Highlights of other experience: Worked in summer jobs performing preventive maintenance, transporting personnel/equipment for a training program, tutoring students, assigning bus drivers, driving a school bus, and assisting high school teachers.

TRAINING

Attended workshops in Word as well as programming. Excellent references on request.

Exact Name of Person
Exact Title
Exact Name of Organization
Exact Address
City, state zip

SECURITY GUARD
&
LOSS PREVENTION
SPECIALIST

Dear Exact Name:

With the enclosed resume, I would like to make you aware of my extensive background in security and retail loss prevention.

As you will see from my resume, I offer a diverse array of skills related to firearms operation, VIP protection, threat analysis, loss prevention, security, as well as reconnaissance and surveillance. For the past few years I have worked for the Wal-Mart organization in the loss prevention field. I have traveled all over the U.S. to set up systems to decrease pilferage and loss.

Systems I have implemented have saved the Wal-Mart organization millions of dollars, and I take pride in my ability to creatively apply my technical knowledge.

I hope you will welcome my call soon to arrange a brief meeting at your convenience to discuss your current and future needs and how I might serve them. Thank you in advance for your time.

Sincerely yours,

Charles D. Clarkson

CHARLES D. CLARKSON

1110½ Hay Street, Fayetteville, NC 28305   •   preppub@aol.com   •   (910) 483-6611

OBJECTIVE   I want to contribute to an organization that can use a hard-working professional who offers extensive experience related to security, surveillance, loss prevention, and private protective services in both military and corporate environments.

CLEARANCE   Maintained **Top Secret** security clearance for 17 years while in military service.

SKILLS   **Firearms:** Expert marksman, small arms and rifle qualified.

VIP Protection: Handled high-risk responsibilities at high-ranking levels.

Threat analysis: Skilled at performing threat analysis in facilities including airports.

Communications: Trained in classified areas of communications.

Medical emergencies: Licensed as a Medic and trained in EMT procedures.

Loss prevention: Skilled in detecting loss prevention including shoplifting.

Security cameras: Install and maintain security cameras and all surveillance equipment.

Classified materials: Proficient at safeguarding classified materials.

Reconnaissance and surveillance: Highly trained in these areas.

Security: Extensive experience in surveillance, undercover tactics, and crowd control.

EXPERIENCE   **LOSS PREVENTION ASSOCIATE.** Wal-Mart, locations throughout the United States (2000-present). Used a variety of methods to detect shoplifters and internal pilferage.
- Set up and monitored cameras.
- Handled invoicing for freight after verifying accuracy of receipts.
- Detected and investigated insurance fraud.
- Assisted in internal and external protection of employees at retail chains, college campuses, high schools, and other areas.
- Worked closely with local and state law enforcement officials.
- Trained in all aspects of fraud and embezzlement in financial offices.
- Maintained and controlled all narcotics in aid station.
- Oversaw daily, weekly, monthly, and yearly paperwork and documents for Wal-Mart.
- Accountable for medical supplies and equipment.
- Supervised and trained in excess of 100 people.
- Excellent analytical and administrative skills: compared freight against invoices for Wal-Mart to detect any freight discrepancies.
- Assisted in organizing, maintaining, and rotating merchandise in stockroom for the world's largest retail organization.

SUMMARY   Offer extensive experience in security and inventory control.
- Honest, loyal, and dedicated with a positive attitude.
- Attention to detail, highly organized, able to work independently.
- Work quickly and efficiently under highly pressured situations and tight deadlines.

CAREER CHANGE

Date

Exact Name of Person
Title or Position
Name of Company
Address (no., street)
Address (city, state, zip)

SPECIAL AGENT

This Master Trooper is attempting a career change into another functional area of the law enforcement field.

Dear Exact Name of Person (or Dear Sir or Madam if answering a blind ad):

I would appreciate an opportunity to talk with you soon about how I could contribute to your organization through my experience in investigative law enforcement, my expertise in building and supervising teams of specialists, and my reputation for finding solutions to difficult problems. I am interested in applying for the position of Special Agent with the Federal Bureau of Investigation.

While serving as a Master Trooper, I have acquired extensive hands-on expertise related to nearly all aspects of law enforcement. I have a great deal of experience in working closely with other law enforcement agencies including the CIA, FBI, and others.

I feel certain that you would find me to be a dynamic and mature professional with outstanding skills as a problem solver and decision maker along with a widely recognized talent for working with others and gaining their confidence quickly.

I hope you will welcome my call soon to arrange a brief meeting at your convenience to discuss your current and future needs and how I might serve them. Thank you in advance for your time.

Sincerely yours,

Will Barton Prosciutto

Alternate last paragraph:
I hope you will call or write soon to suggest a time convenient for us to meet and discuss your current and future needs and how I might serve them. Thank you in advance for your time.

WILL BARTON PROSCIUTTO

1110½ Hay Street, Fayetteville, NC 28305 • preppub@aol.com • (910) 483-6611

OBJECTIVE   To obtain a position as a Special Agent.

WEAPONS   Expert marksman and sharpshooter; qualified with the 12-gauge shotgun and .40 cal. handgun

EXPERIENCE   *Offer a reputation as a quick learner and skilled communicator who relates well to others and possesses a strong ability to work with the public as a member of the State Highway Patrol, Salem, WA, (1997-present):*

MASTER TROOPER. (1997-present). Enforce the laws of the State of Washington and routinely handle investigative duties related to security investigations, intelligence gathering, and criminal prosecution. Routinely work with officials and agencies including local agencies, U.S. Marshals, the State Bureau of Investigation, and others.

Accomplishments:
- As a Trooper, have played a critical role in the detection of criminal activity and in the seizure of illegal substances including alcohol, concealed weapons, drugs, and other items.
- Have seized up to $10,000 in narcotics-related currency.
- Investigated up to 15 deaths; on one occasion, tracked down a felon who fled the scene.

SPECIAL SKILLS
- **Analytical Skills:** Analyze information from automotive accident scenes in order to reconstruct events and draw conclusions; perform detailed analysis of hostage situations to secure the area until hostage negotiators arrive, stationing officers in strategic locations to provide reconnaissance and security to the crime scene.
- **Weapons Skills:** Skilled and qualified in the use of .40 caliber semi-automatic pistol and 12-gauge shotgun.
- **Leadership Skills:** Selected as a Field Training Officer.
- **Communication Skills:** Display my exceptional written communication skills while preparing a wide range of incident, accident, and other police reports. Have built a reputation as an articulate communicator capable of verbally disarming tense situations while responding to traffic/criminal enforcement calls.
- **Defensive Tactics:** Completed training which included preventing an assailant from obtaining my weapon during a struggle.
- **Stress Management:** Demonstrate ability to direct stress in a positive manner and make quick, effective decisions in stressful situations.
- **Staff Development & Training:** As one of only 150 certified Radar Instructors in the state of NC, have trained numerous individuals in radar and in time and distance.
- **Drug Investigations:** Skilled in apprehending criminals, detecting clues and securing evidence.
- **Interview and Interrogation Techniques:** Adept at using communication skills to draw information vital to the investigation from the interview subject. Trained in the psychology of the criminal mind and in detecting leads during the interview and interrogation process.
- **Computer Skills:** Computer literate and familiar with many popular computer operating systems and software, including but not limited to Windows, Corel WordPerfect, and the Mobile Data Terminal systems utilized by the NC Highway Patrol.

PERSONAL   Excellent personal and professional references are available upon request. Non-smoker and non-drinker. Can pass the most rigorous background investigation required for a security clearance. Am a trained and dedicated law enforcement professional.

LACEY D. DOILY

1110½ Hay Street, Fayetteville, NC 28305   •   preppub@aol.com   •
(910) 483-6611

SPECIAL AGENT, CID

OBJECTIVE

To offer a strong background which has emphasized interviewing and communicating with people, conducting investigations, and overseeing administrative operations to an organization that can use an assertive professional who enjoys the challenge of learning new things.

EDUCATION & TRAINING

Earned a bachelor's degree in Business Administration with a major in Management, Maryville College, Maryville, TN, 1993.

- Demonstrated my time management and organizational abilities while earning a degree and meeting the demands of detail-oriented positions.

Completed extensive training in criminal investigative techniques, personnel security, administrative procedures, and postal operations supervision.

SPECIAL SKILLS & KNOWLEDGE

Offer a solid base of experience in specialized areas:

Familiar with **office management and operations**, operate computers for data processing using Microsoft Windows, PowerPoint, and WordPerfect for Windows; type 65 wpm.

Have experience with **postal system operations** and have completed five postal courses at Mosten Technical Community College, Columbus, GA.

CLEARANCE

Entrusted with a Top Secret security clearance with a Special Background Investigation.

EXPERIENCE

Refined analytical, communication, and time management skills, U.S. Army:

SPECIAL AGENT, CRIMINAL INVESTIGATION COMMAND (CID). Germany (2002-present). Was involved in activities related to the conduct of felony investigations which included the collection and preservation of evidence as well as crime scene processing.

- Prepared written reports and was called on to testify in court.
- Conducted crime prevention surveys and drug awareness briefings.
- Displayed diplomacy when dealing with representatives of international law enforcement agencies, executives, and legal professionals including trial lawyers.
- Refined interviewing techniques dealing with witnesses, victims, and suspects.
- Acknowledged as demonstrating sound judgment and the ability to use resources wisely, brought about $388,000 in cost avoidance during four months in the Middle East.

SUPERVISOR FOR PERSONNEL AND INFORMATION SECURITY. Columbus, GA (1998-02). Provided administrative support and subject matter expertise on personnel security issues for a major command which was equivalent to a corporate headquarters.

- Served as liaison for personnel and information security issues

handled in cooperation with the Department of Defense, military units, and law enforcement agencies.
- Controlled and accounted for an inventory of Top Secret documents.
- Handled actions ranging from conducting personnel security interviews, to preparing security clearance packages, to checking local files as well as verifying clearances, determining eligibility for clearances, and preparing interim clearances.
- Maintained a data base of personnel information and records.

ADMINISTRATIVE ACTIONS SUPERVISOR. Ft. Campbell, KY (1994-97). Administered psychiatric testing as well as overseeing the daily operations in the identification card section and processing personnel rosters.
- Contributed my written skills and knowledge to rewrite the administrative division's standard operating procedures (SOP).
- Was awarded a Joint Services Achievement Medal for my accomplishments related to processing in excess of 200 awards during three months in an interim role.

ADMINISTRATIVE SECRETARY Ft. Bragg, NC (1990-93). Provided administrative support for the Secretary of the General Staff (SGS) at a major headquarters.
- Handled the funds and allocation of monies to purchase quarterly supplies for eight offices from a self-service supply center.
- Singled out for my professionalism and briefing skills; was selected to conduct monthly meetings for managerial personnel from throughout the parent organization.

ADMINISTRATIVE ASSISTANT. Germany (1987-90). Handpicked to act as an assistant for the commander of American forces in Europe, provided administrative support while controlling and monitoring the distribution of paperwork and documentation at a major headquarters; became familiar with the Modern Army Record Keeping System (MARKS).

ADMINISTRATIVE SPECIALIST. Ft. Huachuca, AZ (1985-87). Provided administrative support at a training support center during my first military assignment.

PERSONAL   Feel communicating with others is my greatest strength. Offer excellent listening and analytical skills along with a high level of patience and tolerance. Can be entrusted upon to follow through and see that any job I undertake is done correctly with minimal or no supervision.

Date

Exact Name of Person
Title or Position
Name of Company
Address (number and street)
Address (city, state, and zip)

SPECIAL AGENT

Dear Exact Name of Person (or Dear Sir or Madam if answering a blind ad):

I would appreciate an opportunity to talk with you soon about how I could contribute to your organization through my background of outstanding achievements as a Counterintelligence Special Agent.

During the past ten years I earned a reputation as an intelligent quick learner who could be counted on for professionalism as an investigator, analyst, instructor, and agent. Throughout my career, I was based in Washington, DC, where I provided support for Special Forces worldwide missions.

As just one example, I was honored with a Joint Services Achievement Medal for my accomplishments during a special project. Handpicked to support counternarcotics efforts, I analyzed and assessed vital information, operated and maintained computer and communications equipment, and managed the operating budget for a tactical analysis team. Through training and experience I have refined skills in surveillance, countersurveillance, counterterrorism, industrial security, and VIP protection. My skills also include working with safes and locking systems, surreptitious entry procedures, and urban operations.

I am highly self motivated and dedicated to contributing my abilities in the areas of investigations and security matters. An articulate and intelligent communicator, I am comfortable as a public speaker and instructor as well as being effective in debriefing personnel and preparing concise and thorough reports.

An adaptable individual who can handle pressure and get the job done, I am certain that I offer an ability to work well with others as a contributor toward group goals and objectives or in supervisory/managerial roles.

I hope you will welcome my call soon to arrange a brief meeting at your convenience to discuss your current and future needs and how I might serve them. Thank you in advance for your time.

Sincerely yours,

Sam A. Mickey

SAM A. MICKEY

1110½ Hay Street, Fayetteville, NC 28305 • preppub@aol.com • (910) 483-6611

OBJECTIVE
A position in investigative and security operations with an organization that can use a persistent and skilled professional who can provide a background of extensive intelligence gathering and protective services.

EXPERTISE
- Through training and experience, am skilled in countersurveillance, surveillance, counterterrorism, industrial security, photography, evaluating locks/safes/locking systems, surreptitious entry techniques, and basic electronics.
- Operate mainstream computer equipment and software, photo lab equipment, electronic tracking transmitters, direction finders, RF transmitters, and optical systems including 35mm cameras, video, pinhole installations, and telephone intercept equipment.
- Currently hold a Top Secret/SCI security clearance with SBI.

EXPERIENCE
Earned a reputation as a skilled instructor, investigator, and security professional while serving as a Counterintelligence Special Agent, Department of Defense, Washington, DC:
SPECIAL AGENT. (2002-present). Supervised two people involved in a variety of security procedures including processing security clearances, checking local records, and acting as couriers for classified materials.
- Refined skills in areas such as supervising employees and prioritizing the work flow.

COUNTERINTELLIGENCE AGENT. (1995-02). Provided assistance to Special Forces teams while analyzing intelligence data, making determinations on the seriousness and probability of hostile enemy threats, and producing counterintelligence products.
- Participated in activities such as debriefing personnel after the completion of their assignments and preparing detailed reports.

COUNTERINTELLIGENCE AGENT. (1994-95). Developed and enhanced skills in areas such as determining hostile threats, developing counterintelligence products, debriefing personnel, preparing detailed reports following debriefings, providing security for human and materials assets, and ensuring support in the areas of mapping as well as passport and visa processing for elements in preparation for overseas deployment.

COUNTERINTELLIGENCE AGENT. (1991-93). Polished my interviewing techniques and learned to write concise but thorough reports while debriefing Special Forces personnel after they returned from missions. Gained knowledge in functional areas including planning and carrying out exercises designed to locate weaknesses in physical security at key facilities.
- Made recommendations on countermeasures which would help make personnel and physical assets safe from terrorist actions.

EDUCATION
Excelled in a variety of training programs and graduated from the following:
- Graduated #1 from National Intelligence Academy's Technical Surveillance II Course.
- Counterintelligence Agent Course, United States Army Intelligence School.
- Primary Leadership Development Course, Noncommissioned Officer Academy.
- The United States Army Special Operations Command (USASOC) Special Security Office (SSO) Course.
- Excelled in numerous other training programs which were classified in nature.

PERSONAL
Excellent references on request.

Date

Exact Name of Person
Title or Position
Name of Company
Address (no., street)
Address (city, state, zip)

**WEAPONS &
OPERATIONS SPECIALIST**

Dear Exact Name of Person (or Dear Sir or Madam if answering a blind ad):

I would appreciate an opportunity to talk with you soon about how I could contribute to your organization through my experience, knowledge, and skills related to law enforcement.

While serving my country in the U.S. Army, I have become known for my expertise with small arms and light crew-served weapons and am often singled out to give advice on weapons use. As you will see from my resume, I train and provide leadership to Special Forces personnel at Ft. Bragg, NC, the world's largest U.S. military base. During the war in the Middle East, I led a seven-person team in combat operations.

Currently I am studying Criminal Justice and have completed approximately 25 credit hours leading to an associate's degree. In addition to a six-month course for weapons specialists, my military training included such areas as a 400-hour Class II Sniper training course as well as first response, emergency lifesaving, and combat lifesaving programs.

Through training and experience, I have become familiar with a number of specialized areas including many foreign and domestic weapons, airborne maneuvers, reconnaissance, patrolling, and surveillance.

While serving my country, I became accustomed to working in hazardous conditions in which there was "no room for error," and I have earned a reputation for my ability to make prudent decisions under pressure. My temperament and decision-making skills have been tested in combat conditions as well as in routine training activities.

I hope you will welcome my call soon to arrange a brief meeting at your convenience to discuss your current and future needs and how I might serve them. Thank you in advance for your time.

Sincerely yours,

Randy G. Ghostley

RANDY G. GHOSTLEY

1110½ Hay Street, Fayetteville, NC 28305 • preppub@aol.com • (910) 483-6611

OBJECTIVE

To contribute through my strong interest in the field of law enforcement by applying my military training/experience gained as a senior tactical adviser and weapons specialist known for excellent decision-making skills, sound judgment, and unlimited initiative.

EXPERIENCE

Advanced as a manager, senior tactical adviser, and weapons specialist in a Special Forces Group, U.S. Army, Ft. Campbell, KY:
SENIOR WEAPONS AND OPERATIONS SPECIALIST. (2000-present). Promoted based on my expertise with small arms and light crew-served weapons systems, act as an advisor on the use of these weapons in both conventional and unconventional warfare.
- Was handpicked to train and advise the Jamaican military's sniper team which was selected as the honor graduates in international competition.

WEAPONS AND OPERATIONS SPECIALIST. (1995-99). Continued to refine my leadership abilities and weapons proficiency working with a seven-person team.
- Qualified **Expert with the M-16 rifle** and achieved a maximum score in physical testing.
- Singled out for advanced training, completed the 400-hour Class II Sniper Program.

SUPERVISOR, ANTI-ARMOR SECTION. (1992-95). Trained and supervised seven people in an organization which had to remain in constant readiness to move anywhere in the world within 18 hours and be fully capable of going into combat on arrival.
- Applied my instructional skills and knowledge while training personnel, 95% of whom qualified as experts with the M-16 rifle.

COMBAT WEAPONS SPECIALIST. Saudi Arabia (1990-91). Earned several respected medals for my accomplishments during the war in the Middle East.
- Received the National Defense and Southwest Asia Service Medals.

SECURITY TEAM LEADER and **BORDER GUARD.** Korea (1989-90). Supervised a team of six American and two Korean soldiers; saw that they were trained and ready to respond immediately to any threat or hostile action.

RECONNAISSANCE TEAM LEADER. Germany (1988). Became familiar with surveillance and reconnaissance techniques and was selected ahead of ten of my peers to lead a 4-person team; controlled a $1 million equipment inventory.

EDUCATION & TRAINING

Study **Criminal Justice**, Gaston Technical Community College, Gaston, SC; 25 credit hours. Completed the **six-month Special Forces Weapons Sergeant Qualification Course** as well as more than 1,500 additional hours of specialized training programs including the following:

emergency/combat life saving — 44 hours each	Spanish — 510 hours
First Responder Course — 44 hours	leadership training — 200 hours
anti-armor leaders course — 80 hours	driver's training — 40 hours

SPECIAL KNOWLEDGE

Through training and experience, offer special knowledge of areas such as:
Working knowledge of many **foreign and domestic weapons**
Familiarity with **airborne insertion techniques**: parachuting, rappelling, and fast rope
Proficiency with **small arms, air defense systems, anti-armor weapons, and mortars**
Small unit tactics, **reconnaissance, patrolling,** and unconventional warfare

EVAN D. SKINSLOW

1110½ Hay Street, Fayetteville, NC 28305 • preppub@aol.com • (910) 483-6611

WEAPONS SPECIALIST

Here's a final example of a Weapons Specialist.

OBJECTIVE To offer my language skills and technical weapons expertise to an organization that can use a dedicated, honest, and dependable professional with a strong background in international law enforcement and security as well as an eye for details and time management skills.

CLEARANCE Hold a Top Secret security clearance with SSBI.

LANGUAGES Conversant in Russian (Croatian), Polish, and Yugoslavian as well as English.

SPECIAL SKILLS Through experience and training, am skilled at troubleshooting, repairing, and operating weapons including the following:

| M-16A2 | M-203 | M-249 | M-60 | M-9 |
| M-252 | M-1200 | MK-19 | M-2 | AK-47 |

Offer experience in troubleshooting, repairing, and operating night vision devices including the following:

| AN/PVS-7A | AN/PVS-7B | AN/PVS-14 | TVS-5 | GVS-5 |

Am proficient with operation of SINGARS (COMSEC)

EDUCATION & TRAINING Pursuing a B.A. degree in **International Relations**, University of Kentucky. Earned an A.S. degree in **Computer Automation**, Long Island Vocational School, Long Island City, NY, 1990.

EXPERIENCE *Earned a reputation as a self motivated professional who is dedicated to giving time and efforts in order to achieve goals and high levels of productivity, U.S. Army:* **WEAPONS SPECIALIST** and **UNIT ARMORER.** Ft. Campbell, KY (2002-present). Established a solid maintenance program and efficient record-keeping system after taking over this position and quickly reorganizing operations in an arms room.

- Provided advice to the commanding officer as the subject matter expert on weapons.
- Earned a perfect 100% score during an important inspection of operations and security.
- Managed a $2 million inventory of weapons and equipment with such efficiency that the unit saved $10,000 in just a few months by keeping weapons operating and available.
- Was awarded the Army Achievement Medal in recognition of my accomplishments as the battalion's armorer: on one occasion supervised the cleaning of 194 M-16s and 106 PVS-7s; got 82 M-16s, 35 PVS-7s, and five M-2MGs gauged in only three days.

WEAPONS SPECIALIST and **UNIT ARMORER.** Ft. Bragg, NC (1993-01). Maintained, repaired, accounted for, and provided security for $2.2 million worth of equipment while providing technical support and advice on weapons use and maintenance.

- Was promoted based on my performance in this highly visible and critical position.
- Trained incoming personnel in all aspects of technical support for weapons inventories.

PERSONAL Am a reliable, punctual, and creative individual. Use my technical skills with

ABOUT THE EDITOR

Anne McKinney holds an MBA from the Harvard Business School and a BA in English from the University of North Carolina at Chapel Hill. A noted public speaker, writer, and teacher, she is the senior editor for PREP's business and career imprint, which bears her name. Early titles in the Anne McKinney Career Series (now called the Real-Resumes Series) published by PREP include: *Resumes and Cover Letters That Have Worked, Resumes and Cover Letters That Have Worked for Military Professionals, Government Job Applications and Federal Resumes, Cover Letters That Blow Doors Open,* and *Letters for Special Situations*. Her career titles and how-to resume-and-cover-letter books are based on the expertise she has acquired in 20 years of working with job hunters. Her valuable career insights have appeared in publications of the "Wall Street Journal" and other prominent newspapers and magazines.

PREP Publishing Order Form

You may purchase any of our titles from your favorite bookseller! Or send a check or money order or your credit card number for the total amount*, plus $4.00 postage and handling, to PREP, Box 66, Fayetteville, NC 28302. You may also order our titles on our website at www.prep-pub.com and feel free to e-mail us at preppub@aol.com or call 910-483-6611 with your questions or concerns.

Name: _____

Phone #:_____

Address: _____

E-mail address:

Payment Type: ☐ Check/Money Order   ☐ Visa   ☐ MasterCard

Credit Card Number: _____ Expiration Date: _____

Check items you are ordering:

☐ $16.95—REAL-RESUMES FOR MANUFACTURING JOBS. Anne McKinney, Editor

☐ $16.95—REAL-RESUMES FOR AVIATION & TRAVEL JOBS. Anne McKinney, Editor

☐ $16.95—REAL-RESUMES FOR POLICE, LAW ENFORCEMENT & SECURITY JOBS. Anne McKinney, Editor

☐ $16.95—REAL-RESUMES FOR SOCIAL WORK & COUNSELING JOBS. Anne McKinney, Editor

☐ $16.95—REAL-RESUMES FOR CONSTRUCTION JOBS. Anne McKinney, Editor

☐ $16.95—REAL-RESUMES FOR FINANCIAL JOBS. Anne McKinney, Editor

☐ $16.95—REAL-RESUMES FOR COMPUTER JOBS. Anne McKinney, Editor

☐ $16.95—REAL-RESUMES FOR MEDICAL JOBS. Anne McKinney, Editor

☐ $16.95—REAL-RESUMES FOR TEACHERS. Anne McKinney, Editor

☐ $16.95—REAL-RESUMES FOR CAREER CHANGERS. Anne McKinney, Editor

☐ $16.95—REAL-RESUMES FOR STUDENTS. Anne McKinney, Editor

☐ $16.95—REAL-RESUMES FOR SALES. Anne McKinney, Editor

☐ $16.95—REAL ESSAYS FOR COLLEGE AND GRAD SCHOOL. Anne McKinney, Editor

☐ $25.00—RESUMES AND COVER LETTERS THAT HAVE WORKED.

☐ $25.00—RESUMES AND COVER LETTERS THAT HAVE WORKED FOR MILITARY PROFESSIONALS.

☐ $25.00—RESUMES AND COVER LETTERS FOR MANAGERS.

☐ $25.00—GOVERNMENT JOB APPLICATIONS AND FEDERAL RESUMES: Federal Resumes, KSAs, Forms 171 and 612, and Postal Applications.

☐ $25.00—COVER LETTERS THAT BLOW DOORS OPEN.

☐ $25.00—LETTERS FOR SPECIAL SITUATIONS.

☐ $16.00—BACK IN TIME. Patty Sleem

☐ $17.00—(trade paperback) SECOND TIME AROUND. Patty Sleem

☐ $25.00—(hardcover) SECOND TIME AROUND. Patty Sleem

☐ $18.00—A GENTLE BREEZE FROM GOSSAMER WINGS. Gordon Beld

☐ $18.00—BIBLE STORIES FROM THE OLD TESTAMENT. Katherine Whaley

☐ $14.95—WHAT THE BIBLE SAYS ABOUT... *Words that can lead to success and happiness* (large print edition) Patty Sleem

☐ $10.95—KIJABE An African Historical Saga. Pally Dhillon

_____ **TOTAL ORDERED (add $4.00 for postage and handling)**

PREP offers volume discounts on large orders. Call us at (910) 483-6611 for more information.

Would you like to explore the possibility of having PREP's writing
team create a resume for you similar to the ones in this book?

For a brief free consultation, call 910-483-6611
or send $4.00 to receive our Job Change Packet to
PREP, Department SPR2002, Fayetteville, NC 28302.

QUESTIONS OR COMMENTS? E-MAIL US AT PREPPUB@AOL.COM